African Spiritual Traditions in the Novels of Toni Morrison

UNIVERSITY PRESS OF FLORIDA

Florida A&M University, Tallahassee
Florida Atlantic University, Boca Raton
Florida Gulf Coast University, Ft. Myers
Florida International University, Miami
Florida State University, Tallahassee
New College of Florida, Sarasota
University of Central Florida, Orlando
University of Florida, Gainesville
University of North Florida, Jacksonville
University of South Florida, Tampa
University of West Florida, Pensacola

African Spiritual Traditions in the Novels of Toni Morrison

✿

K. Zauditu-Selassie

University Press of Florida
Gainesville/Tallahassee/Tampa/Boca Raton
Pensacola/Orlando/Miami/Jacksonville/Ft. Myers/Sarasota

First cloth printing, 2009
First paperback printing, 2013

Library of Congress Cataloging-in-Publication Data
Zauditu-Selassie, K.
African spiritual traditions in the novels of Toni Morrison / K. Zauditu-Selassie.
p. cm.
Includes bibliographical references and index.
ISBN 978-0-8130-3328-0 (cloth: alk. paper)
ISBN 978-0-8130-4952-6 (pbk.)
1. Morrison, Toni—Criticism and interpretation. 2. Morrison, Toni—Spirtualistic
interpretations. 3. Morrison, Toni—Knowledge—Africa. 4. American literature—
African influences. 5. Yoruba (African people) in literature. 6. African Americans in
literature. 7. Spirituality in literature. 8. Africa—In literature. I. Title.
PS3563.O8749Z97 2008
813'54—dc22   2008040296

The University Press of Florida is the scholarly publishing agency for the State University System of Florida, comprising Florida A&M University, Florida Atlantic University, Florida Gulf Coast University, Florida International University, Florida State University, New College of Florida, University of Central Florida, University of Florida, University of North Florida, University of South Florida, and University of West Florida.

University Press of Florida
15 Northwest 15th Street
Gainesville, FL 32611-2079
www.upf.com

Parts of chapters 2 and 3 were published previously in "I Got a Home in Dat Rock: Memory, Òrìsà, and Yoruba Spiritual Identity in African American Literature," in *Orisa: Yoruba Gods and Spiritual Identity in Africa and the African Diaspora*, edited by Toyin Falola and Ann Genova. Trenton, N.J.: Africa World Press, 2005.

Parts of chapters 1, 4, and 5 were published in "Women Who Know Things: African Epistemologies, Ecocriticism, and Female Spiritual Authority in the Novels of Toni Morrison." *Journal of Pan African Studies* 1, no.7 (March 2007): 38–57.

Contents

Acknowledgments

This project was completed over many years of shifting jobs, attitudes, and cities, and also old and new colleagues and friendships. Many people have helped me along the way; I regret that I cannot thank each one individually. While in graduate school at Clark Atlanta University, I was blessed to have dedicated professors, all intellectuals, who believed that it was important to be creative and to think thoughts outside the main of literary criticism. I would like to thank them all. Additionally, I am grateful to Dr. Jean Billingslea Brown, Dr. Ernestine Pickens Glass, Dr. Janice Liddell, Dr. Charlyn Harper Browne, all colleagues of mine from the Atlanta University Center.

To my former students at Morris Brown College, where I taught for fourteen years, you inspired many of the formulations presented in this book, especially members of my seminar course, the Novels of Toni Morrison. To my former students at Bowie State University, I thank you for bearing with me as I rehearsed my ideas with you in African American Seminar. I am also indebted to members of the Toni Morrison Society, Dr. Carolyn Denard, Dr. Marilyn Sanders Mobley, Dr. Deborah Barnes, Dr. Angelyn Mitchell, and Dr. Adrienne Lanier Seward, for support over the years including critiques of papers presented at society meetings. Some extraordinary colleagues, Dr. Mario H. Beatty, Dr. Valethia Watkins, and Dr. Marimba Ani have enriched my intellectual and personal life with their strong and focused vision for the development of African people. Additional gratitude is extended to Ras Michael Brown, for sharing information on Central African spirituality and its impact on African Americans in the low country of South Carolina and Georgia. Thank you to Nobel laureate Wole Soyinka, for encouraging me to pursue my ideas on Morrison's encoding of Yoruba Òrìsà and to Dr. Richard Schechner of New York University's Tisch School of Performing Arts who asked the pivotal question: "Why write an article on Morrison when you could write a book?"

I am thankful to my editor at the University of Florida Press, Amy Gorelick, for her patient and unwavering support for this project. Additionally, a generous grant in 1993 from the National Endowment for the Humanities contributed to some of the ideas foundational to this current study.

viii ∗ Acknowledgments

Thank you to my mother Marcelite Dolores Landry-Evans, mother of seven, who taught me the supremacy of belief in God, devotion to Yemonja, and faith in the ancestors. Thanks for supporting my need to dance. Because you drove me from dance to dance and created unique dance outfits for me every week, I learned at an early age the value of soul freedom. I also express appreciation to my grandmother, Esther Dolores Rabb (Moms) who continues to mentor me in the understanding of the spirit world. While on earth, she taught me to consider that although everything that exists is not visible, it still exists. To my husband, Mahseeyahu, for the emotional and financial support to walk the African world, from Atlanta to Addis Ababa, from Brooklyn to Brazil, from Memphis to Mali, and from Los Angeles to Lomé in search of the manifestations of spirit, may you always be blessed for the encouragement you have given me. To my son, Angola, who has shown me the importance of doing things that honor a commitment to happiness, as well as for sharing with me the importance of having a dream, I offer my appreciation. To my twin, Isoke, and to my other sisters, Rochelle, Stacie, and Thia, I appreciate your encouragement. Much love and respect to my elders, my Ojubona, my godchildren, and my daughters, Yaba, Ifetayo, and Titilayo. To my Iyalosa, Oseye Mchawi, I express my gratitude for your having crowned me Omo Obatala. May all the Òrìsà and spiritual forces of the universe sustain you and bless you. Your spiritual brilliance and ethical resolve provide sturdy examples of how to live in truth. Finally, I would like to thank my father, Lawrence J. Evans, Abbasante Shabaka, who made his spiritual transition into the world of the ancestors while I was completing this book. You taught me the beauty of language, the value of humor, and the promise of knowledge. Continue to walk in light and love on your journey.

Preface

Dancing between Two Realms

That we the black people are one people we know. Destroyers will travel long distances in their minds and out to deny you this truth.

—Ayi Kwei Armah, *Two Thousand Seasons*

Make a drumbeat, Put it on a record, let it whirl, And while we listen to it play, Dance with you till day—

—Langston Hughes, "Juke Box Love Song"

In one of my earliest recollections of myself, I am dancing. Yes, when I was young, I was that little dancing girl. On various holiday occasions, when my friends' relatives would visit them, they would send for me, saying, "Go get that little dancin' gal." Honoring their requests, I would perform dances such as "Mickey's Monkey," accompanied by Smokey Robinson and the Miracles as the 45 rpm record circled clockwise around the record player's turntable. Over the years, I danced Marvin Gaye's "Hitchhike," Archie Bell and the Drells' "Tighten Up," The Capitols' "Cool Jerk," the Orlons' "The Wah Watutsi," and the Knickerbockers' "Twine Time." I especially looked forward to the imported dances my junior aunt would show me upon her return to Los Angeles from her yearly summer trips to Chicago. Out on the dance floor, even though most of the dances I did were performed with one dance partner, there was a sense of community, because of the collective performance of other dancers sharing the dance space. Wearing our favorite dance "faces" (mine was hanging my tongue out of the side of my mouth, while my sister's was biting her bottom lip), we chanted dance sounds, communicating a sense of well-being summoned from the energy and force manifested by the unity of music and movement. I did not realize until many years later that most of the dances we did were accompanied by songs that oftentimes provided explicit instructions to ensure a uniform presentation of the dance. I also was unaware that having a particular dance to do with a specific song was a unique cultural representation of African people.[1]

Having come of age as a "Negro" in Compton, a suburb of Los Angeles, California—also called "New Orleans West" because of the large numbers of immigrants from the Crescent City—I never considered what other people did. In my all-black part of the city, I was taught by the Sisters of the Holy Family, an order of African American nuns from New Orleans, went to school with other black Catholics, and tried to snatch the meaning out of words spoken in Creole language when grown women were talking amongst one another within ear shot of my friends and me. I ate gumbo, savored red beans and rice with Pete's Louisiana hot sausage, and devoured hot monkey bread straight from the oven of Walker's bakery. In this highly segregated environment, I danced exclusively with other black people in an all-black world of culture.

In this world, my favorite dance was, "The Bus Stop," known by many names, such as, "The Madison," "The Hustle," or "The Electric Slide," depending on the locale. We called it "The Caswell," after my father added a couple of new steps and renamed the dance after our street in Compton. In our collective movements, dancing this re-codified ring dance, we claimed the power emanating from the circle. Rooted in traditions characterized by spiritual considerations whose provenances are anterior to the American experience, this line dance is actually a circle dance performed only in a community of dancers, never by a solo performer. The dancers trace the Kongo cosmogram, the *dikenga dia* Kongo, a symbolic representation of the soul's movement in a counterclockwise fashion through the various stages of life.[2] Representing the cyclical journey of the soul as it moves from birth to puberty, to maturity, to eldership, to begin the cycle of re-births again, the dance is structured in four parts.

One of the key symbols representing Kongo beliefs, *dikenga dia* Kongo is depicted as a circle intersected at the midpoint by two lines: one vertical and the other horizontal. The space above the line is the upper world and the physical world and below the line is the lower world or the spiritual world, the abode of the ancestors. As a result of these two intersecting lines, four quadrants are formed epitomizing the four suns constructing the journey of a human being on earth. The participants begin the dance at the midpoint of the cross on the horizontal line dissecting the circle known as *kalunga*, the "balancing plane for all existence" (Fu-Kiau, *African Cosmology*, 23).

As they move three steps to the right on the *kalunga* line, they journey toward, *kala*, corresponding to birth, symbolized by the color black. From there, they trace the *kalunga* line three steps to the left arriving at the quadrant known as *luvemba* characterized by the color white and representing the death of an individual. Executing this step prepares them to walk three steps backwards toward the southern axis into the realm of the ancestors to begin again at *musoni*, which represents beginnings, seeds, and the color yellow. From there, the dancers move three beats consisting of a pause at the *kalunga* line, one small step back *retracing* their steps toward *musoni* and one down, which is actually the northern axis to collect the power at the zenith of the circle or *tukula*, the sun of maturity, signified by the color red.

Finally, the dancers make a counterclockwise turn to trace the circle again. The circle will be traced four times until they arrive at the same point again to complete/begin the dance's symbolic journey. The dams of time described in each of the cosmogram's quadrants are delineations within the cosmic realm. These mythic symbols hidden in dance steps of the ring shout encircle and contain the spiritual ethos of Kongo derived beliefs. From a Bantu perspective, Bunseki K. Fu-Kiau asserts that nothing exists that does not follow the cosmogram (African Cosmology 27).

My introduction to the dance as a child and my initiation as a Mama Nganga into the mysteries of the Kongo spiritual system as an adult, speak to the ways in which sacred reenactment has the power to knit together time and space in order to establish the self. From an African aesthetic, Geneviève Fabre explains dancers not only communicate with spirits, but also can impersonate and incorporate them through the repetition of specific body movements ("Slave Ship Dance" 33). Mircea Eliade explains that sacred time is not only recoverable, it is also unchanging, and perpetual (*Sacred and the Profane* 69). Performing the ritual dance through the repetitive movements of tracing and retracing the four quadrants of the circle, I recovered sacred time and re-claimed my Kongo spiritual heritage.

This ritualized return to forever allows for continuous time consistent with the Bantu notion of *hantu*, which is time and space unified. Over time, my body performed the dances my soul remembered, as I practiced how to step between modernity and mythical time. Moreover, in my journeys throughout the African world I have danced counterclockwise honoring the ancestors (*Egun*) Òrìsà, the Vodun Gods (Loa), and the Minkisi (Bantu/Kongo). The spiritual awareness I have gained concerning the power of dance and ritual has led me to the goal of this present study, which is to locate spiritual traditions in the novels of Toni Morrison. My uncharacteristic approach, which straddles two realms, is at once divinatory and analytic, representing the duality of my critical trajectory in literary endeavors. Speaking specifically about central African culture, Wyatt MacGaffey notes that to discover trans-Atlantic connections one must recognize that "each word, idea, or object is embedded in matrices of language and ritual practice ("Twins, Simbi Spirits, and Lwas" 211). I extend that search in orders to decode the embedded spiritual ideas from a variety of traditions. The individual chapters in *African Spiritual Traditions in the Novels of Toni Morrison* affirm and demonstrate the power of Morrison's prose to re-codify these Central African beliefs along with other African-derived belief systems and sacred memories. These spiritual ideas dance among oral narratives, folklore, myth, and African derived spiritual principles. Through close readings, I examine how her novelistic figurations impart vital information and reinforce historical and spiritual consciousness.[3]

There's a Little Wheel a Turnin' in My Heart

Cultural Concentricities and Enduring Identities

> Kidnapped by bandits and transplanted to North America, they
> became HooDoo men, maintaining the faith of the old religion.
>
> —Ishmael Reed, "19 Necromancers from Now"

> We have been believers believing in the black gods of an old
> land, believing in the secrets of the seeress and the magic of the
> charmers and the power of the devil's evil ones.
>
> —Margaret Walker, "We Have Been Believers"

Toni Morrison declares that the "forced transfer" of African people is the
"defining event of the modern world" ("Home" 10). The arrival of captive Africans to North America, their enslavement, and their continued
survival, represents a journey of remarkable resiliency. Besides enslaving
African people, the deliberate mission of Europeans included efforts to
destroy them by attempting to wipe out their traditions, substituting their
languages, and desecrating their cultures. To reiterate, this experience of
Africans in America has been a quintessential example of adaptation in the
face of adversity.[1] That they managed to continue on with any measure of
psychic integrity is a tribute to the dynamic role that culture plays in the
lives of people.

A necessary element of life, culture is the medium through which humans exercise their humanity and express and affirm their view of reality.
For members of the African diaspora, culture surpassed its role to provide
self-definition and sustain the group ethos; it became a way to physically
survive. As a site of cosmic connection, identity, meaning, and values were
made and remade in order to resist. Through the tenacious practice of culture, Africans endured in America. This worldview bears witness to the
strength of the survivors of one of the cruelest systems of human oppres-

sion witnessed in human history. Because of this, African culture became stronger as the group faced cultural extinction from external forces.

In "Theatre in African Traditional Cultures: Survival Patterns," Wole Soyinka explains the nature of this fortification. He argues, "The commencement of resistance and self-liberation by the suppressed people is not infrequently linked with the survival strategies of key cultural patterns manifested through various art forms" (89). In *The Afro-American Novel and Its Tradition*, Bernard Bell notes patterns of conditions and circumstances that produce the shared experience of culture, he says, "The network of understanding that defines black American culture and informs black American consciousness has evolved from the unique pattern of experiences of Africa, the trans-Atlantic middle passage, slavery, Southern plantation, tradition, emancipation, Reconstruction, Post Reconstruction, northern migration, urbanization, and racism have produced a residue of shared memories and frames of references for Black Americans" (5). In this study, I am not attempting to present African culture as a monolithic idea. Cheikh Anta Diop underscores this idea of unity across African cultures in the introduction to his authoritative work, *The Cultural Unity of Black Africa*. He writes, "I have tried to bring out the profound cultural unity still alive beneath the deceptive appearance of cultural heterogeneity" (7).

As a response to challenges insisted on by the harsh environment, the brutal physical abuse by their captors, and the psychological disintegration produced by the chaos of the unfamiliar, Africans reached deep within themselves where the roots of culture abide. This protracted struggle and accompanying cultural resolve has allowed them to maintain the deep structure of their cultural distinctiveness. Moreover, dynamic cultural processes allowed enslaved Africans to establish familiar and intelligible patterns through maintaining and preserving their identities and renewing spiritual and ancestral forces. Many of the Africanisms were codified in the folkways of African people, especially the expression of spirituality. The intense need for the expression of spirituality reflected the continuity of beliefs transported from Africa. This spiritual aspiration was encoded in the folklore. In *Puttin' On Ole Massa* Gilbert Osofsky affirms this adaptability, stating, "If one is to ever know about their visions, their quests, their mind, it is necessary to turn to the oral folktales that were collected in the nineteenth century and remain alive at this very moment" (45).

Maintaining cultural continuity was difficult and fraught with many sacrifices and adaptations. It is well documented that the drum was outlawed, names were changed, and many traditional practices had to be adapted in such a way that their meaning was not recognizable by the enslavers.[2] However, in many cases, domination demanded cultural denial and a mass forgetting in order to achieve the self-serving objectives exacted by the oppressive system. In his germinal text, *The Falsification of Afrikan Consciousness*, the late Amos Wilson argues that social amnesia is the root cause of many of the dynamic problems beleaguering the African American community. Defined as the repression of historical and cultural realities, ahistoricity compromises the present and hides individual and group futures. In fact, as Wilson asserts, the fear and shame of memory signify destructive forces that "open the personality up for self-alienation, self-destruction" (36).

In concert with Wilson, I contend that loss of memory, as a result of harsh assaults and cultural contestations, has challenged the ontogeneic agency of the person and covered it with the shroud of self-constructed otherness. Adding to this sense of bereavement is the internment of religious ideas, at times so deep as to render them irretrievable and unrecognizable to the conscious mind. M. A. Oduyoye comments that the identity crisis for African people "may be attributed to the loss of a dynamic perspective on life, which comes from knowing and living one's religio-cultural history" (59). Given this diagnosis of the traumatic effects of repressed memory, it would follow that recovery of memory is an essential first step in the process of recovering identity.

Morrison's use of images, archetypes, and values are reflective of and consistent with a compendium of African spiritual worldviews. With them, she exhumes spiritual rudiments resurrecting and highlighting African deities and mythic ideas, which lead her heroic characters to epic completion. Daniel P. Biebuyck says that because of various connections among different groups, African heroic epic tradition, though diverse in many ways, shared enough common elements to have facilitated transformation under the appropriate circumstances ("African Heroic Epic" 28). Using the performative ideas associated with ritual, Morrison ferries her readers to archetypal spaces where "communality, coherence, connectedness, collective conscience, and efficacy characterize the social order" (Drewal xv).

In this introductory chapter, I examine the cultural agency informing Toni Morrison's artistic vision, explore the African worldview, and lay the foundation for the subsequent examination of these cultural principles within the text of the novels to be discussed in this study. For Morrison, who employs the self-authenticating trope of the Black Arts Movement writers, blackness and culture are not expendable, nor are they negotiable.

They are located in the subterranean structures of culture and must be discussed within the realm of spirituality and African components of the living memory.[3] Comparable to the mnemonic devices employed in traditional African cultures such as the *lukasa* sculptures of the BaLuba (a subgroup of the BaKongo) each of the novels is a commemorative site where readers can participate in re-collecting buried knowledge to refortify and restore a sense of identity and cultural connectivity to the village—the community as Morrison expresses. To illustrate, in southeastern Congo, ancestor societies rely on the use of hierarchical figures inscribed in the hand held objects, which present a conceptual map of fundamental aspects of Luba culture in order to trace memory and recall genealogies and arcane knowledge to pass on to subsequent generations (Roberts and Roberts, *Memory*, 140). With her cataloging of memorates, myths, cosmologies and enduring cultural ideas, Morrison revives a dynamic cultural and spiritual history challenging the myth of being "stripped" and dispossessed of memory as a result of the Middle Passage and subsequent traumas, an account repeatedly narrated by the larger American society.

Morrison is a memory keeper and an historian. As she remarks in an essay titled, "Behind the Making of the Black Book," "the artist is the true historian who does not need to make new myths, but needs to re-discover the old ones" (89). Defining myth as a concept of truth or reality that a whole people has arrived at over years of observation, Morrison comments that this myth has to be communally accepted by the group as truth (89). Furthermore, in an essay titled, "Memory, Creation, and Writing," Morrison discusses the cultural agency framing her literary agenda. She writes:

> I simply wanted to write literature that was irrevocably, indisputably Black, not because its characters were, or because I was, but because it took as its creative task and sought as its credentials those recognized and verifiable principles of Black Art. (389)

What are these verifiable principles? I believe the ideas correspond to a compendium of culturally constructed deliberations imagined, sculpted, and fashioned from the shared memory of spiritual culture.

Toni Morrison's insistence on accompanying her nationalistic impulses with panspiritual ideas helps to restore the respect and identity of a people whose very existence in the western hemisphere has been threatened by European hegemony, Christian imposition, and its accompanying spiritual imperialism. I am using the term *panspiritualism* consistent with John Henrik Clarke's definition of *pan* as any movement by an ethnic group to recover and reclaim their history, culture, and national identity, after slavery, war, or migration, forced or otherwise (26). As Frantz Fanon explains in *The Wretched of the Earth*, "The nation gathers together the various indispensable elements necessary for the creation of a culture, those elements which alone can give it credibility, validity, life, and creative power" (245). These elements that breathe life are available as Soyinka asserts, "Within our African consciousness and at the horizon of our intellection is the possibility to re-constitute ourselves."[4]

African Americans or American Africans continue to demonstrate Africa's enduring power, its flexibility, and vitality. Whether this power is inscribed in dance movements, articulated in the oral tradition of the blues or hip-hop music, or performed in a plethora of stylistic sensibilities, the manifestation of this power in these aforementioned expressions are "legitimate and important modes of comprehending and operating within a universe perceived in sacred terms" (Levine 56). Fundamental to that sense of sacredness is the idea that the material and phenomenal world is endlessly affected by unseen powers (93).

Toni Morrison, one of the ancient mothers described by Alice Walker, helps the reader to find her own "garden" where haints, mojos, fixing folks, and root-workers are significant features of the spiritual universe and are considered requisite components of the cultural and spiritual arts. Affirming reality in culturally determined ways, Morrison authenticates histories and traditions that are not available for participation and acceptance by those who stand outside the culture. What do these spiritual universes look like? What is contained within them? To consider the worldview, one must also examine the accompanying ethos, as they are not separate, but represent the two halves of the primordial gourd of existence. Referencing more than the consideration of nature, self, and society and the comprehensive order of things, this worldview pertains to the moral and aesthetic nature of life. All is contained within this frame and all elements mutually confirm each other.

I argue that although Morrison uses the genre of the novel, her narratives, like the epic, present one metanarrative in episodic installments. Her prose reiterates that we have not stopped being what we have preserved in cultural forms. I began this study asking one big question: To what extent does Toni Morrison inscribe specific African spiritual ideas and traditions in her novels? What I found was a complex and highly textured assemblage of spiritual ideas and diverse forms demarcating and situating core cultural representations and social interactions. Of particular interest are Morrison's inscriptions of the ways in which oppression and belief interact to solidify and strengthen spiritual practices. All of these cultural elements find points of synthesis and emerge through the dynamics of language, which sustain the deep-core values and cosmological structures. Subsequent inquiries guiding my exploration concern the ways in which African people in North America redefined, restored, and reclaimed the African spiritual personality and recovered identity. Finally, throughout this study I examine the functions of women healers to keep the community's spiritual circle intact as they traverse spiritual landscapes emblematic of Yoruba, Kongo, and other African spiritual systems.[5] Testimony to this ancestral heritage is observed, most notably, in the spiritual practices as well as music, dance, and language.[6] It is the continuity of African culture coupled with the arduous experience of struggle in America that informs poems, prayers, and groans of the African American. Heard in the work songs of laborers, the conjures of root-workers, and sermons of the preachers, African culture also makes its presence known in the written literature.

Although I volley back and forth from discussions grounded in Yoruba ideas to Kongo traditions, to Dogon spiritual ideas to Bantu ideas, my approach is not characterized by a mere cataloguing of ideas in a erratic way, but is an encircling of the spiritual traditions that have coalesced and reconciled with one another in the Americas to find common ground in shared beliefs and African sensibilities. At times, the Bantu approach dominates this fused identity. Joseph E. Holloway explains that the Bantu of Central Africa possessed the largest homogeneous culture among the captured Africans and had the most influence on African American culture and language (Introduction to Africanisms" xiii). Lawrence Grossberg concurs that displacement challenges a culture's equation with location or place. He explains, "Politics of identity are synecdochal, taking the part (the individual) to be representative of the whole (the social group) defined by a common identity" (169). Through this process that Grossberg outlines, it is logical that Bantu culture became the superstructure to house the mores of various African nations that ultimately developed into contemporary African cultural practices in America (Holloway 17). The potency of Bantu culture is attributed to the strength of their mutually intelligible languages, the homogeneity of their culture, and the fact that the Bantu who were field hands had little contact with the European Americans. These continuities were maintained in "religion, philosophy, culture, folklore, folkways, folk beliefs, folktales, storytelling, naming practices, home economics, arts, kinship, and music" (Holloway 17).

This deliberate act of remembrance of Africa in America also emerges in the Yoruba example. Michael A. Gomez notes that with the Yoruba, "ethnicity was more consciously operative in the Americas than in Africa" (55). Juxtaposing the loyalty the Yoruba had with towns and regions in Nigeria, Gomez argues "within the context of New World enslavement, however, their common language (with dialects), culture, and religion (featuring a shared Oyo, Ile Ife centered cosmology) combined to erase former boundaries of locality" (55). In this way, the Yoruba were able to emerge as a "nation" in North America, the Caribbean, and Brazil (55).

To understand the process of African American identity formation, Gomez observes: "it is essential to recover the African cultural, political, and social background recognizing that Africans came to the New World with certain coherent perspectives and beliefs about the universe and their place in it" (4). Furthermore, he argues that notwithstanding the *Maafa*, the Yoruba nation emerged as a dominant force in conjunction with the Bantu influence.[7] Despite the distinction and uniqueness of individual traditions, originating in the respective source cultures, Africans have sustained both awareness and appreciation by practicing these spiritual ideas although thwarted by attacks and negative judgments relative to being African heathens, devil worshippers, and conjurers. To illustrate further, having been baptized and confirmed as a Catholic, I am a fully initiated priest of Obatala in the Lukumi Yoruba spiritual tradition and a Mama Nganga in the Kongo-derived tradition of Regla Congas or Palo Monte.[8] Although, I have a blood lineage connecting me to the Ba Kongo, I function ritually in both systems.

I am not unique in my practice of the two systems. Having arrived from Africa unwillingly from a variety of cultures to the western hemisphere, African people have planted many different seeds to produce a variety of collective identities. My understanding of how these mutually inclusive identities cooperated and forged is situated beyond ideas of creolization as I locate Africans and their descendants at the centers of their own historical narratives. I agree with James H. Sweet who argues:

The African impact in the diaspora went far beyond culturally diluted "survivals"; Africa arrived in the various destinations of the colonial world in all of its social and cultural richness, informing the institutions that Africans created and providing them with a prism through which to interpret and understand their condition as slaves [*sic*] and as freed peoples. (2)

Resisting attempts to dispossess them of their spiritual and cultural identities and traditional ways of life, notwithstanding their removal from the geopolitical homelands on the continent of Africa, African people continued to attach importance to communal values, family, and land, members of fictive kin, ancestors, and neighborhood as the foundation for community.

This interconnectedness of community depended upon the quality of human relationships in association with shared knowledge located within the traditional community identity and structures.[9] For instance, the African communal psyche is demonstrated by intersubjectivity, mutuality, and interdependence illustrated by the core values expressed in the Bantu expression *umuntu umuntu nagabuntu*, which translates as "a person is a person because of people." This corporate identity accompanied them to the Americas. Collectively uprooted and removed, this living culture maintained its integrity by forging new alliances consistent with these worldviews. Ras M. Brown suggests that these alliances were "ultimately expressed in the idioms of West-Central Kongo Culture (5).

Furnishing people with a design for living and a sense of group identity, worldviews offer shared meaning and collective consciousness, self-authentication, and give a context and perspective for living. The goal of enslavement was to divorce people from themselves, make them outcasts to themselves, annihilate their ancestors, and remove them from the circle of perpetuity. The pervading idea is that displaced from their homelands and ancestral beliefs, customs and ritual enactment of those belief systems would eventually die. I propose that displaced Africans maintained their existing core values to ensure their psychic and spiritual integrity and created a nation out of many people.

My position is suggested by what Sweet calls the revisionist school of diaspora scholars who supplant the notion of the "Atlantic World" and accompanying conversations of creolization (8). Additionally, like Gomez, I reposition Africa and her descendants at the center and look at specificities of homogeneous concepts, not survivals. The creolist argument that Sidney W. Mintz and Richard Price premised on the idea of fixed traditions and the implausibility of direct transmission due to the heterogeneity of Atlantic African cultures and the lack of prior contact, removes Africans from the center and places them on the margins of reality (8).

To argue that a homogenous European culture served as the foundational core of African culture removes the African ontological impulse to re-create and birth culture from African people and empowers their captors to be the parents of an established spiritual lineage. I assert while not homogenous, the core ideas and spiritual manifestation resemble each other with enough shared features to rule out European parentage. The creolists' stance suggests insubstantiality in African core beliefs that would allow superimposed religious principles to supplant their spiritual centers. Their argument removes the ontological agency necessary for self-regeneration.

By standing their spiritual ground, Africans maintained and created an enduring identity instead of succumbing to a perishing personhood under the dehumanizing system of chattel enslavement. Additionally, the assumption that the essence of African American culture and identity dances along the fault lines of American racial history in black/white terms is a deeply ingrained yet limited view of the African's American experience. In order to emphasize the uniquely "American" experience of African people, the African cultural background has been historically constructed as either empty of meaning or irreparably severed during the Middle Passage, ostensibly ushering in the creation of an identity fundamentally distinct and new, albeit with feeble traces of cultural memory conceptualized as retentions, syncretism, hybridity, creolization, and the like. In these normative readings of African American culture, I contend that the full past and present significance of Africa is suppressed and rendered anomalous.

Contemporary scholars such as Sheila Walker and Teresa N. Washington have challenged these limited models of interpretation and have begun the intricate process of formulating alternative ways to view the presence and power of the cultural homogeneity of a composite African worldview on the American landscape, taking into account the modifications and elaborations occurring over time and space. While Washington invokes the presence of the Yoruba concept of the Ajé, Walker introduces the concept of "Afrogenic" to circumnavigate the consensus paradigm as a means to allow African understandings to play a central, not a peripheral, role as the proper framework of analysis for understanding African diasporic experiences.[10] Walker asserts:

> Afrogenic simply means growing out of the histories, ways of being and knowing, and interpretations and interpretive styles of African and African Diasporic peoples. It refers to these communities' experiences, priorities, and styles, and their articulations of them while

acknowledging that most human behavior is not intellectually articulated by the actors who perform it and that plural interpretations of
similar behaviors are obviously possible.(8)

In the case of Central Africans, core beliefs and practices include a religious cosmology based on the distinction between the world of the living
and the world of the spirits with particular emphasis on the importance of
ancestral spirits.[11] Additionally, beliefs, which John Blassingame pejora-
tively refers to as superstitions, allowed the enslaved African to construct
"a psychological defense against total dependence on and submission to
their masters" (Blassingame 45).

Religion is a key constituent reinforcing these spiritual networks of relationships through its dynamic corporate structures and communal rituals
and sacrifices. My idea of religion is consistent with Margaret Washington
Creel's notion of religion as the category of behavior and experiences providing belief systems, sacred symbols, and images of cosmic order and logic
framing human existence and processes (*A Peculiar People* 59). Employing
the terms *spirituality*, *spiritual impulses*, and *spiritual traditions* coterminously with religion, I account for the remembrance of one's ancestors
and God, which have as their sacred agency practices and epistemological
considerations anterior to African people's western hemispheric realities.

Creel notes that this idea of sacred extends to an explanation of behavior, the nature of human relationships and communality. In speaking of the
Central African influence on corporate behavior and collective necessity of
inhabitants of the low country or Gullah region, she writes:

> Traditional African spiritualism was an individual as well as col-
> lective experience. It encompassed the total well-being of the com-
> munity, but each person had a role in society, guided by spiritual
> forces. . . . The sacred was not set apart from the temporal, indi-
> vidual, communal, material, or even political concerns, and religion
> assumed a meaning outside of the "holy" building, a "sacred" day of
> the week, or a set of dogmas and creeds to be accepted at face value.
> (*A Peculiar People* 59)

Extending Creel's findings beyond the unique world of the Gullah communities, it is not conceptual within an African ontological frame to live
separate from the sacred world.

African culture demonstrates that it is meaningless to talk about art di-
vorced from spiritual intent since it points to a meaning beyond the imme-

diate situation of culture. Toni Morrison's novels speak to common cultural and spiritual concerns as she constructs imaginative scaffolding of symbols and codes consistent with African values. Like all artists, Morrison taps into this intuition using symbols to point beyond her literary excursions to a wider reality. My reading alongside ethnographic texts provides the necessary cultural frame to understand her novels' deeply embedded spiritual ideas.

Troublin' the Waters: Critical Revisions and Theoretical Necessities

My exposition of African spiritual traditions in the novels of Toni Morrison represents an endeavor to revise theory and re-align the trajectory of criticism for reading African American women's literature. Guiding my approach—which I call "tracing memory"—is a consideration of African spiritual ideas that engender community cohesion and collective remembering. By collective remembering, I mean the relocation and reclamation of the conscious spiritual, and historical, and cultural knowledge common to African Americans informed by African spiritual ideas. This shared knowledge transmitted intergenerationally through the use of traditional oral forms reiterates identity and engenders the cultural integrity of the group. Necessary to the revitalization of literary criticism, my endeavor in this study, is to provide a matrix to read African American women's literature in novel ways.

Morrison's corpus of work presents African spirituality with its accompanying ideas of deities, emphasis on nature, representations of ancestor communication, and the importance of community responsibility—core elements of spirituality and the backbone of African culture. Given the historical experience of African people in this country, a significant way to live in a world of change is to hold onto something that is a constant. Spirituality provides that constant and is an active principle that influences all aspects of daily life. African American literature testifies to belief in the faithfulness of the spirit. I attempt to traverse new intellectual terrain and make connections that rely on African spiritual traditions as the foundation for critical endeavors relative to African American literature. Moreover, advancing African-centered ideas beyond the frame of structuralism, poststructuralism, and postmodernism, which have preoccupied the interpretation of African American literature, I seek to elevate African intellectual thought that does not originate nor serve as a point of departure from a European-constructed critical vantage point.

In addition to ferreting out the remembered idea of African deities and sacred phenomena, I also explore ritual as the primary structure of plot stressing the communal and performative nature as well as the spiritual exclusivity of the belief systems highlighted in novelistic figurations. In an interview with Thomas LeClair titled, "The Language Must Not Sweat: A Conversation with Toni Morrison," Morrison reminds us that these rituals are grounded in the African traditions and have a level of cultural specificity. Ralph Ellison records in *Shadow and Act* that myth and ritual are used in literature "to give form and significance to the material" as they are true portraits of how people function in everyday life (174). He continues this analysis noting that the "rituals become social forms, and it is one of the functions of the artist to recognize them and raise them to the level of art" (174). This explanation not only accounts for myth as a basis for engaging life, but also as a means to remove the yoke of cultural estrangement and negation. Albert Murray echoes the importance of these restorative and subversive elements as a means of psychic survival. He writes:

> What must be remembered is that people live in terms of images, which represent the fundamental conceptions embodied in their rituals and myths. In the absence of adequate images they live in terms of such compelling images (and hence rituals and myths) as are abroad at that time. (*Hero and the Blues* 13)

Far from being easy reads, Toni Morrison's novels are not accessible to all readers; only to the initiated. By initiated, I am referring to those readers who are willing to acknowledge the cultural and spiritual ideas originated by African people. In most spiritual and religious practices, certain rituals are restricted to priests or other adepts who have mastered the foundational knowledge and spiritual insight to comprehend the significance of the intended ceremonial activity. In Morrison's novels, concepts of time and space, alongside their association with the natural world and notions of ancestral remembrance, are prominent cultural features that for some readers may seem eccentric and out of the main of rationality. Morrison, however, is quick to point out their location in contemporary African American life.

In an essay titled, "The Site of Memory," Morrison defends the cultural legitimacy of this stance. She states: "The work that I do frequently falls in the minds of most people, into that realm of fiction called the fantastic or mythic, or magical, or unbelievable. I'm not comfortable with these labels" (302). Morrison sees these events as everyday happenings and over time has "taught readers to rediscover, reassess, and reclaim the human values signified by folk community in Black fiction" ("Site of Memory" 129). This encoding of messages to the village is the primary purpose for her writing. What is in need of rediscovery is the cultural locations that characterize and situate her novels—where gossip is "truth," numbers are played according to dreams, play names are given to children in order to protect them, illness is viewed as a bad spirit to be rebuked, pain may be accompanied by laughter, language is for conjuring, and where women would never fathom buying a plant when all they have to do is get a cutting before leaving a friend's house in order to propagate life and the circle of community.

In an essay titled "Beyond Realism," Keith Byerman says these African penchants position Morrison's writing "beyond realism," in some fantasy-land, or netherworld, as witnessed by the reporting of "extreme events" (100). Byerman's reductive comments are further illustrated in his observations of Morrison's characters as being in "pursuit of some black folk value, such as true community, true family name, or authentic black history" (100). Comfortable in dismissing the agency of cultural items such as the quest for family, identity, irretrievable names, and history in the lives of African people in America, his critical efforts work against the significance of their retrieval and reclamation. For Byerman, this quest is realized only after the "loosening of the control of logocentrism so as to achieve a black selfhood that negates that control" (100). In this seemingly benign and objective literary statement, Byerman points out the Eurocentric intent of his essay, that is, to move Morrison and, by association, African people, out of the arena of logicality by claiming that the content of her work is shaped by emotionalism. The assumption in his remarks is that inclusions of culturally specific items that do not necessarily appear as motifs in the European American literary canon are not logical, are not real, and are out of control.

Cultural critic Marimba Ani suggests that rationality is the basis for European cognitive behavior, which is based on lineality. In that model, the knower of objectified facts is able to achieve the ultimate in European culture. It follows, according to Ani, that the denial of spiritual reality is the premise for the devaluation of the African self and beliefs, which in turn, leads to exploitation and enslavement (xxix). For Ani and other African-centered critics, African cosmologies and accompanying axiological ideas that do not exist as values for Europeans are rendered ineffective in the minds of critics. Carlyle Stewart discusses the threat to white (cultural) supremacy arguing that "Black spirituality supplants the untruth embodied in those systems of devaluation that preclude black [*sic*] ascendancy and empowerment" (60).

Most critics suggest that ideas of the conjurer in literature belong solely to the domain of folklore and therefore are not credible realities. The underlying idea of European solipsistic thinking reinforces the hegemonic notion that reality is solely a construction of European values and ideas and accordingly relegates spiritual ideas of others to a liminal realm. Morrison's narratives re-situate these ideas beyond the limits of ordinary experiences, into the cosmic realm where many of the Africanisms were codified in the folkways, especially the expression of spirituality. Perhaps Morrison's own words express it best when she says, "When I wrote I wanted not to have to explain. Somehow, when black writers wrote for themselves I understood it better . . . when the locality is clear, fully realized, then it becomes universal" (Ruas 96). Pointing out this culturally proactive stance that governs her artistry, she states:

> We are the subjects of our own narrative, witnesses to and participants in our own experience, and, in no way coincidentally, in the experiences of those with whom we have come in contact. . . . And to read imaginative literature by and about us is to choose to examine centers of self and to have the opportunity to compare these centers with the "raceless" one with which we are, all of us most familiar. ("Unspeakable Things" 9)

Toni Morrison's careful placement of spiritually significant emblems is suggested by W. Lawrence Hogue who explains the idea of literature being a textual system that "transposes one or more systems of signs into another" (330). Like Hogue, I challenge universalism and read Morrison's texts within a cultural or ideological context. He argues that "literature is a social institution which reproduces certain codified values, conventions, or worldviews" (338).

Additionally, Morrison describes the exclusive audience for whom she writes and to whom her language provides the requisite access codes, stating that "there is a level of appreciation that might be available only to people who understand the context of that language" (LeClair 373–74). Dismissing universalism as a term to apply to what she does, noting the cultural impulse, she says, "Behind this question is the suggestion that to write for black people is somehow to diminish the writing. From my perspective, there are only black people. When I say, 'people,' that's what I mean" (LeClair 374). She sees universality as a burden for the black writer, meaning they are writing for someone outside of themselves. Just as she is clear that when she writes, she deliberately invokes Nommo ("Unspeakable Things" 229). A Bantu concept, Nommo refers to the power of the spoken word with all its vital essence to bring things into existence, accompanied with the innervating force of *ntu*, which refers to being (Jahn 101).

Not limiting her cultural determination and ideas of cultural specificity to her own production, Morrison extends this inclination to critical endeavors. In an interview with Nellie McKay, she bemoans their failure to match their critical impulses with her literary figurations. Morrison laments:

> Critics of my work have often left something to be desired, in my mind, because they don't always evolve out of the culture, the world, the given quality out of which I write. Other kinds of structures are imposed on my works, and therefore they are either praised or dismissed on the basis of something that I have no interest in whatever, which is writing a novel according to some structure that comes out of a different culture. (425–26)

For example, modern literature exemplifies African people's deep reverence for the power of nature. Jean Toomer's novel *Cane* stands as a classic ecological text, with its imagistic musings on pine needles, flowers, sugarcane, and golden sunsets representing the beauty of nature and its mythic potential to save African people from the traumatic terrain of American racial landscapes. He writes, "The sun is hammered to a band of gold. Pine needles, like mazda, are brilliantly aglow. . . . Smoke curls up. Marvelous web spun by the spider sawdust pile" (*Cane* 10). Additionally, Toomer takes into account the connection between Africa and the South. He writes, "She does not sing, her body is a song. She is in the forest, dancing. Torches flare . . . juju men, gree gree, witch doctors . . . torches go out. . . . The Dixie Pike has grown from a goat path in Africa" (10). In this significant literary passage, Toomer links Africa with America intimating that Africa has extended to America through the mediating forces of African people and the culture that they transported with them.

However, contemporary critical interpretations fall short of acknowledging Africa as the foundation for both identity and culture of African people. To illustrate further, Philip Page, a critic who has written numerous critical essays on Morrison's work, overlooks this connection in his book of critical essays, *Reclaiming Community in Contemporary African American Fiction.* He attributes the South as "the site of the birth of African American culture, the locale of one's ancestors, and therefore the source of one's collective and individual identity" (7). This statement in the introduction to his book, in a chapter ironically titled "At the Crossroads" (the vertical and horizontal intersection, where a person's contact with the divine takes place), diminishes the possibility of the interspatial self and the collective self. Implicit in his words is a dissection of cosmic continuity, which defines African identity. His comment dismembers time, causes a cultural truncation, and severs the possibility of African deep thought with regard to his literary analysis.

As a critic he is not alone; many have neither considered the idea of African temporality, nor African identity. Because of Christian imposition and its superimposed worldview that has asphyxiated African notions of belief systems, what has been presented in literary analyses are fragments of spiritual systems, usually reduced to the realm of superstition and/or folklore.[12] Morrison argues that these conflicts are spiritual at the core. Bemoaning these critical practices, Morrison says she distrusts the "capacity of the literature and the sociology of other people" to reveal the truth of her own "cultural sources" ("Memory, Creation, and Writing" 386).

African American critics, also, are not exempt from missing the literary mark. Morrison notes that she learns most from the texts after the critic enters it and comments on the African culture without resistance. Conversely, she states: "I learn nothing from those who resist it, except of course, the sometimes fascinating display of their struggle" ("Unspeakable Things" 229). Morrison hopes that critics who do embark upon the journey would respect the "already legitimatized" cultural "sources and predecessors" (229–30). For example, when referring to folklore as a foundational idea informing the African American literary tradition, Houston Baker asserts that one needs to gain more knowledge of folklore to better understand the literature (*Long Black Song* 41). However, twenty years later in *Workings of the Spirit*, Baker shifts his thesis to include a consideration of African sacro-religious tradition informing the soul of the literature. He advances the notion of spirit work as generic, tropological, and analytical. That is, *soul searching* becomes a heuristic approach to understand African American literature's accretive textures and highly nuanced meaning. In an attempt to locate folkloric and mythic elements in Toni Morrison's novels and to establish the relationship of these two components as extensions of African American antecedents and African world thought, one must look beyond the geophilosophical and geophysical boundaries of Western culture. For when the connections are extended beyond their Western frontiers and the sources of these African components are discussed, one can render a more complete portrait of African spiritual archetypes and images in not only Morrison's works, but in the corpus of African American literature as well.

To achieve this clarity, there must be a departure from the realm of the universal and a reorientation to the particular. To illustrate, most myth critics usually skirt the issue of African cultural heritage and instead emphasize mythic foundations informed by a European worldview. They usually refer to Jungian classifications suggested by a European perspective and bolstered by Greek and Judeo-Christian sensibilities. An example of this culturally contextualized perspective guised as a universal truth can be found in Northrop Frye's *Anatomy of Criticism*. Based on Jungian principles, his book is considered to be a stellar reference point for myth critics. In speaking on the theory of archetypal meaning, demonic images in particular, Frye says, "In religion the spiritual world is a reality distant from the physical world" (38). This statement, accepted a priori, guides the direction of criticism of many myth critics who proceed from this "truth" and posit archetypal interpretations of literature based on these kinds of faulty universal suppositions. In most African traditional religions, the delineation between the spiritual and material world is not arranged in such a truncated and mutually exclusive framework.

Another illustration of Euro-solipsistic myth criticism in distinctions made by Jung concerning the "primitive" and "civilized" orientation is evidenced in the following statement:

> Primitive mentality differs from civilized chiefly in that the conscious mind is far less developed in extent and intensity. Functions such as thinking, willing etc. are not yet differentiated. . . . [The primitive] is incapable of any conscious effort of will . . . owing to the chronic twilight state of his conscious, it is often next to impossible to find out whether he merely dreamed something or whether he really experienced it. (35)[13]

In *Myth, Literature and the African World*, Wole Soyinka notes this differentiation in the nature of archetype between the primitive and civilized mind misrepresents the universality of a collective consciousness, the premise of Jung's argument (35). Given the kind of hierarchical distinction suggested by Jung's statement, I would argue the need of reference points for African-based literature to be drawn from the culture. The African centered focus that I am suggesting does not preclude the inclusion of mythic ideas and ideas espoused by thinkers such as Jung or Frye, but instead situates these perspectives within the cultural frame of the African worldview wherever appropriate and applicable.

This political critical stance works in consonance with Morrison's literary polemics. For Morrison, there is no contradiction in the work's being political and artistic. To her, art is political. What makes it political is her obstinacy in documenting the ethos of her own culture. As Fanon would argue, Morrison's novels represent "a literature of combat" as she molds "the national consciousness, giving it form and contours, and flinging open before it new and boundless horizons" (240). In an interview with Claudia Tate in *Black Women Writers at Work*, Morrison expresses this cultural vision, stating, "When I view the world, perceive it and write about it, it's the world of black people" (118). She continues her exploration of cultural specificity in her interview with the late literary critic, Nellie McKay:

> Because my books come out of those things and represent how they function in the black cosmology . . . I am yearning for someone to see such things—to see what the structures are, what the moorings are, where the anchors are that support my writings. We have no systematic mode of criticism that has yet evolved from us, but it will. (426)

This clarion call for criticism from an African diasporic perspective is reiterated in "Negotiations of Power: White Critics, Black Texts, and the Self-Referential Impulse," where Michael Awkward details the consequences of not having African American constructed criticism. He also notes the critical tendencies of "white-authored analyses" to be inconsistent with the "interest of the discourse" (583). In order to ensure greater cultural equity in the interpretation of African American literature, Awkward asserts that "it is the responsibility of Afro-Americanist scholars to examine and expose those consequences" (583). Moreover, he remarks:

> Even in self-reflective white critical acts, racial privilege may create interpretative obstacles or, more importantly, points of resistance that color, in racially motivated ways—perhaps even in hegemony-maintaining ways—the effects of an exploitation of blackness. In other words, white reading can mean the adoption of a posture antithetical to Afro-American interests. (583)

In the interest of African American representation, my goal in this book is to define and interpret a few underlying spiritual realities that transcend the written word and provide a context for the deeper meaning beyond literary events in the novels of Nobel laureate, Toni Morrison. Consequently, my theoretical endeavor is born from the lack of authoritative exegesis concerning the spiritual nature of African American literature in critical circles. Having failed to establish that spiritual expression is an essential principle in the lives of African people, critical models inbred from linear worldviews are inadequate tools to examine African American literature. As an African and a critic, I am exercising my prerogative to construe and negotiate what signs are to be seen as spiritually symbolic within an African frame.

I am not alone. Simon Bockie decries the Western world's insistence on explaining African existence. He asserts, "The time has come for Africans themselves to set forth their values and identities as only they are capable of doing" (ix). Similarly, in *Myth, Literature and the African World*, Wole Soyinka chides African people for accepting ideas originating from cultural spaces outside of themselves. Providing the rubric for cultural interpretation, Soyinka asserts that African people should check to see if they can elicit those ideas from their own cultural frame (xii). Morrison echoes Soyinka's ideas, reclaiming African culture's cogency. She states in an interview with Christina Davis: "There's a great deal of obfuscation and distortion and erasure, so that the presence and the heartbeat of black people has been systematically annihilated in many, many ways and the job of recovery is ours" (142).

These determined critical trajectories juxtapose critic Sara Blackburn's limited idea of the magnitude of African thought. She writes, "Morrison is far too talented to remain only a marvelous recorder of the black side of provincial American life" (3). Her remarks seem to indicate that even when gender corresponds, the default perspective for critics continues to be issues of race informed by hegemony. In an essay titled "Home" Morrison remarks, "I have never lived, nor has any of us, in a world in which race did not matter. Such a world, one free of racial hierarchy, is usually imagined or described as dreamscape—Edenesque, utopian, so remote are the possibilities of its achievement" (3). Because Morrison's adventure in novel-writing has been "explorations of seemingly impenetrable, race-inflected, race-clotted topics" ("Home" 9), to not take into account race and its accompanying signs and sentiments would be intellectually irrational and academically dishonest. I am also unsympathetic to African cultural critics and others who feel that any allegiance to African people serves to thwart the possibilities of an objective critical stance, or a common humanity, thereby damaging a presumed social progress amongst the races.

This intellectual supervision and suppression of memories guised as the need to counter essentialisms, seeks to determine what can and should count as valid. Additionally, these stances continue to justify the intervention of those outside the circle of cultural production to determine and control critical thought. In short, they become recodified judging "eyes" simultaneously gazing and denying.

In addition to considerations of race, I submit that by not taking into account the role of beliefs and spirituality as legitimate ways for groups of people to sculpt identity, critics bent on renouncing the grand narratives of the past have unwittingly displaced Africans further in their intractable pursuit to maintain their dispassionate un-raced criticism, which eschews the narrative of blackness. In my analyses, I am not willing to disengage or compromise the integrity of cultural matrices on which traditional ideas are formulated in order to be in accordance with current theoretical trends. Coupled with her polemic sensibilities, Toni Morrison is clearly a "representative of the tribe" who does not see any incongruence with an artist having a "tribal or racial sensibility and an individual expression of it" ("Rootedness" 339); I extend that perception to criticism of her work.

Writers create in this cultural stance, to both preserve culture and protect the group from cultural annihilation. This worldview provides the group shared meaning and collective consciousness and gives the context and perspectives for living, or as she remarks, "Black people take their culture wherever they go" (*Black Women Writers at Work* 119). In her literary, as well as critical works, Morrison has employed a cultural-nationalist agenda consistent with principles illustrated by Ngugi Wa Thiongo, expressed in *Writers in Politics*. He asserts, a nation's literature reflects the summative products of the individuals as well as the collective, and represents the "people's collective reality, collective experience," and "embodies that community's way of looking at the world and its place in the making of that world" (Wa Thiongo 7). Morrison contends:

> In the Third World cosmology as I perceive it, reality is not already constituted by my literary predecessors in Western culture. If my work is to confront a reality unlike that received reality of the West, it must centralize and animate information discredited by the West—discredited not because it is not true or useful or even of some racial value, but because it is information held by discredited people, information dismissed as "lore" as gossip, or "magic" or "sentiment." ("Memory, Creation, and Writing" 388)

The present study is simultaneously theoretical and historical, attempting to explain the literary and the African spiritual bases for characters, plot, symbol, and theme. Undergirding my theoretical approach is the notion that African American literature—like dance, music, and other cultural forms—houses the beliefs and values and challenges the reader to interrogate his or her attitude about the nature of God, existence, the idea of the person, the role of community, and the transformative power of ritual. As Morrison remarks in "A Slow Walk of Trees," African people are "suffering from racial vertigo that can be cured by taking what one needs from one's ancestors" (152). Cosmological knowledge is augmented through spiritual insight and communication with the ancestral words (language) by which people construct identity and accompanying life philosophies mediating the distance between African belief systems and western hemispheric realities of Africans in America. A prominent way the Òrìsà were remembered and celebrated in America has been through folkloric frames and subsequently their inscription in literature.

The first critic to recognize the African origin of the trickster was Julien Hall. In an 1897 essay titled "Negro Conjuring and Tricking," appearing in *The Journal of American Folklore*, Hall notes the tenacity of the trickster idea in the cultural inventory of the enslaved African. He says these beliefs were brought here from Africa by the first comers and continue in full force to this day notwithstanding the Negro is a free man and living amongst the white people of the United States of America" (241). As a modern literary study of the trickster, Henry Louis Gates's *The Signifying Monkey* is an important text, wherein he establishes a theory of African American literary criticism based on the hermeneutical possibilities offered by the Yoruba Òrìsà, Eshu. Gates asserts to the literary world that Eshu or Elegba allows for a multiplicity of meanings out of which we find significance; he is the master interpreter. It is appropriate that Eshu should represent the first named incorporation of Yoruba belief into literary analysis, since all communication with the Òrìsà must first pass through the master of divine speech.

However, critics, including Gates, have not examined the trickster's spiritual dimensions; their literary essays have confined him to the cultural boundaries of North America. For instance, H. Nigel Thomas argues that the trickster is necessary for African American survival, but does not discuss his ancestry or draw parallels to Eshu, the Yoruba deity of randomness and uncertainty. In *Long Black Song*, critic Houston Baker Jr. fails to discuss the origins of the trickster; instead he advances that the trickster tales begin to appear after the Civil War. Furthermore, when John Roberts does acknowledge an African provenance for the trickster in *From Trickster to Badman*, he is reluctant to explore the ideas with adequate depth. Moving Elegba from Gates's rhetorical consideration of him, a fundamental matter that I address is the uncovering of and recognition of other Òrìsà to whom Eshu or Elegba communicates on behalf of his devotees. My close readings of Morrison's novels extend Gates's theoretical initiative that is locating other Òrìsà who rely on Elegba's assistance to facilitate their devotee's spiritual balance.

The Journey

The chapters contained in part 1 introduce the concept of nature, the healer, and other spiritual manifestations mediated through the ritual activities. Essays in this section are titled "I's Got the Blues: Malochia, Magic, and the Descent into Madness in *The Bluest Eye*" and "Always: The Living Ancestor and the Testimony of Will in *Sula*." In my discussion of *The Bluest Eye*, I consider the importance of the community in ensuring the wellness of its individual members. Additionally, I discuss spiritual ideas such as malochia or the "evil eye" and the role of ritual leaders in mediating life's spiritual dilemmas. My discussion of the Òrìsà, Oya, the concept of Egungun, and the living ancestor are the foci for Morrison's second novel, *Sula*.

Part 2, Psychic Domains and Spiritual Locations, focuses on the connection between identity and the concept of home. I begin with a chapter titled "I've Got a Home in Dat Rock: Ritual and the Construction of Family History in *Song of Solomon*," where I examine the importance of family history in aligning oneself and achieving his or her spiritual destiny. At the heart of my interpretation of *Song of Solomon* is an examination of Morrison's epic reconstruction and invocation of the Kongo ritual specialist, the Nganga, in the character Pilate Dead. Additionally, I examine Elegba, the divine spokesperson of the Òrìsà relative to Milkman's search for familial identity. In "Dancing with Trees and Dreaming of Yellow Dresses: The Dilemma of Jadine in *Tar Baby*," I investigate the relationship of human beings to nature, the divine mothers represented by the Ajé, and the trope of spiritual transformation with an examination of Shango, the Òrìsà of redistributive justice, and the Òrìsà of beauty and regeneration, Oshun. In "In(her)iting the Divine: (Consola)tions, Sacred (Convent)ions, and Mediations of the Spiritual In-between in *Paradise*," I discuss the nature of spiritual balance by examining the Yoruba deities Ibeji—the primordial twins, representative of balance and spiritual abundance. Additionally, I examine the ways in which Morrison structures the narrative according to the spiritual, aesthetic, and social principles of Yoruba belief and Dogon sensibilities in her exploration of spiritual dualities.

Part 3, titled "Remembrance Has Not Left Us: What the Record Shows," addresses historical records and the need to trace and record memories to ensure a viable future. The first two chapters are "Living with the Dead: Memory and Ancestral Presence in *Beloved*" and "Tracing Wild's Child Joe and Tracking the Hunter: An Examination of the Òrìsà Ochossi in *Jazz*." In these essays I explore Morrison's dogged insistence in countering America's recurring bouts with memory loss regarding the spiritual, political, and cultural realities of Africans in America. Morrison's use of memory, a phenomenon of primary importance in oral culture, helps to relocate ancestral images and recollect African spiritual ideas. As Morrison depicts the characters in the novel, a distinct picture of their allegiance to African spiritual beliefs emerges reinforcing key cultural values and the necessity of maintaining harmony. In my examination of *Beloved*, I begin with an analysis of memory as the major conceit and then move to an examination of the Yoruba Òrìsà Oya and Aganju, as I explore the ways in which characters come to terms with remembering, healing, and recovering spiritual balance. In *Jazz*, Morrison warns about stepping out of the tradition represented by Southern values represented by nature. I examine these ecocritical and historical ideas with a focus on the Yoruba Òrìsà Ochossi, the archetypal Òrìsà of the hunt, and his stalking accuracy illustrated by the character Joe Trace described as the best "hunter in Vesper County" as he searches for reconnections with his mother, nature, and family—a pursuit that defines the major breaches that have had a deleterious effect on African people in America. I conclude with a chapter titled "If I'd a Knowed More, I Would a Loved More: *Love* and Spiritual Authorship," a coda using *Love*, Morrison's eighth novel, to catalogue the spiritual ideas invoked in her previous novels.

I

⁜

Ancestral Echoes Positing a Spiritual Frame

I's Got the Blues

Malochia, Magic, and the Descent into Madness
in *The Bluest Eye*

What shall I tell my dear one, fruit of my womb, of how beautiful they are when everywhere they turn they are faced with
abhorrence of everything that is black?

—Margaret Burroughs, "What Shall I Tell My Children
Who Are Black?"

At the conclusion of Toni Morrison's first novel, *The Bluest Eye* (1970), the
protagonist, Pecola Breedlove, has descended into a world of madness.[1] In
this realm, her ruptured personality has not divided into the Duboisian notion of "warring souls" but into an amicable split—a way to exist in a land
where the "soil is bad for certain kinds of flowers" (*Bluest Eye* 206). Key to
understanding Pecola's dilemma is a consideration of the debilitating effect
of white supremacy and the negative aesthetic cast by its malevolent eye.
Before her descent into madness, Pecola's de-centering primarily relates to
the transference of the aesthetic negation of blackness from her mother,
her other mothers, her age-mates, the community at-large, and the hostile
environment of a racialized America. Pecola Breedlove is shunned by her
community and is not given the protection of an individual consistent with
African cultural values. Since a person is not only an individual but also an
integral member of a community, the notion of this young girl not being
protected transgresses African morality and ethics. Claudia, a friend of
Pecola's and witness to her destruction, narrates alternate stories. She and
her sister Frieda are saved a similar fate by a strong and supportive family
unit.

Culturally and spiritually there is no space for Pecola to exist alone, outside the circle of community support. In speaking of normative behavior
of the Ba Kongo, a Bantu people occupying most of what is known today
as the Democratic Republic of Congo and Angola, Simon Bockie describes

the first level of many initiations that will occur in a child's lifetime to bind her or him as an individual to the circle of community. He notes that an individual's existence begins on the day of birth and moves from being the property of the parents to being a part of the community through a series of initiations into his or her new world. After being born, the child is taken by the Nganga or the ceremonial priest who introduces the child to the community. The process of the child's development is to be guided by every member of the community who helps to prepare the child for all the collective expectation the community has for them (Bockie 32).

In traditional life, the individual does not and cannot exist alone. He or she must exist corporately, constructing one's existence through connections with other people, including one's contemporaries and those of past generations. Individuals are part of the whole. John S. Mbiti explains that physical birth is not enough; the child must go through the rites of incorporation to become fully integrated into the entire society (108). Among the Yoruba, a similar formal introduction to the community occurs at the naming ceremony where blood sacrifices are offered to the ancestors, a divinatory reading for the baby is performed, and the baby—along with her or his name—is presented, completing the individual's entrance as a member of the community.

An African view of an individual demands a balance between the collective identity as a member of society and the personal identity as a unique individual. In general, African philosophy tends to define persons in terms of the social groups to which they belong. A person is thought of first as a constituent of a particular community, for it is the community that defines who he is and what he can become (Ray 132). In Pecola's case, it is not only the external white community of Lorain, Ohio, America, that has determined who she is and who she could possibly be, but also the African community that has limited her as well. Having internalized the aesthetic view of white people themselves, the community has also prescribed the contours of existence for Pecola.

Consequently, Pecola's "step over into madness" (*Bluest Eye* 206) represents a way for her to be whole and allows her an alternate way of traversing reality. Pecola still exists, but in a world more compatible with the internalized messages forming her consciousness since her birth. Additionally, this split in Pecola's personality coheres to Bantu cosmological concepts, which do not accommodate the notion of individuated things existing by themselves. Isolated from other witnesses, Pecola's need for psychic alliance is logical. Extending the discussion of what constitutes a person, Benjamin

C. Ray notes, "The African concept of the person never approximates the Western notion of individualism—the idea that someone's identity exists as a private self essentially independent of family bonds and local roots" (*African Religions* 92). These aforementioned philosophical ideas highlight the value in maintaining socially harmonious relationships; that is, each person must relate to each element in the concentric circles of life. In this cyclically constructed novel, Morrison invites the reader to examine the ways in which the ring/*eye* of community, vital to a people's survival, has been replaced with the axiological imperative to possess whiteness. The desire for blue eyes is not only emblematic but also symptomatic of a de-centered worldview.

In this omnisciently narrated chapter, which begins with the last of the seven primer phrases, Morrison employs a double-voiced narrative to illustrate the two discrete halves that now make up Pecola's fragmented mind. Reflecting upon the value as well as the validity of her eyes, one of the voices queries, "Are they really nice?" The other voice responds, "Yes. Very nice" (194). It is only the imagined self, created in the darkroom of abnegation, that allows Pecola to find both voice and vision. For Pecola, her "blue eyes" replace the center or nucleus of community. It is her eyes that nurture her and affirm her. What has happened? Morrison observes that silence is at the center of Pecola's "unbeing" (215); I add that Pecola's invisibility is at the core of her "unraveling."

However, Toni Morrison does not bait the reader into castigating Pecola for any perceived individual weakness, instead she holds both communities, those without and within, responsible for their complicit actions. They allowed Pecola to be vulnerable to their gazes. In the afterword to the 1994 Plume edition of the novel, attempting to expose the wrongdoers, Morrison raises the following questions: "Who told her? Who made her feel that it was better to be a freak than who she was? Who had looked at her and found her so wanting, so small a weight on the beauty scale?" (210). Morrison interrogates the most essential ideas of white supremacy: aesthetic and spiritual negation. Continuing, she remarks, "The novel pecks away at the gaze that condemned her . . . the damaging internalization of assumptions of immutable inferiority originating in an outside gaze" (210). Not only has this malignant viewing aesthetically displaced African people in North America, but also the internalization of the gaze has created new cosmologies—new ways to imagine self and to be in the world.

The concerted effort to negate the African self or personality has been well documented. The judging eyes, defining gazes, malevolent eyes, turned inward on Africans made them see themselves in the same manner as their captors and armed them with the same soul-extinguishing aspirations. Morrison raises the same question that Ayi Kwei Armah asks in his novel *Two Thousand Seasons*. What does it look like in the mind to have "our very colour turned into the predator's name for evil?" (39). In part, the answers are rooted in the historical practices reflected in the principal narrative structure of the novel, the primer excerpts. Framing the novel's omniscient narration, as well as providing the categorical ideas that deviate from the African constructed worldview, the words sting with a haunting familiarity of worlds never imagined or seen by little African boys and girls in North America. In her eulogistic poem "For My People," Margaret Alexander Walker elucidates the role that the American educational system plays in erasing the African personality. She writes, "For the boys and girls who went to school to learn the place where and the people who, in remembrance of the times when we discovered we were black and poor and nobody cared and nobody understood" (6–7). The primers used ostensibly to coax literacy from emerging readers were replete with images of white people, their world, their homes, their activities, and their values. In these images of the insular, prototypical nuclear family, African children saw no representations of themselves in the stories or in the situations highlighted in the books. By presenting this alternate and unattainable world of "whiteness" early in the introductory educational experience of African children, the students learned very early, as Walker asserts, that their world was marginal. And as a result, they as a people were either placed on the edge or not considered at all.

However, there is a different way to look at the concept of the edge and the demarcation of the seven central elements of the plot—the *house*, the *family*, the *cat*, the *mother*, the *father*, the *dog*, and the *friend*. In an African sense, these delineations cohere to the seven concentric circles constructing the Bantu cosmology. Fu-Kiau notes that in the center of the seven-ringed circle is the person (*muntu*), followed by the family (*buta*), motherhood (*moyo*), extended motherhood (*mwelo-nzo*), community (*kanda*), land (*nsi*), and the universe (*nza*) (*African Cosmology* 41). This matrix describes the cosmic order of life that all human beings must connect with in order to achieve balance. Moreover the demarcation of these seven components corresponds to the thematic ideas of the novel: self-awareness, self-knowledge, self-fulfillment, and self-love. Fu-Kiau explains the idea of walking inward, or self-knowledge:

The Bantu people, in their teaching, believe that the human being suffers mostly because of his lack of knowing how to walk towards this seventh direction, the innerwards direction. Their own words put it so perfectly well: *kani ka bwe, kana lu lumoso-ku lubakala-ku n'twala-ku nima-mu zulu evo mu nsi ukwenda, vutukisa va didi i yand* (No matter what you may walk leftwards, rightwards, forwards, backwards, upwards or downwards, you must come back to the core/center. The human being is nothing unless he discovers how to walk towards the seventh direction, the center [*didi*], the inner world, which represents the essence of his being) (*African Cosmology* 134–35).

Pecola's failure lies in her inability to meet her healthy "self." What she does meet is the societal constructed self, antithetical to her being. The lack of punctuation of any kind in the last repetition of the primer indicates the dissolve of the spiritual space in which to grow. Not having access to the spiritual power that resides at the interstices diminishes the possibilities of ritual contact with the realm where guardian spirits could assist her to be well. Additionally, the primer categories adversely and inversely define Pecola's reality—creating a world where black people are nothing and white people are everything.

Toni Morrison is quite aware that African people in North America reside in two separate antagonistic worlds, no matter the political rhetoric used to bolster theocratic and democratic vistas, like "one God," "one country," and "one people" with liberty and justice for all. Written in turbulent times when African people in America affirmed in strident voices, "Black is Beautiful," Morrison added her strident voice to the continuous narrative of what it means to be black in racist America. In *Visions of a Liberated Future*, Larry Neal describes this methodology. He states, "The main tenet of Black Power is the necessity for black people to define the world in their own terms. The black artist has made the same point in the context of aesthetics" (62). For Pecola, desperately trying to rid herself of the mantle of "ugliness" imposed upon her by society, possessing blue eyes is the result of having succumbed to the malochia or *evil eye* of white supremacy. With its fixed gaze towering over her omnisciently, at once defining and delineating the lives of those whom it captures in its sight, the eye hypnotizes all in its view, coaxing them from their own sense of center into the abyss of annihilation.

Using the idea of the eye as the central metaphor—the mirror reflecting a white supremacist aesthetic—Morrison challenges imposed definitions. With its ideas of dualities, spiritual sites and in-sights, Morrison's first novel illustrates the ways in which the power of images outside the cosmological frame of blackness disrupts and destroys the worldview of people, and the people as well. My reading of *The Bluest Eye* is not an attempt to further reprimand African people, but seeks to investigate the deep structure or core processes facilitating this type of psychic decline for the Pecolas of the world. These mental lapses are predictable, since "no sane society chooses to build its future on foreign cultures, values, or systems" (xi).[2]

In *The Bluest Eye*, Toni Morrison presents the cosmology of otherness alongside assemblages of African frames to highlight the process of psychic destruction and to point out the deleterious effect of not maintaining balance. Her literary construction of this balance suggests the idea that something must bridge the ruptures and close the interstitial gaps between the two polar realms of whiteness and blackness, ugliness and beauty. Alternatively, she illustrates that, notwithstanding similar social circumstances and even when faced with cultural aggression, characters attain stability; given similar social circumstances, balance is possible. Their accounts affirm the role of culture to protect against malochia and counter the negative effects of the malevolent eye.

Morrison suggests that one should fix a proactive gaze from one's own eye—whether the eye be worn around the neck as a talisman or wielded through deliberate and cultural practices. Terry Otten notes that in order for Morrison's protagonist to survive, she must "somehow violate the rule of the oppressive system, reject the values it venerates, and recover the human potential denied to blacks" (3). The twin narrative accompanying Pecola's tale of destruction is a story of Africans who have insisted on remaining whole by adhering to traditional African culture as the blueprint and primary source of information for a variety of political, gender, and social issues. Additionally, there are testimonies of African people who have found agency and refashioned their identity from a wellspring of cultural and spiritual items to help them navigate "the unheimlich terror of the space or race of the other"—those denied "the comfort of social belonging" (Bhabha 3).

Even though she has informed readers on the very first page what has happened, Morrison invites them to participate in the novel through a series of narrative flashbacks. Besides the use of doubling, the cyclical cosmogram provides the structure for the novel, two groups of four: the

Breedloves and the Macteers. Another grouping of fours consists of the three whores and Pecola. Using this number of cosmic completion, Morrison is able to move the microcosmic individual story of Pecola to the level of the macrocosm, leaving her reader with a sense of epic fulfillment and reconnection.

The Bluest Eye begins in autumn, the season of dissolution, with its images of "dead grass in the field" and actions such as gleaning in urban coal fields, juxtaposed with the cosmic event of the protagonist, Pecola Breedlove, getting her first menses. The reader is primed to traverse the cosmogram from maturity in a counterclockwise back/toward to the novel's prologue signifying the death of Pecola's baby. Understanding the worldview of a people is the basis for understanding their culture. And key to this consideration of time is the language employed to navigate their respective environments. For example, the prologue to the novel begins, "Quiet as kept, there were no marigolds in the fall of 1941." Fu-Kiau says that when African people speak in proverbs, a special and sacred language, they prevent the "leak of very fundamental principles of the society" and thwart outsiders from having access to its secrecies (93). There is a level of appreciation that might be available only to people who understand what the expression "quiet as kept" signifies within the context of African expressive culture (*Bluest Eye* 215).

Toni Morrison states that she chose the opening line for the novel with great care, preserving the speakerly quality of speech familiar to her. She expresses her choice of anecdotes to make the reader lean into the story. Morrison's word choice reflects "black women conversing with one another" (*Bluest Eye* 212). Additionally, the opening line signifies that African people still believe in signs and the principles of causality relative to the natural world. The epistemic idea that ethics and morality have a correlation with natural phenomena is conveyed by Claudia and Frieda's reading of the earth and paying attention to its rhythms, patterns, and secret language. The pair attributes the absence of marigolds to Pecola's incestuous impregnation. The significance of signs for African people from a historical perspective must be considered. Mary Frances Berry and John Blassingame note:

> One of the major functions of the signs was to enable the slave to deal with the ever present and always specter of death. Seeking control over a harsh world where masters and overseers were capricious and irrational, the slaves developed an unshakable belief in the infallibil-

ity of dreams and signs as predictors of future events on the plantations. (250)

Another cultural idea useful to interpret both the narrative and thematic structure of *The Bluest Eye* is the Yoruba idea of complementary
opposition. The Yoruba argue that anything that does not contain an element of opposition is incomplete, for God (*Olodumare*) is a combination
of opposites (*Black Gods* Mason and Edwards 3). Corresponding to this
spiritual rubric, the novel's dedication page reads, "To the two who gave
me life and the one who made me free." The Yoruba divide reality into two
parts: forces that build up and forces that tear down.

Morrison presents the following twin ideas to advance the idea of America's negation of the African aesthetic. Her use of doubles includes positive
and negative maternal roles; positive values and negative values; two black
families; the white world/black world; Hollywood representations and reality; Claudia and Frieda; Pecola and Sammy; Cholly and Pauline; the narrative voices of Claudia and Frieda; and Pauline Breedlove's twin siblings
Chicken and Pie. Additionally, Cholly and Pauline live in two rooms and
have two children, and Pauline's cognomen, Polly, implies parroting or the
doubling of words.

Ultimately, the mirror that negates and affirms beauty represents another type of doubling. For the Yoruba, the individual consists of complementary pairs of the exterior—what the Yoruba call *ode* and *innu*, referring
to exterior and interior (Drewal and Drewal 73). In *Gelede: Art and Female
Power Among the Yoruba*, Henry and Margaret Drewal note that the exterior is just the outward physical appearance (*ori odi*), whereas the inner
head (*ori inun*) controls thoughts and actions, as well as the character, personality, and mind (73). In the case of Pecola's internalization of the gaze,
the exterior world has replaced the interior and subverted any attempts to
recover her true self. A balance must be maintained between internal and
external to be "well."

The imbalance, which has diminished Pecola's vital life forces, leaves
her unbalanced. These dualities as philosophical ideas can be traced to the
kala and *zima,* or the notion of duality in the Kongo tradition. Giving and
receiving are not really opposites; they are reflective and reciprocal—the
balance of life. Like the Yoruba, the union of cosmic forces should serve to
unify the person with his or her destiny and life incarnation objective; in
short, they should allow the person to meet "self" in the physical realm, in
order to have the same recognition in the spiritual world once they detach

from the physical body. Other dualities expressed in spiritual-religious terms are the Yoruba notion of the two souls. The Yoruba believe that individuals have at least two souls: *eleda* (the ancestral guardian soul associated with the head) and *emi* (the breath, lungs, and chest), as well as a third soul *ojiji* (the person's shadow).

Dualities also exist as the Yoruba in the proverb—*tibi tire* (good and bad luck together). Balance, the goal of life, is achieved by the recognition of the elements of bad, which complement the elements of good to achieve the idealized state of coolness. Joy and pain are the human experience as the Yoruba name *Ekundayo* expresses. J. Omosade Awolalu states, "The Yoruba world does not know of totally opposing forces—one representing evil and the other good" (28). This balanced worldview allows the Yoruba to find fulfillment. The Yoruba traditional belief system underscores the importance of balance as a primary spiritual idea. To illustrate in nature, the rainbow's arc touching the earth represents completeness and the joining of heaven (*orun*) with earth (*aye*). This union of cosmic forces also symbolizes the cooperative and complementary nature of men and women as the basis for family, community, and nationhood. As the poet/activist Ayi Kwei Armah states in the prologue to *Two Thousand Seasons*, "All in life is twinned, receiving and giving are one."

The varying spiritual traditions of Africa attest to the unifying idea of complementary pairs. Departure from this intimate balance splits the two mutual halves that frame African ontology. Although the Dogon and Yoruba are two autonomous cultural groups, I am extending the idea of "African-European cultural confluence" used by Michael A. Gomez to describe how one reconciles distinct spiritual traditions (*Exchanging Our Country Marks* 3). I term my interpretative approach African *global mutuality*. This idea allows for the interchange of cultural and spiritual ideas across geopolitical borders in order to enhance the potentiality of the person.

Consigned to the script of the world in which she was born, Pecola's mental descent leads the community, including the readers, to resolve their own issues. In *The Bluest Eye,* Morrison presents the cosmology of *otherness* alongside an African frame to highlight the process of psychic destruction and to point to the deleterious effect of not maintaining balance. Her literary construction of this balance advances the idea of interchange between the interstices of the two polar realms of whiteness and blackness: ugliness and beauty. Alternatively, Morrison argues that finding a balance is possible, even when faced with cultural aggression. In *The Bluest Eye* there are testimonies of African people who have found agency and refashioned their identity from a wellspring of cultural items transported with them: proverbs, religion, medicine, social organization, and ideas of justice, morality, and ethics.

Toni Morrison's inscription of ritual performance establishes continuities in belief using a gathering of cultural symbols and invokes the spirits into the circle engendering mythic memory of belief revealed in Aunt Jimmy, M'Dear, and Cholly Breedlove. Aunt Jimmy, Cholly Breedlove's great-aunt, belongs to a group of women easily identified in fiction as one of the wise women tied to an African past. She is described as a woman "eating collard greens with her fingers, sucking her four gold teeth," and wearing an "asafetida bag around her neck" (*Bluest Eye* 132). The wearing of the asafetida bag is a visual signifier of her traditional orientation.[3] Another practice of Aunt Jimmy's that indicates her African cultural orientation is her remembrance of traditional naming practices. When Cholly asks why he wasn't named after his father, she replies, "Your mama didn't name you nothing. The nine days wasn't up before she threw you on the junk heap. When I got you I named you myself on the ninth day" (133). Evident in her response is that even though there was a disruption indicated by his mother's abandonment of him, traditional practices are still upheld in naming practices and order can be restored through ritual and ceremony.

After having established Aunt Jimmy's spiritual nature, Morrison sets the stage for the intervention of a group of women to assist in her healing when Aunt Jimmy takes ill. "Friends came to see about her. Some made her camomile [*sic*] tea" and offered advice: "Don't eat no whites of eggs," "Drink new milk," "Chew on this root" (135–36). When none of these remedies worked to alleviate her suffering, they send for M'Dear. Displaying the dynamism of African culture, Morrison employs the idea of the Iyalorisa or female ritual officiant, reinforcing the idea of African spiritual continuities in America.[4]

In *The Bluest Eye,* Morrison reinscribes the concept of female healer illustrating how African women continue to remember and, as a result, heal one another. Morrison advances how the power of African indigenous culture, healing, and female authority combine to chart a course toward new levels of liberation; hypnotized by the vibration of the "hum-song" and the power of continuous spiritual journeys, characters traverse the past in search of the meaning of the present. Linking the narrative to ritual is an attempt to restore balance in both the visible and invisible realms through the harnessing of spiritual energy. Reminding African people about the power of believing, Morrison locates M'Dear as a woman connected to the spiritual arts. Displaying the dynamism of African culture, Morrison employs the idea of M'Dear as a Mama Nganga or female ritual officiant.

One of the timeless earth mothers, Morrison describes her as a "quiet woman who lived in a shack near the woods" a clear sign of having the ability to access the spiritual realm. As an abode for the invisible powers consistent with West and Central African spiritual traditions, as a literary trope, M'Dear's proximity to the woods is identifiable spiritual indication of her ability to access the spiritual realm. Morrison also inscribes her as a midwife with a timeless presence to be summoned to perform healing that could not be handled by "ordinary" means (136). In this description Morrison depicts this ageless women as the repository of indigenous knowledge. A competent midwife and healer, M'Dear is spiritual pillar of her community. Able to cure any sickness "that could not be handled by ordinary means—known cures, intuition, or endurance—the word was always, "Fetch M'Dear" (136).

African cultural and spiritual resistance was deliberate and determined. Beneath the façade of apparent assimilation, African people in America sustained practices and beliefs using African spirituality as the vehicle for validating and articulating a unique history and culture. These remembered beliefs punctuated practice while publicly accommodating the impositions of various Christian denominations. This knowledge is augmented though spiritual insight and communication with the ancestral world—including the ancestral words (language) and spiritual forces by which people construct identity and accompanying life philosophies and practices. These healers have maintained traditional knowledge, despite the physical, psychic, cultural, political, economic, and spiritual censure of European Americans. As spiritual and cultural providers, they protect the community and officiate at a variety of community gatherings.

M'Dear's physical description further confirms her identity: over six feet tall with hair arranged in "four big white knots" (136). As a spiritual idea, the four knots correspond to the cosmological idea of the Kongo number of the cosmos and the Yoruba division of the world into four categories— Òrìsà (deities), *osain* (plants), *eniyan* (human beings), and *egun* (ancestors). Additionally, the color white conveys the Yoruba concept of coolness that "characterizes covert power and action as well as affirms ritual purity, calmness, and patience—soothing feminine qualities" (Drewal and Drewal 74).

From a Kongo perspective, MacGaffey records whiteness as a spiritual metaphor that conveys the clairvoyance associated with an *Nganga* who is able to mediate between the worlds of the living and the dead (*Kongo Political Culture* 85). Morrison opens up literary spaces where black beliefs and culture are the forms of influence. Conscious reflection on characters and imperatives of Black experience helps readers to reclaim, reconcile, renew, and recover cultural identity. Also, by pairing M'Dear with the preacher who accompanies her, Morrison indicates the ways in which African people move comfortably between African spiritual spaces and Christianity without conflict. Morrison expresses the power of M'Dear as a spiritual diagnostician consistent with her ritual posture and prognostications, "Standing straight as a poker, she seemed to need her hickory stick not for support but for communication. She tapped it lightly on the floor, as she looked down at Aunt Jimmy's wrinkled face. She stroked the knob with the thumb of her right hand while she ran her left one over Aunt Jimmy's body (137).

With the spiritual stick, M'Dear is able to tap into the spiritual core of memory and communicate with her ancestors much as current practitioners of the Yoruba religion tap the *egun* (ancestor) stick on ancestor altars when placing food and when ritually communicating with the deceased. Drewal and Drewal note the dimensions of spectacle as a fleeting transitory phenomenon that may be a "display or performance for the gods, ancestors, or the mothers; but it may also refer to mental images" (1). They note that the Yoruba word for spectacle *iron* is coterminous with the words for mystical vision—*ojuu iron* (remembrance), *inuron* (a mental recollection), and *iruron* (the act of seeing visions). By tapping into these spiritual codes, M'Dear gains access to the root cause of Aunt Jimmy's dis-ease and immediately works toward the cure. Having pulled the information from the spiritual realm, she leaves Aunt Jimmy in the hands of the women.

The women tending to Aunt Jimmy structure their lives using the African concepts of intersubjectivity and mutual interdependence. This description coincides with that of Ronald L. Grimes, who notes that the ritual field is both "the locus of ritual practice and the totality of a ritual's structures and processes" (39). According to Grimes, "Ritualization is not just a symbolic way of pursuing survival, but is a quest for a specific style of being in our bodies and world" (57). Serving in the capacity of healers under the guidance of M'Dear, these women had lived extraordinary lives that taught them to lie on the edge. Morrison describes the transition from being young when "their laughter was more touch than sound" to being mature women. "Then they had grown. Edging in life from the back door. Becoming" (138). These women had transcended from servility to a space of spiritual elevation and had become the caretakers of the spiritual semiotics. I argue that the domain of the *edge* indicates their having access to the spiritual power resident at the interstices between the *kalunga* line and the world of the *bakulu* (ancestors), and their inclusion serves as a counter to the spiritual assaults internalized by other characters.

This circle of women surrounding Aunt Jimmy and M'Dear proffering gifts of the earth or *aye* portray village values that help protect the village from spiritual threat. In ritual, human beings are able to transcend themselves and communicate directly with the divine and petition or effect solutions with their proactive actions. Regarding the notion of communitas, Richard Schechner argues that rituals are more than functional; they are also experiences where people feel expanded in contact with others (8). Having reached old age, the women are now situated to be spirit workers—a way to be different in the world. Ritual action is a primary way to denote difference as it is non-ordinary, done at special times in special places taking place "betwixt and between" life stages serving as transformative bridges from one stage to the next. In these spaces between structure and antistructure there is a dialectical space to access different identities, meanings, values, behaviors and power.

This literary inscription of difference is usually a reference to possessing the ability to see and to appreciate the value of signs. For instance, after Aunt Jimmy dies, the women set out to reconstruct the signs that should have provided foreknowledge of her "passing": "'What did she die from?' 'Essie's pie'" (140). In *Self-Healing*, Fu-Kiau takes into account that a person's vitality may be affected by "what we are taught, what we see, and through what we eat" (80). In spiritual culture, adepts are particularly vulnerable to certain foods that may be prescribed as taboo. For example, in the Yoruba traditional spiritual practices, most practitioners are generally cautioned against eating pumpkin because it is a plant or *ewe* used to heal a variety of illnesses. One woman recalls that when Aunt Jimmy had been feeling better prior to her death, "She was doing fine, I saw her the very day before. Said she wanted to bring me some black thread. . . . I should of known just from her wanting black thread that was a sign" (141). For these women, black thread was a sign of death that they should have paid more attention to. They recall, "Just like Emma." "Member? She kept asking for thread. Dropped dead that very evening" (141). These women, much like those in Toni Cade Bambara's *The Salt Eaters*, believe in the power of signs. Bambara writes "Every event is preceded by a sign," and Cora Rider, "whose bed, kitchen table and porch swing were forever cluttered with three Wise Men, Red Devil, Lucky Seven, Black Cat, Three Witches, Aunt Dinah's Dream Book, and other incense-fragrant softback [*sic*] books that sometimes resulted in a hit" (*Salt Eaters* 13).

Unsuccessful in their endeavors to heal Aunt Jimmy, the women enter into the next phase of service: preparing for the funeral by cleaning the house and sewing funeral clothes for Aunt Jimmy to wear. In this final ceremony, the women attempt to restore order and close the spiritual ruptures caused by her passing. One of the ways in which the women begin to cement Aunt Jimmy's memory is to begin to tell stories about her testifying to her life, such as how well she was liked and how she would be missed by all.

✳　　✳　　✳

"A whistling man and a cackling hen, both come to no good end."
—African American proverb

Cholly Breedlove's behavior contrasts with the positive energy exchanged at the margins or edges of life, which the older women are able to access. Abandoned by his mother on the junk heap by the railroad when he was four days old, Cholly is described as the "whistling stranger." Toni Morrison writes, "He came strutting right out of a Kentucky sun on the hottest day of the year. He came big, he came strong, he came with yellow eyes, flaring nostrils, and he came with his own music" (Bluest Eye 114). Pauline recounts, "He used to whistle and when I heerd him, shivers come on my skin" (115). Added to his correspondence with Elegba, whose spiritual sound is whistling, Cholly is also a person who walks on the margins indicated by "his heavy lidded light-colored eyes" (116), a prefiguring of the two-eyed male characters in Morrison's subsequent novels.

Mentored by Blue Jack, who provides him with history, Cholly admires Blue's facility with language and storytelling. Blue tells ghost stories and "about how he talked his way out of getting lynched once, and how others hadn't" (134). Similar to the Yoruba idea *adahunse*, "possessors of great knowledge of things not known to ordinary people" (Awolalu 113), Blue's spiritual presence often referred to in the folkloric tradition as "root man," "conjure man," or "two-headed snake doctors," causes Cholly to wonder if Blue could be God. Cholly's physical description of God that follows his musing doubly signs his personal construction of God and the deleterious effects on self-esteem when African people incorporate the physical idea of God separate from their own physical makeup. He thinks, "No, God was a nice old white man, with long white hair, flowing white beard, and little blue eyes" (134). Almost immediately, he modifies his perception that Blue could not be god, but instead he remarks that Blue resembles the devil.

Here Morrison affirms that maybe an alternate view of God is needed, one that aligns itself to the image of the person, one who reflects the image in the mirror that would yield the self-acceptance to assist not only him, but all African people. Providing the mental trauma and the deleterious effects of this self-destructive perception on the psyche, Frances Cress Welsing states:

> To be Black and accept consciously or unconsciously the image of God as a white man is the highest possible form of self-negation and lack of self-respect under the specific conditions of white domination. Such perception, emotional response, and thought are therefore insane. This logic circuit ensures that Black people always will look up to white people and, therefore, down on themselves. (172)

Consistent with this illogicality, Cholly would align himself with the devil if the white man is what the world said God was. His rejection of the image of God motivates him to search for his own father.

While on this search, Cholly experiences a sense of emptiness and another rejection. Participating in a rebirthing ritual helps him to mend his divided mind and restore order to the world. His rebirth takes place in "the beginning of open space at the Ocmulgee River" where "Finding the deepest shadow under the pier, he crouched in it, behind one of the posts. He remained knotted there in a fetal position, paralyzed, his fists covering his eyes, for a long time" (157). At the river's edge, through the rush of tears, Cholly emerges, leaving his vulnerable side behind. He is now "dangerously free. Cholly was truly free. He was alone with his own perceptions and appetites, and they alone interested him" (160).

This godlike state of self-absorption, characteristic of Elegba, leads him to Pauline. Cholly tricks her with his loud whistling and "yellow, heavy-lidded eyes" that took away "the gloom of setting suns and lonely river banks" (115–16). Once they move to the North, unlike Elegba, the Òrìsà of beginnings and openings, Cholly is not able to provide Pauline access to nature or protection from the black folks who were meaner than white people. Instead of recovering self with his new attitude of being free, he snares himself in a trap of self-absorption, having internalized the oppressive view of African people as antithetical to God. Being selfish and self-absorbed like Cholly, and mean like the northern people, has no place in communal structures where one's continued existence is intimately connected to the aforementioned concepts of mutuality and intersubjectivity.

Consideration of the interests and needs of others is important for community stability and development. One of the first examples of this breach takes place early in the novel when Pecola is temporarily placed in the Macteer household because her father has burned down their house. Even though Mrs. Macteer uses indirect speech, "Mama never named anybody—just talked about folks and some people" (24), an African rhetorical practice of not directly aiming hurtful language at a person, the intent of her words invariably demonstrates her lack of hospitality. Mrs. Macteer's refusal to be hospitable at a time of crises for Pecola destroys the "communitarian purpose of the universe and is immoral" (Magesa 63). A Yoruba proverb asserts, "The generous man meets amiable people." This is essentially a restatement of the Yoruba spiritual objective, which is the cultivation of good character (*iwa pele*), an objective for all human existence. Because there is no ritual redress for the harsh words spoken to Pecola, she is removed from the circle of community.

Besides community abandonment, Morrison also explores the psychic breach of having been looked upon with the evil eye. The African idea of being spiritually vulnerable to the glance of the evil eye or malochia and the accompanying protection from it is well documented in African culture. The many talismans worn for this purpose demonstrate this phenomenon. Laurenti Magesa explains that the eye frequently plays a part in the "destruction of the life force." Quoting C. Maloney he mentions the seven features:

> (1) Power emanates from the eye (or mouth) and strikes some person or object or person; (2) the stricken object is of value, and its destruction or injury is sudden; (3) the one casting the evil eye may not know he has the power; (4) the one affected may not be able to identify the source of power; (5) the evil eye can be deflected or its effects modified or cured by particular devices, rituals, and symbols; (6) the belief helps to explain or rationalize sickness, misfortune, or loss of possession such as animals or crops; and (7) in at least some functioning of the belief, everywhere, envy is a factor. (164–65)

During the Black is Beautiful movement of the late 1960s, all the problems were not solved; in North America, black had not always been beautiful. This novel is about cultural beliefs, spiritual beliefs, as well as the patterns and behaviors that have had a negative impact on African lives. Having inherited the cosmology along with attendant aesthetic considerations, the Breedloves of the world can only ride it out to its logical conclusion from Pauline Breedlove's imitation of the women in the movie to the fantasy of establishing order in the Fisher household, to Pecola's quest for blue eyes. Having blue eyes means having everything. Having blue eyes is the metaphoric representation of having love, acceptance, friends, and family illustrated by Pecola's ritual request for blue eyes. The blue eyes become a magical amulet for Pecola, who believes that if she had blue eyes, the boys would not shout names at her.

Frieda employs another type of eye in order to defend Pecola from the boys. She uses her own eyes; mirroring a look she had seen her mother use to keep Cain at bay. Claudia notes that Frieda defends her with "set lips" and "Mama's eyes," which explains why Woodrow Cain is frightened into stopping. Claudia speculates, "Maybe he had lost because he saw her eyes" (66). Here Toni Morrison employs the notion of eyes as also having the ability to ward off the evil eye by returning it in kind. The casting of the "evil" eye by the boys reflects white supremacist aesthetics turned inward on African people. As a result, the target of the malevolent eye ends up internalizing the gaze and projecting it on others with evil intent.

If not deflected, the gaze creates shame and ultimately the dissolution of the personality. John Bradshaw describes the deleterious effect of shame:

> Shame is the source of the most disturbing inner states, which deny full human life. Depression, alienation, self-doubt, isolating loneliness, paranoid and schizoid phenomena, compulsive disorders, splitting of the self, perfectionism, a deep sense of inferiority, inadequacy or failure, the so-called borderline conditions and disorders of narcissism, all results from shame. Shame is a kind of soul-murder. Once shame is internalized, it is characterized by a kind of psychic numbness, which becomes the foundation for a kind of death in life. Forged in the matrix of our source relationships, shame conditions every other relationship in our lives. Shame is total non-acceptance. (*Bradshaw on the Family* 170–71)

The most damaging of these encounters with shame occurs with Pauline Breedlove, Geraldine, and Mr. Yacobowski (representatives of the family, community, and the society at large, respectively). Pecola is entrapped in a web of shame and white supremacy. As a political idea, white supremacy is the foundation for all America's institutions and systems. Explaining white supremacy as an ideological tool, Ani notes its systematic nature. She says, "Europeans have constructed a system of institutions which depend on and encourage a particular pattern of behavior" (*Yurugu* 459). These systematic manifestations can be seen in the historic practices of enslavement, segregation, and other forms of government-sanctioned oppression.

Ideas of beauty are also contextualized in culture and politics. In *Black Skin, White Masks,* Frantz Fanon identifies how this epistemic violence is internalized perceiving the self as the other. In this manner the other only reflects its image on the object that receives the gaze. Clearly one is subject, replete with power, and the other is object, to be dominated and cut off from authenticity. For Pauline, white valuation is a function of the popular media. The way we see things is affected by what we know or believe. How the Breedloves felt about themselves became the reason why they lived in the storefront. Their *ugliness* encircled them even if they did not generate it. Even though that ugliness did not belong to them and was instead the ornamentation of racist assumptions, they donned it, accepted it, and therefore became it. For Pauline, romance is substituted for love and standards of white beauty for self-worth.

Since the source of their ugliness is mythic, constructed in the individual mythemes of the white supremacist cosmology, there is nothing to figure out. They internalize and accept this imposed reality "leaning at them from every billboard, every movie, every glance" and wear the reality as a "mantle" (*Bluest Eye* 39). Pecola employs her veil as a mask. The narrator reports that Pecola "hid behind hers. Concealed, veiled, eclipsed—peeping out from behind the shroud very seldom, and then only to yearn for return of her mask" (39). Instead of finding the power and transcendence associated with a mask, from an African perspective, Pecola is content to employ the mask for concealment—not of power but of shame. This indeterminate identity and the accompanying spiritual and psychological liminality find their origin in the external representations of whiteness presented as the trope of ultimate value.

Pauline further negates her daughter's blackness in her positive consideration of the little white girl in the Fisher household. However, Pauline does not act alone in the destruction of Pecola's psychic wholeness. Other adult women or "other mothers" contribute to Pecola's emotional despair. The three prostitutes—China, Poland, and the Maginot Line (Miss Marie)—are middle-aged women who supply the only nurturing models of motherhood for Pecola. The composite character descriptions of the women—Marie cooking and addressing Pecola with sweet epithets and references to food, China making available representations of beauty complete with information on grooming and hygiene, and Poland working and singing—provide Pecola with motherly representations lacking in her own home. As a composite or merged mother, the three prostitutes fulfill the role of "other mother" necessary for the child to become whole in the society. Morrison describes the connection of beauty with *Oshun*, the river deity of laughter and beauty, and *Yemonja*, the Òrìsà of the sea and motherhood. She writes, "All three of the women laughed. Marie threw back her head. From deep inside, her laughter came like the sound of many rivers, freely, deeply, muddily, heading for the room of an open sea" (52). The women take time to talk with Pecola, affirm through loving eyes her value: they "did not despise her" (51). Countering the assaults that Pecola faced daily, their affection toward her and their geniality made Pecola question whether they actually existed.

The women are unlike the broader community who treat Pecola with indifference, especially Mr. Yacobowski, the storeowner from whom Pecola buys her Mary Jane candy. Unlike Mary Jane's eyes, described as "petulant" and "mischievous," his eyes are unresponsive. The omniscient narrator asserts, "At some fixed point in time and space he senses that he need not waste the effort of a glance. He does not see her because for him there is nothing to see" (48). Mr. Yacobowski does not see Pecola as a person. The narrator notes Pecola's assessment of her "invisibility" in his eyes and describes his glance as "suspended" (49). The mirror of his eyes and those of other white people become the inverted reflection through which Pecola sees herself and the world. "She would never know her beauty. She would only see what there was to see: the eyes of other people" (47). The natural world, signified by the "clump of dandelions," which she once thought could be her allies would also conspire to reflect Pecola's shame. After the visit to the store, the dandelions reflect Mr. Yacobowski's apathetic response to her presence as she transfers her disdain for herself onto the dandelions.

This imposed contempt parallels the burden of bearing the white aesthetic projected as the source of all value, like the white baby dolls given as Christmas gifts, which Claudia observes, were given to fulfill their "fondest wish." Claudia reveals her true feelings regarding this gift in her rejection of its value. Claudia's reaction to the doll represents her desire to determine and control the contours of value. In her refusal to accept the doll's beauty, she notes the conspiratorial nature of the world to cast its gaze and for African people to agree to their own devaluation. Her dismembering of the doll is done to destroy not only the doll but also what the doll represents.

Her analysis takes into account the socialization of African people and their willingness to adopt—or at least their willingness to surrender to—the dominant discourse of whiteness.

What saves Claudia from these cultural impositions is her valuation of blackness. She chides her parents for attempting to rob her of her "tribal" identity. Having to take a bath, she laments, "Gone the ink marks from legs and face, all my creations and accumulations of the day gone." These ink marks are recodified warrior marks and ethnic inscriptions attesting to choices not given to her by society and her parents. She laments her lack of choice and the resulting de-centering. Her choice would be one not equated with an imposed material value characterized by the white dolls, but relates to the African value of the social realm of human relations possessing the highest significance.

Claudia notes, "I want to sit on the low stool in Big Mama's kitchen with my lap full of lilacs and listen to Big Papa play his violin for me alone" (22). Claudia's insistence on sitting on low stools is a metaphor for black traditional beliefs. In *The Salt Eaters*, Bambara suggests that a belief in the "reliability of stools" (6) is a way to connect with the eldest members of her community, those who remember the old ways, like the women in Aunt Jimmy's community. The enumeration of cultural items such as food and music coupled with the primal senses of olfaction and audition underscore Claudia's cultural appreciation. Otten notes that in order for Morrison's protagonists to survive, they must "somehow violate the rule of the oppressive system, reject the values it venerates, and recover the human potential denied to blacks" (3).

✳   ✳   ✳

Magic mirror come and search my heart can you tell me what you see?
—Earth, Wind, and Fire

Against this backdrop of cultural despair, social inadequacy, and spiritual sterility, Toni Morrison initiates a discussion of another cultural resource in the form of magic, which Pecola seeks to help her with her dilemma of being ignored by an indifferent "God." After the rape, Pecola requests that the town's mystic or "root man," Soaphead Church, give her the "blue" eyes she needs to cope with her shattering life. Soaphead Church is a "Reader, Adviser, and Interpreter of Dreams" whose clients find their way to request services like "Keep my baby's ghost off the stove. Break so and so's fixing"

(172). Having failed in her attempts at prayer, Pecola seeks his assistance for the desired blue eyes. An ineffective charlatan, Soaphead cannot help Pecola.

Claudia and Frieda's ritual is more in keeping with ritual protocols and is guided by the unselfish, caring intent to help her. In the prologue, Claudia, the novel's first narrator, discloses this concern: "we could think of nothing but our own magic: if we planted the seeds, and said the right words over them, they would blossom, and everything would be all right" (prologue *Bluest Eye*). Claudia and Frieda, although not yet menstruating "women," possess the ability to harness the forces of nature, as Bockie explains: "Generally, any member of the community with unique qualities may be considered *ndoki*, possessing the power to garner the forces of nature and the spiritual world to do good or evil" (43). Claudia and Frieda's ritual planting of marigolds attempts to restore the cosmic harmony for the group.[5] Sacrificing the money saved up for the bicycle, they act on behalf of a community that has no sympathy for Pecola's situation. Claudia and Frieda, confident in their ability to intervene, knew that prayer and being good were not enough. They needed a more concrete exchange—the seeds and two dollars.[6]

Providing the reader insight into their magic, they discuss their plan. The sacrifice (*ebo*) is to bury the money and plant the seeds. In their explication of the ritual, they detail the step-by-step process, including the diligence needed. They also illustrate the way they will determine the ritual's efficacy by the blooming of the flowers. Their ritual is even accompanied by two prominent features to ensure the ritual's efficacy: ritual words and song. Having initiated a ritual with the planting of seeds, burying two dollars in the earth, and reciting special "magic" words, Claudia and Frieda demonstrate their understanding of sacrifice in order to change outcomes.

Magesa notes that magic is the art of causing change in accordance with the will and consciousness. Additionally, the imagination can be manipulated to produce the desired results, whether physical, spiritual, or psychological (46). Claudia and Frieda's actions also correspond to the ideas expressed in Yoruba rites. Awolalu asserts that a magical act has almost always three elements: there are words to be uttered according to a formula or set order, actions to be carried out, and the officiant should be spiritually prepared (78–79).

Throughout the novel, the Macteer girls, Claudia and Frieda, demonstrate their spiritual suitability to be the next generation of women who "dreamed dreams that no one knew—not even themselves, in any coherent fashion—and saw visions no one could understand. They wandered or sat about the countryside crooning lullabies to ghosts, and drawing the mother of Christ in charcoal on courthouse walls" (*In Search of Our Mothers' Gardens* 232). Like these women, Claudia and Frieda demonstrate their awareness of nature. "We always responded to the slightest change in weather, the most minute shifts in time of day. Long before seeds were stirring, Frieda and I were scraping and pulling at the earth, swallowing air, drinking rain" (*Bluest Eye* 64). Additionally, the ritual choice to construct the *ebo* using seeds shows the girls' spiritual sophistication.

Seeds (*ngina* in *Ki-Kongo*) are archetypal symbols, sacred images, models of behavior, as well as modes of thought; all make up the traditional universe mythic symbols and ritual acts expressing the genetic and historical lineage of a community. The death of Pecola's baby and the subsequent inability of the marigold seeds to blossom represent the spiritual and social taboo associated with the breach created by the incestuous acts of Cholly Breedlove. When the ritual does not work and Pecola's baby dies, Claudia accepts the blame that she planted the seeds too deeply. Similar to the wise women who try to reconstruct the signs that foretold Aunt Jimmy's death, Claudia reconsiders her culpability and resigns herself to the fact that something bigger than she caused the seeds to be unproductive—the hostility of the land.

My examination of *The Bluest Eye* has been an exploration of African cosmologies and the nature of spiritual power and beliefs, alongside axiological ideas of beauty and value. Concerning the resultant environmental inversions, I have come to the same conclusion as Toni Morrison, who ends the novel explaining why Claudia and Frieda's well-intentioned intervention does not work. The "unyielding earth" to which Morrison's narrator refers is a metaphor for white supremacy. The inhospitable land is a gaping hole too wide to vault over and surpasses the rupture caused by the perversity of the rape. This unnatural racial structure has marginalized and exiled African people and has thwarted the magic available in the natural world. However, flanking the novel's bleak end, there is hope that Claudia and Frieda will become the next generation of African women who can read and understand the significance of signs. They will continue to wield the power of sacred words and perform sacred deeds to assist the community in deflecting the harmful gaze of the white aesthetic and other assaults to African people.

Always

The Living Ancestor and the Testimony of Will in *Sula*

> I have always been just me, with no frame of reference to any-
> thing beyond myself.
>
> —Bessie Head

Following the success of Toni Morrison's first novel, *The Bluest Eye*, her second novel, *Sula* (1974) received considerable critical attention with approaches varying from dialogues concerning the nature of good and evil to examinations of motherhood.[1] However, the quest motif remains a major critical feature that begs for exploration. The idea of the quest, an essential component inherited from the epic tradition, makes a smooth transition in Morrison's novels.[2] Morrison locates Sula's heroic quest to a psychological mindscape defined by interiority and revises male versions of the heroic journey usually defined by slayings, rescues, and a valiant return to the homeland laden with treasures. Although Sula does venture away from the community, there is little mention of what has occurred on her journey because her heroic action is acted out within the frame of community (Birenbaum 55).[3]

It is in the community where Sula's psyche, spirit, and soul get explored. Karen Stein proposes that the shift in focus by African American women is a conscious attempt to subvert the patriarchal guises of male heroes, creating a new definition of heroism that "encompasses the lives of Black women" (146). One of these redefinitions of heroism is that heroes are not always successful. This is evident in *Sula* where Morrison attributes Sula's failed quest to her detachment from community responsibility, her indifference to guidance offered by archetypal characters, and her excommunication from ancestral forces. Sula's insistence on rugged individualism, an American cultural trait that conflicts with the African communal emphasis, turns the quest into a contest of will and dooms her from the onset. I contend that the thwarted quest that Morrison presents empowers the reader to reverse the heroic character's actions and subsequently obtain a sense of fulfillment and an awareness of African spiritual and cultural values by default.

In this chapter, I chronicle the eponymous character's shortcomings by examining her negligence of these African values. In keeping with Morrison's unyielding cultural perspective, I examine archetypes and symbols that mark Sula's definitions as well as her rejection of the living ancestor's presence and her departure from an understanding of African worldview. In order to fully comprehend the implications of Sula's self-centered actions, it is essential first to examine the community from which she deviates, the archetypal guide whom she fails to heed, and the ancestor whom she rejects.

One of Toni Morrison's recurring literary concerns is the survival of an authentic African American community. From a traditional perspective, Marcel Maus explains that community is the main agent of meaning and that the role of the individual is to act out the life of the clan (5). The importance of the community is evident in the prominence that it is given within the structure of the narrative. Considering the community before the formal introduction of the title character attests to the significance of community as one of the concentric circles that define the individual's existence. From an African perspective, individuals are born into communities and derive their identities from these communities, which inscribe their sense of values, notions of cultural decorum, and ideas of accountability. At once, the name of the town and a metaphor for the foundation of the ancestors on which healthy community is situated, the Bottom functions as a reconfigured African village. Throughout the novel the community functions as a barometer that gauges the moral actions of Sula, as well as other characters.

The novel begins by introducing that community: "In that place, where they tore the nightshade and blackberry patches from their roots to make room for the Medallion City Golf Course, there was once a neighborhood" (*Sula* 4). Morrison's invocation in the opening sentence indicates the endurance of spiritual practices in this community. Giving the readers a glimpse of the end, this ordering of story elements anachronistic to the Western mind but coherent within an African model of time, the narrator alerts readers that something catastrophic has occurred to warrant this destruction and prepares them for a series of flashbacks.[4] Along with African notions of temporality, the narrator advances the idea that members of this community participated in *working* roots, since both of these plants are used by spiritual adepts in the practice of ritual and the making of *minkisi*, or spiritual packets.[5]

Following the introductory statement is a history of the origins of the town. Then the narrator describes the types of places in the "used-to-be-town." There is the Time and a Half Pool Hall, Irene's Palace of Cosmetology, and Reba's Grill. Finally, the types of people who inhabit the community are portrayed: men who wore "long tan shoes," women who had "Nu Nile lathered into their hair," a woman who cooks "in her hat because she couldn't remember the ingredients without it," and people who do the "cakewalk," sing, and laugh easily" (3–4). These descriptions sufficiently define this as an African American community whose mundane façades hint at the most extraordinary inner worlds. The inclusion of the Time and a Half Pool Hall as a place of significance to the neighborhood invites the reader to conjure up familiar scenes of African American men participating in the oral tradition of "big lies" and "signifying," along with accompanying recollections of male-specific gathering places, like barber shops and lodge halls that help define the social realm of men in the African American tradition. In a similar way, Irene's Palace of Cosmetology locates the women in a particular domain designated as a place for the exchange of gossip, the offering of advice, and ritual grooming similar to the kitchens and basements in African American homes. Moreover, the inclusion of an eccentric character who needs a hat to generate memory provides a locale for the discussion of things of the spirit that may not make sense outside the cultural confines of this neighborhood.

Having introduced the community, Morrison then narrows the focus to a consideration of one individual. Shadrack who is shell-shocked from his experiences with the horror of World War I, is one of the village's eccentrics with wild eyes and "long matted hair" (15).[6] One of Morrison's conventional river characters similar to Stamp Paid in *Beloved,* but just a little stranger, Shadrack dared to walk about with his penis out, pee in front of ladies and girl-children, curse white people and get away with it, drink in the road from the mouth of the bottle, and shout and shake in the streets. He also resembles the peculiar Soaphead Church in *The Bluest Eye,* whose business was to "Overcome Spells, Bad Luck and Evil Influences" (137), and he prefigures Robert Smith, the insurance agent who in *Song of Solomon* jumps off the roof of Mercy Hospital in an attempt to fly. He has similarities as well to Son in *Tar Baby,* whose overpowering hair, which was "wild, aggressive, vicious hair that needed to be put to jail," matched his uncontrollable passion (113).[7]

Shadrack was not always this way, but as the story goes, because of his inability to cope with the horrors of war, he ties "the loose cords in his mind" and returns to a faraway time. This excursion through memory is an ancestral flight that takes him "somewhere" where he collects the cultural information needed to reintegrate his shattered psyche. The omniscient narrator reports what Shadrack finds while in this trancelike state, which consists of "more than a year, only eight days of which he fully recollected" (11). During one of these eight days he sees a river and hears someone "speaking softly just outside the door" (10). The river symbolically represents memory—in this sense, the memory of venerated ancestors or *bakulu* in Ki-Kongo language.[8] Furthermore, the memory of the river substantiates Shadrack's identity as a person who has had a spiritual epiphany concerning his role as a river devotee. The soft voices are the whispering of the ancestors, and the door signifies a metaphysical separation between the dimensions of spirit and matter, or what the Ba Kongo call *mwela*, a portal for the soul that allows access from one dimension to another.

The description of his discharge from the hospital further advances the idea of his being a river initiate, specifically a devotee of Oya, the Òrìsà who controls the wind. His departure from the hospital is distinguished by an accompanying wind that makes the "heads of trees toss" and thoughts of making people disappear with "a good high wind" that would "pull them up and away." Furthermore, his first steps toward his new life are referred to as taking "the plunge" and his journey is marked by the images of rebirth and severing of his past life, pointing to another connection with Oya, the guardian of death (10–11). Moreover, the enumeration of items that he does not own include intangible items, such as language, source, and past, as well as personal possessions, to emphasize his separation not only from the military but also from the material world—a significant point that confirms his liminality as an initiate. For example, at times the divination performed after initiation prescribes the relinquishing of all former material possessions to mark the transition from an earthly existence to one determined by spirit. Moreover, his un-tethering from physical phenomena confirms his allegiance with Oya the Yoruba Òrìsà who, like Shadrack, is perpetually transitional—without a past, familial ties, or home. This connection with Oya also relates to the ancestor, since the ontological existence of ancestors in the realm of the invisible represents the idea of an absent presence.

After a short journey, beset by problems, Shadrack comes home to Medallion, to his river. As a river priest ordained by the ancestors and enlightened by discoveries made on the journey, he is free to assume his initiate duties unobstructed by considerations of sanctions from the community.[9] Estranged from others and living in a shack on the riverbank that had once belonged to his "grandfather long time dead," he fashions a way to ritually deal with fear and with the ultimate manifestation of dread: the fear of death.[10] His formulation of National Suicide Day coheres to the function of the *egungun* to remind people about the positive value of ancestors and the circle of perpetuity.

Equipped with his ritual implements—bells, a rope, and a song—he re-establishes the idea of collective rituals. Shadrack's tools reacquaint the people of Medallion with the relevance of ritual in their lives. The bell functions in two important ways. First, it admonishes the townspeople to attend to the spiritual aspects of their lives. Second, the bell spiritually cleans the town of negative influences and restores a sense of balance. In the Yoruba culture, bells are used to communicate with the Òrìsà and to invoke spirit possession. The rope is symbolic of the binding or fastening needed to engender community cohesion. And the song, referred to as a dirge, invites the presence of the deities. By reinstating ritual into the principle of village life, Shadrack binds the people of the community to a set of beliefs that legitimatize their spiritual identities. In the novel, ritual behavior is a manifestation of the will. Ritual is sometimes the only effective manifestation of willful reconciliation of one's perception of reality. Therefore, as a symbol of will, ritual functions as its expression.

His value as a genuine and contributing member of society is apparent in the way Shadrack is *accepted* in the community. For example, even though the people consider him to be *crazy*, they do not summarily dismiss him. His peculiarity "did not mean that he didn't have any sense, or even more important, that he had no power" (15). Over time, the people fit him into the scheme of their lives. "Once they understood the boundaries and nature of his madness" (15–16), Shadrack's fusion into the fabric of life is so exhaustive that people in the town begin to record time by references to these rituals. One character comments to another about the onset of labor pains on Suicide Day. Others make plans with respect to the day: "Let's do it after New Year's." "OK, but make sure it ain't on Suicide Day" (16). In addition, local lore begins to develop around the day. A grandmother reports that her "hens always started laying of double yolks right after Suicide Day." In this manner, Suicide Day has become a part of community life.

The next significant member of the community that the narrator introduces is Eva Peace, who symbolizes the living ancestral presence who heads an earthy home where there "is a constant *stream* of boarders" (30;

emphasis added). This house "of many rooms," where dreams coexist with the mundane, is the home of the matriarch Eve—one of the trio of women who are also occupants.[11] As an ancestral figure, Eva's power lies in her will to survive, clearly seen in her decisive actions. When others in similar situations might have given up, by tapping into the power of the will Eva has become a survivor who outlives all of her children. She is like Toni Morrison's own ancestor, her grandmother, Ardelia, whom Morrison describes as having faith in the magic "that can be wrought by sheer effort of the will" ("A Slow Walk of Trees" 152).

Eva Peace also represents the sacrificing mother. Abandoned by her husband and left to provide for three children, when Eva is down to her last three beets, she leaves her nine-month-old son and two daughters and returns eighteen months later "with two crutches, a new black pocketbook, and one leg" (34). Her homecoming is accompanied by rumors that she stuck her leg under the railroad car in order to collect a monthly pension check. That Eva could leave her three children with a neighbor and return more than a year later to find them healthy and cared for attests to the village values that Africans continue to maintain in the Bottom.

Her maternal sacrifices are not limited to this one act of willful behavior. When Eva's only son, Plum, becomes a drug addict, she sets him ablaze.[12] But before she does, she anoints him in kerosene, rocks him, and loves him. This highly ritualized sacrifice is done not out of anger or malice, but out of Eva's love for him. As Eva pours kerosene over him, the narrator suggests that Eva's actions are a blessing or a ritual to bring things back into balance. Years later, when Hannah confronts Eva about Plum's death, Eva explains she did what she considered motherly by releasing him from his pain. Eva rails, "He wanted to crawl back in my womb and well . . . I ain't got the room no more even if he could do it" (71).

Although some critics have commented on the incestuous nature of Eva's statement, I suggest that a mother's despair, not incest, is her motive. Because of the futility of Plum's addiction, Eva decides to control the circumstances of his inevitable death consonant with the identity of Oya, who is the guard of the cemetery and as such supervises ingresses and egresses to and from the realm of the dead. Eva demonstrates another act of love when she sees Hannah on fire and leaps out of the second floor to the yard below in an attempt to save her daughter.

In addition to her will to survive and her strong sense of self-sacrifice, Eva is also described as a woman who knows things. The omniscient narrator describes Eva as a woman of two voices: "like two people were talking at the same time, saying the same thing, one a fraction of a second behind the other" (71). This description relates to Eva's ability to access both realms in the same manner as the two-headed snake doctors, a concept rooted in the African American folkloric tradition. As such, Eva has the ability to traverse and to spiritually negotiate both material and spiritual realms. The lack of synchronicity of her voice suggests her coterminous presence in both realms of existence.

Eva also has the ability to see things thought to be hidden. Toward the end of the novel when Nell Wright goes to visit Eva in the nursing home, Eva tells her that she saw what happened to Chicken Little. Nell is stunned by Eva's clarity because she has pushed her participation in the event into the deep spaces of memory. Chikwenye Okonjo Ogunyemi credits Eva's knowledge of this event not to her clairvoyance but to confession. He says, "Apparently Sula makes a confession to Eva to explain her distraught state after Chicken Little's death and during the funeral" (131). I disagree. Eva is capable of knowing things through dreams and visions. The importance of her character will be made more evident in the following discussion of Sula and the examination of her failure to endure the trials of her quest.

Jane Bakerman attributes Sula's failed quest to her inability to learn the lesson of true friendship, while others have argued that because of her "evil" nature her quest was doomed (549). Additionally, many critics explain Sula's failed quest for selfhood, with analyses focusing on her insistence upon experimentation. I argue that the self Sula creates results in the breaking of familial, community, and ancestral circles, all of which are foundational to define a complete individual. Consisting of many constituents besides the individual, the circle includes spirit guides, the ancestors, and the community. The relationship between the narrative elements that deal directly with Sula and those that are peripheral is an expression of the balance that must exist between the individual and the community in order to maintain harmony. Sula's departure from community responsibility illustrates this rift. She moves away from the harmony dictated by the principles of community and resorts instead to her preoccupation with physical pleasures, the exercise of an intractable will, and blatant disregard for the community's interests. Left unchecked, Sula's hedonistic tendencies render her incapable of assuming the social responsibility needed to perpetuate the family and to sustain the community members of the Bottom.

Sula is the granddaughter of a woman who cut off her own leg in order to collect a $23.00-a-month disability check and who also poured kerosene on her only son and lit him on fire because she could not bear to see him destroy himself. Sula is also the daughter of a woman known as the town whore, whom she watched get burned alive. In short, Sula is fashioned out of the composite merging of these two bold women. However, she appears to be motivated by a sense of self or "me-ness" as a counter to the narrow strictures that defined life for a colored girl in the early twentieth century. The limitations, which constrained choices for women at the time outside maternal roles, help to move Sula into the realm of marginality where she is neither understood nor accepted.

Sula, a self-created woman, invents her own world defined by self-absorption. The female construct of the free or uninhibited self, Sula's depiction also characterizes Shadrach's self-construction. The omniscient narrator rationalizes:

> Had she paints, or clay, or knew the discipline of the dance, or strings, had she anything to engage her tremendous curiosity and her gift for metaphor, she might have exchanged the restlessness and preoccupation with whim for an activity that provided her with all she yearned for. And like any artist with no art form, she became dangerous. (121)

In *Cane*, Jean Toomer describes Avey in a similar fashion:

> I pointed out in lieu of proper channels, her emotions had overflowed into paths that dissipated them. I talked, beautifully I thought, about an art that would be born, an art that would open the way for women the likes of her. (46)

These two mirror statements explain what is needed to make Sula whole.

The danger and experimentation begins after Sula overhears a conversation in which her mother says she does not like her. After this experience, Sula is let loose, unmoored, and her lack of centeredness wreaks havoc on those who surround her. Morrison's depiction of Sula's individuality and free unrestrained self is not without consequence. Here, Morrison suggests that death occurs when one perforates the circle of responsibility to one's lineage ancestors and ignores the principles of intermutuality foundational to continuity and community.

Even though Sula is paired with Nell Wright, a best friend later to become foe, this relationship still does not provide the necessary structure to regulate Sula's actions. The narrator describes them as inseparable with a friendship that is intense and contained. She continues, "In the safe harbor of each other's company they could afford to abandon the ways of other people" (55). It is only later on in the story that we actually become aware that Toni Morrison has misled us. This friendship is severely limited by Sula's disproportionate taking of more than what she gives. Nell is the giver who provides Sula with a sense of self that Sula is unable to fathom alone, as she has "no compulsion to verify herself—be consistent with herself" (119).

In a *New York Times Magazine* interview, Morrison explains Sula's self-constructed personality stating, "And she had nothing to fall back on: not maleness, not whiteness, not ladyhood, not anything. And out of the profound desolation of her reality she may very well have invented herself" (163). This self-centeredness is made clear upon Sula's return to the Bottom, when her lack of dependency is highlighted against the backdrop of Nell's world defined solely by responsibilities to husband and children. It is only after seeing Sula after a ten-year absence that her ideal situation begins to unravel. A major irony is that although Sula is unable to define her own selfhood, she "helped others to define themselves" (95). Speaking to Diane Cooper-Clark, Morrison says she "found Sula frightening." Morrison explains, "Her definition of freedom is to do anything one wishes, and I personally would be frightened by this freedom" (195).

It is important at this juncture to spiritually identify this woman who wants to make herself. Although this question may be answered from many perspectives, the spiritual and cultural approach initiated earlier offers a clear depiction of Sula's nature. I propose that Sula, one of Toni Morrison's marked heroines represents the river Òrìsà Oya indicated by her physical description, behavior, and her affinity with the archetypal manifestations of this Òrìsà of the cemetery. There are few physical descriptions of Sula, but the ones given provide insight and confirm her spiritual identification. The first portrait rendered is a physical description of her with a birthmark covering her eye, which was shaped like a "stemmed rose" (57). The eye is Sula's mark that designates her as one of Morrison's marked heroes in much the same way as Sethe's back in *Beloved* and Pilate's smooth stomach in *Song of Solomon*. Sula's eye is also a type of scarification indicating her unyielding strength and courage, similar to the Yoruba notion of *gbere,* where a black powder is inserted in incisions to mark identity and status. In another sense, the eye, itself a circle, is symbolic of the many broken circles: the friendship circle between Nell and Sula; between Sula and the circle of community; and between Sula and the family circle represented by the ancestor.

The eye is a fitting symbol for Sula because, like Oya who refuses definition, it defies description as well. Her emblematic eye represents a kind of double sign; it sums up her deviation from the imposed definitions in the eyes of the community and helps to define the character of the perceiver. Teapot's mother sees Hannah's ashes symbolic of her own maternal deficiency. Nell's children see it as a "scary black thing," which foreshadows the chaos caused by their parent's separation. Also, Jude sees the mark over her eye as a rattlesnake revealing much about his fears and sexual attraction to her. Shortly after seeing Sula for the first time, Jude's fears of being dominated by Nell are resolved because he is empowered by his infidelity with Sula to break free from the oppressive bonds of Nell's dependent love. Of primary significance is Shadrack's perception of her eye as a "tadpole": a sure sign of her spiritual nature and connection to him that substantiates her identity as potential spiritual initiate of the river Òrìsà, like himself. For Shadrack, the marked eye (circle) connects her to the ancestors, rivers, and death.

A dominant description of Sula that substantiates her spiritual identity is the physical description of her upon her return to the village of Medallion. Described as a brown woman wearing "a black crepe dress" and "a black felt hat with the veil of net lowered over one eye," Sula's appearance is congruous with the description of Oya, the benefactor and mentor of the *egungun* or masked ancestral spirits who parade through town reminding the villagers of the permanency of life as well as reminding them to attend to their own individual ancestors. Henry Drewal notes that the Odun egungun are "commemorative funeral rites where the living dead appear and are honored though the mediation of the mask" (Drewal, Pemberton, and Abiodun 175). The *egungun* convey the essence of the ancestors to the living, the relationship of the living to each other, and reflect the nature of social relationships (175). Judith Gleason's description of the Egungun illuminates the deeper meaning of Sula's promenade through town. She writes, "The function of the Egungun cult is to bring the Ancestor back to life in masquerade form in order to "legitimate reigning authority"; this is done at the annual festival for the dead (Gleason 70).

The significance of Sula's black dress is suggested by Gleason's description of the cloth as a protective gesture of Oya. According to Gleason, the black cloth "tears social reality to shreds. Like a glandular secretion, it touches us at the instinctual level of defense" (50). Sula's arrival prefigures the social reality to be shred in the community, and the housewives respond to the sign by "throwing buckets of water on their sidewalks" (*Sula* 91).

Another characteristic that authenticates Sula's association with Oya is the phenomenon of death. The novel's prologue and epilogue both refer to death; and death abounds in the novel and serves as the dominant image informing both structure and content. Barbara Christian notes that each death "gives way to a new view of life" (154). Christian's observation can be explained by Oya's enigmatic identity, as substantiated by Gleason, who explains: "Oya is a conundrum. She is a double goddess: not here but there, not there but here; on the side of death, on the side of life" (50). This doubling effect can be seen in the symbolic deaths such as the demise of Nell and Sula's friendship, the dissolution of Nell and Jude's marriage, the separation between Eva and Sula, and the revised image of Sula at the novel's end following Eva's disclosure to Nell. Moreover, there are actual deaths many of which are connected to Sula in significant ways: Hannah and Plum both die by burnings; Chicken Little drowns; Mr. Finley chokes on a chicken bone; and many of the townspeople are killed in a culminating ritual at the end of the novel following Sula's death.

Notwithstanding the prevalence of death, the circles that recur as a leitmotif and encompass the actual deaths symbolize the permanence of life. The circling serves to unite both the presence of the Òrìsà and the idea of the intransience of life. In the novel, right before Hannah's death, the circling motif appears when she is preparing green beans for dinner: "She swirled them about with her fingers, poured the water off and repeated the process" (72). In addition to this image of circling, Hannah's death represents another kind of circle: Eva's love and Sula's indifference. Sula is intimated in her mother's death since she calmly watches her mother's fire dance "because she was interested" (78). This woman—daughter, town whore, and mother—is dead, and it is left up to the reader to reach a conclusion as to the cause(s) of her death. Again, an analysis of Oya helps to explain Eva and Sula's possible participation in this deadly alliance. Gleason explains that Oya, as the deity of women who lead "intense, erotic lives," is the essence of fire in motion represented by one of her major symbols— lightning (291). Hannah's lightning-swift death by fire occurs immediately after she questions Eva's love and after Sula overhears her saying that she does not like her. These actions cannot be overlooked as contributing factors to her demise.

The third ritualized death in the novel—the death of Chicken Little— illustrates Sula's spiritual vocation. Prior to Chicken Little's death, Sula is at an emotional crossroads in her life signified by both puberty and her indifferent mother's lack of maternal affection. She heads down to the river accompanied by her "dark thoughts" (57). Toni Morrison carefully crafts the scene leading up to Chicken Little's death with subtle prose that prepares the reader for the ritual sacrifice. In the preparatory stage of the ritual, before the river is fed, Elegba is invoked as customary in his capacity as a mediator.[13] His invocation is manifested by the activity engaged in by Sula and Nell immediately prior to Chicken Little's appearance, which consists of feeding the earth a variety of organic materials: "rooted grass," "stripped twigs," "cigarette butts" (58–59). After this ritual of stripping symbolic of the preparatory activities to prepare *osain* (herbal fluids) and the feeding of the hole, Sula sees Chicken Little "coming up from the lower bank of the river" and coaxes him to climb the tree with her, and they look out over the "far side of the river" (59).[14] This sacrificial feeding of the bird to Oya at the river also propitiates the ancestors located at the bottom of the river in the realm of the *bakulu*. Additionally, the circular ripples in the river and Chicken Little's having been swung in circles replicate the concentric circles of the living and the dead and the symbiotic relationship and exchange between the two realms from an African spiritual perspective.

Having performed the ritual intentionally or not, Sula is forever changed and heads deliberately toward her own beginning/end. Moreover, entering Shadrack's house binds her to him as she is the only person who has ever crossed his threshold. Additionally, the purple belt she leaves behind is also emblematic of that connection. Later in the novel, Shadrack would confirm that connection speaking his one-word mantra "always" when he encounters her in the street. However, Sula does not heed his exhortation and heads in another direction re-routing her destiny.

As dramatic as the other deaths are, Sula's death and the circumstances that prefigure it point to its primary significance in the novel. The attending details create a surreal atmosphere:

> It would be here, only here, held by this blind window high above the elm tree, that she might draw her legs up to her chest, close her eyes, put her thumb in her mouth and float over and down the tunnels, just missing the dark walls, down, down until she met a rain scent and would know the water was near, and she would curl into its heavy softness and it would envelop her, carry her, and wash her tired flesh always. Always. (149)

"Always," this word spoken on her deathbed recalls the guidance given her by Shadrack concerning the permanence of life. Moreover the water imagery substantiates the locus of *bakulu* or ancestral realties in the Kongo tradition and reiterates the notion of perpetuity.

Finally, the words spoken after her "death"—"Wait till I tell Nell" (149)—attests to her ability to communicate between worlds and demonstrates the possibilities of a future, even at the end, confirming her spiritual affinity to Oya, who is able to transcend death. Sula's death, associated with her rejection of the ancestor, is further explained by the metaphysical cause of illness. It is held that an illness can be symptomatic of an outraged ancestor. Also, illness can be caused by failure to render service and to offer the requisite sacrifices, afford the reverence, and to give the expected offerings. Morrison says, "When you kill the ancestor you kill yourself" ("Rootedness" 344). This ancestral transgression of Sula's can be examined by both her transgression against the ancestral presence represented by A. Jacks's (Ajax's) knowledge of traditional spiritual practices and the rejection of Eva as a familial ancestor.

Because of Sula's failure to recognize the spiritual nature of Ajax, this earthy man with skin of "black loam," she is doomed. Introduced early in the novel as the "twenty-one-year-old pool haunt of sinister beauty" with the most imaginative foul mouth in the town (50), he re-enters her life following her sexual escapade with Jude. For Sula, the memory of his "lemon-yellow" pants, which had caused her sexual excitement some years earlier, ignites the relationship. To Ajax, Sula represents the only other woman who is interesting "other than his mother who sat in her shack with six younger sons working roots" (126). He comes often bringing her various gifts, of which the blackberries are the most significant because of their use in fixing a person.

Once Ajax begins coming regularly, Sula becomes dependent and things begin to change. Suspecting that Sula has put roots on him—this "flying man" and "seventh son of a seventh son" (137) starts to think more and more about "air shows," "planes," and flying with regularity to counter Sula's newly acquired domesticity and the building of a nest (134). This idea of being the seventh son of a seventh son is a recurring trope in African American literature signifying one whose life is charmed. Fearing domination, Ajax seeks help.

The following passage, which describes his mother, indicates Ajax's access to the resources to secure his release:

> She was an evil conjure woman, blessed with seven adoring children whose joy it was to bring her the plants, hair, underclothing,

fingernail parings, white hens, blood, camphor, pictures, kerosene and footstep dust that she needed, as well as to order Van Van, High John the Conqueror, Little John to Chew, Devil's Shoe String, Chinese Wash, Mustard Seed and the Nine Herbs from Cincinnati. She knew about the weather, omens, the living, the dead, dreams and all illnesses and made a modest living with her skills. (126)

Whether acting alone or in collusion with his mother, Ajax is able to free himself from Sula's influence. Shortly after he leaves, Sula dies.

Sula's death at such an early age and without reference to a previous illness alerts the reader that a major spiritual transgression has occurred to cause her death. Margaret Washington Creel notes that in traditional African societies, "Punishments and retribution for breaches in morals and ethics were not the province of a future world judge but were dealt with on earth" ("Gullah Attitudes" 72). In African culture, it is not uncommon to examine a series of events precipitating the death of a person who predeceases her elders. In these instances there is a search for the signs, not the cause.

The next transgression that Sula commits is directed at Eva. Sula exhibits blatant disrespect for Eva by word and deed. Sula's verbal misbehavior indicates her incapacity to grasp the hierarchy of the relationship that situates Eva before her as a representation of the ancestor to be duly honored and revered. Sula's cursing of Eva is a misuse of the spoken word (*nommo*) or verbal *asé* that tears down any spiritual protection and power Sula might have had. One of the profound aspects of Oya's personality is her sharp tongue symbolized by the machetes—Oya's major symbol. The following conversation highlights the rupture in this intergenerational relationship caused by the sharpness of Sula's double-edged weapon. When questioned about getting married, Sula responds, "I don't want to make somebody else. I want to make myself" (93). The notion of "make" is significant used in this context. The Yoruba refer to initiation as making a person. The fact that Sula does not refer to initiation or re-connection to her spiritual personality, but to separation, cuts herself off from the ancestor. Eva cannot depend on Sula to call her name into eternity, and Sula will leave no offspring to call her name either.

Soon after, Sula, devoid of familial loyalty, puts the matriarch of the Peace family in a senior citizen home. This serves as her final breech with the ancestor. In *The Forest of Symbols: Aspects of Ndembu Ritual*, Victor Turner identifies the ancestors and the consequences of not duly honoring

them: "These ancestors are always the spirits of those who played a prominent part in the lifetime of the persons they are troubling" (10). Turner
submits that the reason these ancestors trouble the person(s) is because
they have been forgotten. What is paradoxical about Sula's behavior, however, is that she is the person who is punished for neglect of her ancestral
duties, and she is also the person who is chosen to be the intermediary in
future rituals that would connect the living with the dead. She earns this
distinction because she represents spiritual strength in the same manner
as Eva. In fact, Sula could have been as strong as Eva and a replacement for
her had she the ability to sacrifice for others.

For instance, like her grandmother, Sula amputates a piece of herself
when she cuts off part of her forefinger to frighten the white boys who
torment her on her way home from school. Her self-mutilation acts as an
initiation rite establishing her courage much in the same way as her grandmother's amputation of her own leg. However, Sula fails because she has
no ancestor to invoke and no one to intercede on her behalf to ensure her
fulfillment. Properly invoked, the ancestor secures spiritual and psychic
protection for a person. Because of Sula's excommunication from the ancestor, she cannot fulfill her heroic mission—and the community is further
disintegrated.

The group integrates individuals. And in turn, the individual members
must submit to the will of the group in order to have integrity. In African
world thought, the needs and concerns of groups surpass those of individuals. The individual who breaches this order by placing personal advan-
tages at the expense of others may cause others to experience misfortune,
disease, and death. Denial of her ancestor and community accountability
makes Sula a scapegoat and a misfit in the community. This judgment is
rendered from a traditional group of people who do not "believe doctors
could heal" or that "death was accidental" (90). Morrison does not let their
assessments of Sula become dismissed as small-town meddling: Sula is different. Sula's independence is not seen as a desirable trait to possess in the
mid-twentieth century as evidenced by other character's reactions to her.

Similarly, as with Shadrack, a body of lore develops around Sula. In this
way they incorporate her into the community. When Mr. Finley chokes on
a chicken bone and dies, this too, is attributed to Sula—more specifically to
her using the evil eye. Likewise, when a woman gets a sty on her eye after
Sula looks at her, Sula is blamed (117). Moreover, similar to Baby Suggs who
is judged by the community in *Beloved*, Sula is considered to have powers
superior to mortals, which places her under the highest suspicion. The

townsfolk note that she is impervious to insect bites, had "no childhood diseases," and it is said that "when Sula drank beer she never belched" (115). Here the idea of an individual person distinguishing herself and exceeding the allowable community norms is seen as a potential to destabilize the collective's balance.

In keeping with the inherent contradictions espoused by the idea that the "dead are alive," Toni Morrison presents another equally conflicting one; Sula has both a destructive and a constructive presence. While Sula's behavior upon her return to the Bottom outrages her community, making her a pariah, ironically, her presence generally has a beneficial effect on the Bottom. Sula's malevolence highlights the community's munificence. Her influence is not totally evil as the people of Medallion re-direct their scattered energies and reinvest it into family matters using Sula's lack of familial concerns as catalyst. Without Sula as a scapegoat they are free to revert to their previous indifferences and slackness.

After her death, even though the community assumes its former shape, the village is troubled. This trouble is attributed to many things, but more specifically to the cultural ruptures that have occurred in the novel. These ruptures are represented by events such as people going to white folk's hospitals or placing elders in nursing homes, and seers not attending to the importance of dreams. What the community needs is the harnessing of forces to balance the negative influences in the form of ritual acts. Since ritual is designed to keep the believers spiritually clean, renewed, and centered they appeal to the voices of nature. They are compelled to act in a communal way to fashion a proper burial for Sula to create harmony and repair the disjunction. When something happens to one member of the community, a comprehensive redress of these abnormal circumstances is indicated.

The need to propitiate the forces responsible for the malaise that causes a "restless irritability" is of chief importance in the minds of the community members. The townspeople misinterpret the signs that appear after Sula's death. The first sign indicates *life* represented by the construction of the New River Road tunnel. The second sign suggests the *death* of cultural values indicated by the building of a senior citizen home to place the elders of the community. The third sign is the "freezing rain" emblematic of stasis or *stillness*. The narrator explains the obfuscation of the signs: "Still it was not those illnesses or even the ice that marked the beginning of the trouble that self-fulfilled prophecy that Shadrack carried on his tongue . . . there was something wrong" (153). I submit that because there is no rebirth in the community, one of the prerequisites for eternity and continuation of the ancestral line, this collective ritual provides the renewal necessary to re-establish harmony, since the central purpose of ritual is to impose patterns of behavior upon the individual in the interest of the whole group.

Benjamin C. Ray notes that restitution needs to be made to compensate for diminution of vital force by means of propitiatory offerings and ritual purification of the village and its inhabitants (referred to by the BaLuba as *koyija kibundi* [washing the village])(Ray 149). Having no other resources except National Suicide Day to deal with the evil visited upon the town by the harsh winter, they shape their exigency into this established ritual. The purpose of the ritual is not only to pacify the spirits for relief for the winter; it is also a ritual sacrifice or *ebo* for Oya.

As a spiritual officiate, Shadrack is called upon to adjudicate the improprieties of the community. He recognizes that although Sula has crossed over into "a sleep of water always," there is still need for a culminating ritual. Funerals as culminating events are equally as important for the living as well as the dead. Sula was not *funeralized* properly; there was no wake-keeping and other ritual activities. The community overlooks this important activity. They do not participate by sending "yellow cakes" for the funeral repast, nor do they "leave their quilt patches in disarray to run to the house" (172). Additionally, there were those who said when they heard she was dying, "She ain't dead yet?" (172). Not contributing to the ritual meal after the burial constitutes a major cultural and spiritual breach. Moreover, turning her body over to a white funeral home where she has a closed coffin funeral signifies the harshest of all spiritual trespasses. From an African American standpoint, the dressing of the body is a skill that can be only done by black morticians, who know how to ready the person's body for viewing. The ultimate compliment to honor the deceased is to remark, "She looks just like herself." Additionally, having a closed casket does not provide the cultural closure needed to substantiate the death.[15]

The importance of rites for the dead relate not only to the deceased individual, but to the community as well. The funeral is attended by a few who are brave enough "to witness the burial of a witch" and sing "Shall We Gather at the River?" for politeness's sake (150). The song, "Shall We Gather at the River?," had become a question no longer linked to the spiritual realm associated with ritual and the former worship of the *bisimbi* or water spirits, but instead prefigures the ritual at the mouth of the cave where members are sacrificially killed in the baptism of water. Also, the song's inquiry is a question of vital importance. Shall Africans, as a people, gather/collect the continuous flow of spiritual-cultural ideas represented by the river, the ancestors?

So, Shadrack accompanied by Tar Baby and the Deweys who represent the lesser spirits—the intermediaries that give "assurance of human perpetuity beyond the grave"—send Sula off in traditional fashion (Creel, "Gullah Attitudes" 73).[16] However, he is not able to persuade those "who understood the spirits touch which made them dance, who understood whole families bending their backs in a field while singing as from one throat, who understood the ecstasy of river baptisms under suns just like this one" (160). Those that went meet their end while Shadrack stands there ringing his bell. Robert Farris Thompson explains this idea from a Kongo perspective: "The death of an important person occasions a split within the community. The crown of bells militates against this possibility: I am the bell that sounds within the town. I sound for unity. You have to remain united even as I remain here forever bound to you" (Thompson and Cornet 147). Shadrack's bell attempts to engender this accord. However, having forgotten the other ritual implements, it does not have the efficacy needed to be successful.

Toni Morrison leaves readers with a formidable picture of cultural and physical death by reiterating the true powers available to African people if they listen to ancestral voices, practice their cultural traditions, and accept responsibility for one another. At the novel's end, half the town is dead, there is limited hope for the future, and Eva's life has been rendered finite as the sole survivor of the Peace family. Because Sula has failed to fulfill her destiny there is no one to call Eva's name into eternity. Moreover, Sula's excommunication from the community, the ancestor—and her inability to understand the concept of intermutuality—leave behind "circles and circles of sorrow" (174).

II

�֍

Psychic Domains and Spiritual Locations

I've Got a Home in Dat Rock

Ritual and the Construction of Family History
in *Song of Solomon*

I've got a home in a that rock
Don't you see? Don't you see?

—Traditional spiritual, "Got a Home in That Rock"

When I die, my spirit shall return
to its place of birth
Africa is my home
This mortal, fragile body
will roam no more
Lifted and free
of earthly ties and bonds
Transported back to my land for eternity
Africa is my Home.

—Abbasante Shabaka (Lawrence J. Evans), "Injustice Reversed"

Ontological Considerations

On the page following the dedicatory inscription to her father, Toni Morrison writes, "The fathers may soar and the children may know their names." In these prefatory annotations, Morrison informs her readers of the novel's twin themes: freedom and identity. For Morrison, identity continues to be indispensable to the integrated cultural and spiritual personality and it is connected to knowing one's name.[1] The protagonist has two names—Macon Dead III and Milkman—one of which is his given name and the other a nickname that socially establishes him. At the end of Morrison's third novel, *Song of Solomon* (1977), Milkman comes to the end/beginning of his protracted search, enlivened by the discovery of his great-grandfather's name and identity.[2] A symbolic healing of the trauma associated with the assignment of names by European Americans during enslavement that disconnected African people from the souls of their ancestors and caused great spiritual distress, the discovery of his ancestor's name helps Milkman to regain a sense of self beyond his individual representation of self and the limitations associated with the meaningless names given by the oppressors.

Ralph Ellison reminds us that names are "our masks and our shields and the containers of all those values and traditions" that we learn and/or imagine as being the meaning of our familial past (*Shadow and Act* 148). And in an interview with LeClair, Morrison iterates the importance of names and their connection to the ancestors, stating, "If you come from Africa, your name is gone. It is particularly problematic because it is not just *your* name but your family, your tribe. When you die, how can you connect with your ancestors if you have lost your name? (LeClair 126). In the Bantu philosophy the first criterion is the name.

Ostensibly, on a search for gold, Milkman exchanges the material object of his quest for knowledge of his family history, despite his indoctrination by his father, Macon Dead. Tutored on the preeminent value of the material world with advice such as "Money is freedom," Milkman achieves cosmic wholeness on his epic journey through his connection with his African ancestors and the recovery of their names and family narratives. Rejoicing in Solomon's transcendence from enslavement to flying home to Africa, Milkman shouts, "The son of a bitch could fly! You hear me, Sweet? That motherfucker could fly!" (332). On his spiritual trek, a series of concentric circles of rituals reconnect Milkman, just as Solomon's individual remembrance of Africa links him with the larger group of African people who made promises in the putrid holds of ships to return home to Africa.[3]

In this chapter, through a close reading, I trace Milkman's reiterated self to African provenances, as he becomes an heir to continuous historical and spiritual consciousness.[4] I examine African symbolic codes that guide Milkman toward his destiny and explore the role of archetypal helpers, principally the Kongo spiritual officiant or Nganga ritual expert characterized by Pilate and the Yoruba Òrìsà Elegba depicted in Guitar Bains, both of whom assist Milkman in his epic quest. Additionally, I consider the ways in which ritual engenders Milkman's new corporate identity, values, and behaviors. To frame my analysis of Milkman's quest I employ the structure of the Middle Passage conceived as: departure, passage, arrival, deprivation, and transformation.[5]

In *Song of Solomon* Toni Morrison argues that ruptures of time and identity can be repaired and recovered respectively through *willed* memory. As Maria Diedrich, Henry Louis Gates Jr. and Carl Pedersen remind us, "The Middle Passage emerges not as a clean break between past and present but as a spatial continuum between Africa and the Americas, the ship's deck and the hold, the Great house and the slave quarters, the town and the outlying region" (*Black Imagination* 8). In *Song of Solomon*, Morrison affirms that this topography not only extends from "the interior of Africa across the Atlantic and into the interior of the Americas" (*Black Imagination* 8), but also maps the spiritual terrain of African people in their imagination of freedom in the course of their experiences under the yoke of oppression.[6]

This historical continuity undermines statements by literary critics such as Houston A. Baker Jr. who asserts, "Black folklore and the black American literary tradition that grew out of it are the products of a people who began in slavery and who, to a large extent remain in slavery" (*Long Black Song* 11). Although the Middle Passage was a space of indeterminacy, resistance and spiritual resoluteness created a reconfigured African identity whose spiritual equation can be re-inscribed as passage, reclamation, and recovery.

Epic Topoi

Ideas of identity and nationhood are important ideas on which to reflect, especially as they relate to the epic. Epic is particular and cosmic is universal. Particular cultural nuances team up with ritual performance as the narrative achieves "cosmic entirety" (Soyinka, *Myth* 2). Wole Soyinka further states that the epic celebrates the victory of the human spirit over forces inimical to self-extension concretizing in the "form of action the arduous birth of the individual or communal entity" (2). This self-extension is related not solely to the individual but also to corporate interests allowing for the type of efficacious healing transcending both liminal and spatial time.

In *Song of Solomon*, Toni Morrison's literary considerations are modifications of the genre of African epics and as such accomplish the reclamation of African heritage including features such as ancestor worship, the invisible world, and African spiritual traditions. These epic factors, thought to be lost en route to America via the Middle Passage, are recovered through Morrison's revision of epic realities, which incorporate the cornerstone of the African tradition with the enlivened annexation of New World and womanist concepts. Her reconstruction is seen in her addition of a female hero to accompany the male hero, typical in both African and European epics.

In *Song of Solomon*, the interplay between ancestral and living spheres is highlighted by performance elements with respect to epic ideas, African archetypal deities, and Pan-African spiritual traditions. These elements characterize the mending of breaches and ruptures at the micro level represented by the narrative and at the macro level represented by the larger historical narrative of the African Diaspora. This change also indicates a shift in public to private considerations of the heroic quest. The village setting is translated into the community or neighborhoods, the supernatural forces are supplanted by their syncretic manifestations, and the battles shift from physical to psychological and are not confined to the home (the Western world's construction of a woman's domain). Epic fulfillment is achieved when the heroine acknowledges her identity complete with a past and unites herself with other members of the community. In this transformation of self, gained through the challenges of the journey, the veil, which had separated the hero from cosmic wholeness, is lifted.

In the novel, this resolution is accomplished in various ways through healing and/or transition or transformation of the individual and/or community. The achievement of heroic completion of the characters during the "return" phase is usually accompanied by a highly stylized ritual, which re-consolidates the psychological with the social dimension of being.[7] Geneviève Fabre argues that the celebratory spirit of Africans accompanied them to the Americas, and the Africans reinvented both ritual and forms "to alter the time space framework prescribed or suggested by whites" (72).

Preserving "historical truth" rooted in cultural landscapes, primarily archetypes, allows both the hero and reader to find their way on their respective journeys. Since traditional expression can be interpreted through a variety of cultural vehicles and ideas, it is significant that the novel opens/closes with the classic metaphor of flight signifying freedom.[8] Additionally, epic ideas of circularity structure *Song of Solomon* as Morrison begins and ends the novel with flight and song. I read the flight of Robert Smith from the roof of Mercy hospital and Milkman's flight at the novel's close as recovery of African ontology: "At 3:00pm on Wednesday the 18th of February, 1931, I will take off from Mercy and fly away on my own wings. Please forgive me. I love you all" (3).[9] Signaling a departure from the trope of Christian salvation in her inversion of Phillis Wheatley's thesis about the redemptive value of Christian mercy illustrated in her poem, "On Being Brought from Africa to America," Morrison prepares the reader for a flight from America to Africa.[10] Moreover, Smith's final words concern the primacy of love as a universal force, both human and cosmic. Sharing the same name as the biblical book, "Song of Solomon," an anthology of Hebrew love poems allegorical to God's relationship with the soul, Pilate will echo Smith's legacy of love at the novel's end when she speaks of love's enduring legacy.

Toni Morrison communicates this epic theme, as well as others, using one of the epics' primary resources, the bard. Providing space for the employment of call and response, the narrator encourages the reader's involvement. In an interview with Nellie McKay, Morrison explains this participatory approach asserting that "readers who wish to read my books will know that it is not I who do it, it is they who do (403). Besides eliciting participation from the audience, Isidore Okpewho notes that one of the bard's most prolific skills is the "flexible technique of improvisation" (*The Epic in Africa* 40). Most assuredly, Morrison echoes this epic imperative in language that mirrors musical improvisation as "she performs words" (LeClair 369).

In *Song of Solomon* Morrison inscribes excursions mimetic of jazz:

> He knew her face better than he knew his own. Singing now, her face would be a mask; all emotion and passion would have left her features and entered her voice. But he knew that when she was neither singing nor talking her face was animated by her constantly moving lips. She chewed things. As a baby, as a very young girl, she kept things in her mouth—straw from brooms, gristle, buttons, seeds, leaves, string, and her favorite, when he could find some for her, rubber bands and India rubber eraser. (30)

The narrator starts with the idea of Pilate's face then moves to her lips, then to specific movements of her lips, then continues on to a more focused look:

> Her lips were alive with small movements. If you were close to her, you wondered if she was about to smile or if she was merely shifting a straw from the base line of her gums to her tongue. Perhaps she was dislodging a curl of rubber band from inside her cheek, or was she smiling? From a distance she appeared to be whispering to herself, when she was only nibbling or spitting tiny seeds with her front teeth. (30)

Morrison ends the foray, this variation on a theme, with a return to the beginning in much the same manner of a jazz musician who rejoins the melody after a protracted wandering up and down the scales and beyond in search for that new combination of sounds. The reader's attention, once again, is directed to a consideration of the mask: "Her lips were darker than her skin, wine stained, blue-berry-dyed, so her face had a cosmetic look—as though she had applied a very dark lipstick neatly and blotted away its shine on a scrap of newspaper" (30).

The ideas of masking and music represent prominent epic elements. In traditional cultures of Africa, masks are used ceremonially to promote well-being and community. This motif is usually employed as an ironic device, and clearly the heroes of the African epics *Sundiata* and *Mwindo* begin their heroic adventures as masked heroes. For example, Sundiata's late physical development and the accompanying derision masks the possibility of him emerging as a great conqueror whose name is destined to be remembered in perpetuity. In a similar fashion, Mwindo is a baby when he undertakes his heroic journey; a baby is hardly the heroic idea of authority.

In Morrison's revised epic, she introduces the idea of marking as a correlate of masking. Her protagonists Milkman—who walks with a limp because one leg is shorter than the other—and Pilate—who has a smooth stomach sans navel—are both physically marked, helping to substantiate their positions as heroes. Pilate's face illustrates Morrison's use of masking. When Pilate's face is in motion she is safe like the Dogon masks, which come alive when they are being danced. Lifeless masks are taboo. At various times in the novel, Pilate's immobile face expresses notions of unconcealed danger, such as when Milkman returns home to Michigan after discovering his family history. Pilate is angry because of Milkman's culpability in Hagar's recent death, and her face is described as "still" (337). Informed later that day that the bag of bones she has been carrying around for many years belongs to her father and not to the white man that her brother had killed, the narrator says, "She seemed happy now. Her lips [were] mobile again" (338).

In addition to the unique function of the epic bard and the concept of masking in the African epics, there are also differences in the heroic attributes that serve to further distance them from their European cognates. Although African epics contain rudiments of the basic epic formula—auspicious births, a sense of the quest, and engagements in battles—possessing these universal elements does not diminish the uniqueness of the African epic tradition.[11]

Equally characteristic of the African epic is the prominence of music. Christiane Seydou notes, "Music is an essential feature common to all epics in West Africa" (312). And Isidore Okpewho recognizes that along with formulae, epithets, topoi, repetition, call and response, and digression, an intersection of songs throughout the narrative define the African epic. To this list, Daniel Biebuyck adds the emphasis on performance, the prevalence of occult forces and heroic manipulation of these forces, an amalgam of music and dance, the audience's interaction with the bard, and the use of a rich and highly poetic language (*Hero and Chief* 23–25).[12] As the novel begins with Pilate singing a song heralding the birth of Milkman, the novel ends with Milkman becoming a singing man. Following the song he joins eternity, or as the Zulu elders express, he becomes "a song which is sung again and again" (Mutwa 185).

Another essential feature of the African epic is the type of characters depicted in the narratives. According to Biebuyck, the following types of characters are found in the Nyanga epic *Mwindo*: heroes; people in special roles, such as ritual experts; divinities that live in the air and subterranean worlds; spirits of the dead, extraordinary beings who live in the forest, sky and caves; animals, birds, and insects; and the fabulous (*Hero and Chief* 28–32). Of these characters, the hero is of primary importance. In both epics, *Sundiata* and *Mwindo*, the heroes share similar traits. For example, they are both born to suffering women, their fathers are chiefs, and the heroic sons are destined to become chiefs as well, which provides a source of tension to their enemies. Similarly, in *Song of Solomon*, Milkman is born to a suffering mother who grieves for the affection of her deceased father and entrusts all of her attention to her son Milkman whom she nurses until his "legs dangled to the floor," which recalls the eponymous hero of the Malian epic *Sundiata*, who did not walk until nearly his adulthood. Additionally, Milkman's father, an owner of multiple properties and a luxury automobile, is the modern equivalent of a chief.

Toni Morrison recovers these features, thought to be lost en route to America via the Middle Passage, through her revision of epic realities, incorporating the cornerstone of the African tradition with the enlivened annexation of the New World symbols. As models for behavior, archetypal symbols represent the sacred symbols of a group or groups of people, including an assemblage of deities, ancestors, spirits, and other phenomena constructing the sacred world. Symbols also inform myth and rituals through a web of representation. This network of symbolic forms representative of specific cultural systems bind together beliefs about the nature of social relations, ecological interactions, and the manner in which characters recognize and categorize patterns and events to meet their present needs. Symbol and myth are complimentary ideas. For instance, myths primarily influence spiritual archetypes, which in turn form the basis of myth. For African Americans, both symbol and myth continue to advance African belief systems, because of their shared agency. Rodney Needham notes the importance of symbolism as being necessary to "mark what is socially important, and to induce men to conform in recognizing the values by which they should live" (5).

In *Song of Solomon*, the primary motif in the novel concerns the ability of Africans to fly. The preservation of this mytheme is significant chiefly because of the political freedom that has eluded Africans in America since their arrival. Flight becomes a significant statement about spiritual power and the endurance of African belief systems. In his recounting of the story of his great grandfather's flight, Milkman comments that flying is a form of resistance against hegemony and its socially reductive roles for Africans in America. He exclaims, "No more orders! No more shit!" (332). In *Song of Solomon*, Morrison develops this idea of flight and its constituent goal, spiritual transcendence, using the symbols of gleam and language as major conceits.

Birth of the Hero

Milkman's arduous birth and the prebirth rituals prepare the reader for his spiritual distinction. Wyatt MacGaffey notes that among the BaKongo a child that is born abnormally is referred to as *baana ba nlongo* and has precocious spiritual sensibilities ("Twins, Simbi Spirits" 213). As a child, Milkman was called "deep" and "mysterious," which makes the women ask, "Did he come with a caul?" They tell Ruth, "You should have dried it and made him some tea from it to drink. If you don't he'll see ghosts." The ability of the women to maintain tradition through ancestral speech consistent with what the old people believe, while purporting to have Christian beliefs distinct from these folk ideas, is reminiscent of the type of dissimilitude recorded throughout African American literature from the enslavement or captivity narratives to the present.[13]

The conversation about the caul being a spiritual mark is consistent with folkloric ideas expressed in African American literature. In an interview with inhabitants of White Bluff, a community of four hundred African Americans located southeast of Savannah, researchers with the Georgia Federal Writers Project queried the oldest citizen, Sophie Davis, who was eight at the end of the Civil War. When asked if she saw spirits, she replied,

"I caahn see spirits cuz I ain bawn with a caul" (*Drums and Shadows* 76). In the appendix to *Drums and Shadows* the authors record various attributes for babies born with a caul. The foremost trait is being able to see spirits and to not be harmed by them.

Pilate understands the presence of *kimyumba* or deceased spirits echoing the perception of the Kongo subgroup, the Ba Manianga. For example, both Pilate and Macon Dead II see Macon Dead I after his death. Once they saw him on a stump, as well as in various locations including at the entrance to a cave. His appearance at the cave—a symbolic womb—is emblematic of the deceased's ability to be reborn. In addition to a visual presence, the spirits also have the ability to communicate with the living. For example, having made his transition, Macon Dead I appears to Pilate and informs her about responsibilities to the dead. His name is a metaphor for the spiritual regeneration of the ancestor, which is to make the dead significant in the lives of the living.

In *Death and the Invisible Powers*, Simon Bockie explains the Bantu-Kongo philosophy about the nature of the human being, which consists of three basic elements: *nitu* (the physical body); *kini* (the invisible body); and *mwela* (the soul) (129). When the *nitu* or physical body dies, the other two components exit and begin their journey to the other world. The *kini* and the *mwela* join and become the "life body" that continues to live as opposed to the death body *nitu*, which has been left behind by its former occupant (131). It is important to point out that the invisible body or *kini*, which is a shade or reflection of the physical body, looks identical. Since *kini* has eternal life, the soul never leaves it; actually, *kini* is the "visible body of the other world" (129). Mary Frances Berry and John Blassingame discuss the significance of these beliefs within an African American context, noting, "The slaves believed that a person's soul remained on earth three days after death, visiting friends and enemies, and that the ghosts remained near graveyards, communicated with and could harm or help the living, and might return to claim property which had belonged to them" ("Africa, Slavery" 248).

According to Bockie, belief in the existence of the invisible realm supports the notion of survival of the community or *kanda*. The Bantu community consists of the individual, the total living community, the recent dead, those who are in the process of becoming ancestors, those who have achieved the status of ancestors, and good spirits. This community of the dead is called Mpemba and its residents are called *bakulu* (Bockie 131). Death is not a permanent separation: "From time to time the deceased return home to warn, inform, or give instructions to the *kanda* or an individual member regarding an upcoming event looming large (*lwengisa*), or to reprimand or punish (*semba*)" (83). Additionally, the Yoruba believe that the deceased can appear in dreams or trances, where they impart valuable information, explanation, or instruction. The dead are reborn as ancestors who guide the living to help them remember the nature of their respective destinies and the power of their names.

Through his interaction with Guitar and Pilate, Milkman is taught the power of reclaiming his name along with the power of spiritual awareness. His predilection for looking skyward also marks him as a person in search of his spiritual lineage connecting him with the flying African. When he learned at four "that only birds and airplanes could fly—he lost all interest in himself" (9). Learning early lessons about the limitations of the physical world, Milkman begins his search for the spiritual realm in order to garner more meaning beyond his individual self, which is limited by space, time, and earthly boundaries. Milkman must be initiated to undertake his mission as a spiritual being and recover himself and his familial past.

✳   ✳   ✳

> One Bright morning when my work is over,
> I'm going to fly away home.
> —Bob Marley, "Rasta Man Chant"

The spirits summon Pilate to facilitate Milkman's birth. As a prelude to his birth, the ritual she performs prepares him for subsequent rituals enacted on his journey toward epic completion. Pilate represents the continuation and resonance of African culture, imagination of homelands, a sense of tradition, and history. Toni Morrison constructs her, not as a private self or individual, but as a symbol of the community in which Milkman needs to reconnect. Bunseki K. Fu-Kiau discusses the symbolic idea of community consisting of both living and dead:

> The community is a channel: people go (die); people come (are born). The community renews perpetually its members and its principles accordingly to its (*fu*) systems, conforming to the natural laws that of birth and death, the theory of (*makwendamakwiza*), what goes will come back, the perpetual process of change through (*dingo-dingo*),

the constant back and forth flow of (*ngolo zanzingila*) living energy. (*African Cosmology* 100)

Wielding the power of ritual to harness spiritual energy, Pilate is the matrix for purposeful existence and the archetypal help essential to the success of Milkman's quest. As Milkman's spiritual guide and double, Pilate teaches him how to soar utilizing the three processes of cultural transmission suggested by Robert N. McCauley and E. Thomas Lawson, which are: (1) the generation of representation, (2) the retention of those representations, and, (3) the communication of those representations (45). In her narratives of the past, Pilate illuminates the shared patterns of familial history and supplies the fundamental stability for Milkman's unbalanced psyche. Only with a true knowledge of the past can he re-create the consciousness and sense of community needed to imagine a future. In fact, Milkman's penchant for "riding backwards" and "flying blind" (32), and his habit of concentrating "on things behind him" (35), signals his bond with Pilate, who will connect him to the past and deliver him from his spiritual dilemma.

After having his first conversation with Pilate, Milkman is primed with enough background information about his family to elicit a story from his father. Finding out that Milkman has spent the afternoon at Pilate's house, Macon begins to tell him things about their ancestors. Reuniting him with the stories of his ancestors and reconnecting him with his living relatives bridges the gap in Milkman's familial narrative and introduces him to a larger community of people to whom he has a collective responsibility. Using this formulation, one can see that ancestors are not just past constructions but, as Nkira Nzegwu reminds us, they are also aspects of future generations (182).

Pilate is his *ndoki* and the author of those essential lessons. Fu-Kiau discusses the notion of *ndoki* as one who knows man's higher principles or knowledge. The manipulation of knowledge is "to assist one to become a winged person, a flier" (*African Cosmology* 33). As an archetypal companion, Pilate helps to coordinate the experiences and spiritual opportunities that Milkman agreed to before his physical birth. For the Yoruba, destiny refers to the "pre-ordained portion of life wound and sealed up" in an *ori*— or bearer of destiny. However, a person arrives at a destiny whether it is received or chosen; destiny "determines the general course of life" (Gbadegesin 47).

Born to the Dead

> Some I know were lovers of the moon who would
> pierce their ears on full moons.
>
> —Robert Hayden, "Full Moon"

> I was born in the Congo
>
> —Nikki Giovanni, "Ego-Tripping (There May Be a Reason Why)"

Toni Morrison depicts Pilate as having an aura of spirituality and establishes her as a pilot for Milkman's flight to self-hood and social incorporation. Remembered by the people of Danville for her closeness to nature, they recall Pilate as a "pretty woods-wild girl that couldn't nobody put shoes on" (236).[14] Macon comments on her earthiness. "Seeing the pine trees started him thinking about her mouth; how she loved, as a girl, to chew pine needles and as a result smelled even then like a forest" (27).

Additionally, a description of Pilate's blackness is highlighted. Macon tells Milkman that Pilate looks and acts like an African. While in Shalimar, Milkman reflects that Pilate must have looked like the young girls—with "wide sleepy eyes that tilted up at the corners, high cheekbones, full lips blacker than their skin, berry-stained, and long long necks" (266). Disrupting the meaning of black as being bereft of light, Pilate's blackness leads Milkman into the light of self-realization. The Ki-Kongo term *kala* is associated with blackness. Furthermore, the idea of spiritual Nganga connects with this force of blackness expressed in the following expressions that define Pilate's character: *Kala/ba muntu* (be a human being, a helpful being); *kala/ba n'kisi a kanda* (be the community's medicine); *kala/ba nganga* (be a specialist, a true knower, a master, a doer); *kala/ba n'kingu a kanda* (be the principle of the community); *Kala/ba lembabzau kia kanda* (be the strongest of the community) (*African Cosmology* 27).

Furthermore, Bockie corroborates this identity, employing the concept of Nganga or bridge between the communities of the dead and the living. He expounds on the idea of the Nganga:

> As used by BaManianga, [a subgroup of Kongo people], the term *nganga* denotes a physician or medical man, pharmacist, prophet, seer, visionary, fortune-teller, priest, and ndoki. He uses his kindoki to provide help rather than harm. . . . Working closely with an an-

cestral spirit, he sits above any imaginable kind of human power. He thereby becomes the factotum and guardian of the community secrets. To some degree he lives in a world of his own. He is the last hope to whom the individual and the entire community turn in the time of despair. (67)

Fundamental to Pilate's spiritual identity as an Nganga are the circumstances attending her birth. Macon's description of Pilate's unusual birth illustrates her spiritual distinction. Not only was Pilate born to a dead woman, but also she birthed herself. Further substantiation of this spiritual inclination is Pilate's being physically marked. The unmarked stomach is a type of scarification conveying the spiritual significance of Pilate being "otherworldly." Henry John Drewal and Margaret Thompson Drewal remark that the cutting of the umbilical cords "gives us life apart from our mothers" (349). Even though Pilate does not know her mother or her mother's name, she remains attached to her in the ancestral realm signified by her unmarked stomach. Her mother's name, Sing, becomes the primary and most efficacious means to facilitate ritual outcomes, evidenced by singing Milkman to life and Hagar onward to the afterlife. Furthermore, the piercing of her own ear affirms her spiritual courage. She confirms herself at age twelve by piercing her ear, putting the slip of paper bearing her name in a brass box, and hanging the brass box in her lobe. Beyond being an accessory, by wearing the container bearing her name, Pilate marks a critical stage of life. This self-confirmation occurs after her father's murder. The idea of courage is an essential feature of an Nganga, who is expected to be courageous in order to protect the family as well as the community.

Another verification of Pilate's spiritual status occurs when Guitar first brings Milkman to her house. She is described as having "one foot pointed east and one pointed west" (36). In many Bantu cultures the concept of spirituality manifests in one's ability to dwell concomitantly in both the material realm and the spiritual realm. This duality is expressed in African American culture as being "two-headed." The description of Pilate's feet going in two distinct directions is indicative of her two-headedness. According to the Zulu of South Africa, the description of a *sangoma* or female spiritual healer is a person whose feet turn backwards.[15] The Akan concept of *sankofa* is the spiritual metaphor representing the fluidity of past and present, translating to the imperative to return to the past to fetch the cultural and spiritual memorates and bring them forward to the present. Symbolized by a bird whose feet are facing forward and whose head is turned looking behind him, the description of the Sankofa bird is similar to Pilate's feet, pointing forward and backward and establishing her ability to assist people in their spiritual and cultural recovery.

Additionally, this spiritual/material orientation finds fusion in Pilate's attraction to rocks. She states, "Everyplace I went I got me a rock" (142). J. Omosade Awolalu explains the significance of such a connection: "Rocks are witnesses; they were there from the beginning." Moreover, the Yoruba have a proverb, *Ota o ki iku* (the rock never dies). In South Africa, the Bantu describe stones as the living bones of the earth and people are initiated into the spirit of the stones. The geography book that she carries with her for most of her life confirms Pilate's role as earth mother. Representing spiritual topography and her connection with the feminine principle of the earth and natural forces, the geography book is a metaphor for the earthy woman whose voice "made Milkman think of pebbles" (40).

Pilate has been rejected and marginalized by the community at large because of the absence of a navel. In fact, it is Pilate's remoteness and separation from others that facilitates the symbolic sight and self-mastery that she possesses. Additionally, this spiritual partition has allowed her access to the archetypal language needed to understand herself along with the spiritual clarity needed to access the ancestral realms. Unhampered by any responsibility to please others, she can devote her physical energies to listening to the voices of her spiritual guides, the *Ajé* or earth mothers and the ancestors. In previous novels, Toni Morrison establishes the significance of liminality in defining the space to access spiritual phenomena.

Pilate's liminality is facilitated by her initiation. Preparing her head, she cuts off her hair. Her next steps are to determine the contours of her life and to continue communication with the dead. Having been trained by a rootworker, she is a natural healer and a midwife. In Africa, the female healers were also midwives. Midwifery was one of the few spiritual roles permitted and reinforced during slavery. While African people were moving in the direction of individualism consistent with the values of American (white) cultural identity, Pilate remains linked with other black people through a deep and abiding love and sense of hospitality—twin values indicating an intact sense of African morality and ethical consciousness. Pilate's happiness in Virginia comes from being in the company of so many Black people. Later on his journey, Milkman will come to the same conclusion about the level of African generosity, hospitality, and genuine concern for the welfare of others. For example, while in Shalimar, with the absence of white people, he discovers the comfortableness and ease in which the community members functioned with each other and the sense of intermutuality that defines their lives. He even wonders why they ever left the South in the first place.

Described as having palm oil flowing in her veins and being generous, Pilate retains the African traditions of offering food "before one word of conversation—business or social began" (150). Regarding generosity, a Kongo proverb states, "He who holds out his hands does not die." African sensibilities are further illustrated in the smell of ginger associated with her presence and indicated by her preparation of hot nut soup, a dish of West African origin. Musing on her openhandedness, Milkman notes, she has "cooked him his first perfect egg," has "shown him the sky," has told him stories," "sang him songs," "fed him bananas and cornbread," and "hot nut soup" (211). Offering him an egg is a spiritual gesture suggestive of the incomplete nature of his life at that time. Since Pilate is Milkman's spiritual double, the symbolic gesture of offering him an egg is significant. For the Dogon, Amma, the Creator, originally created eight human beings. He created four pairs of twins—female and male. These Nommo or twins refer to mythological ancestors and to one's own lineage. In this offering of an egg, Pilate underscores the necsssity of balance and communication between the living and the dead—a metaphor for his initiation on the journey.

The description of Pilate's house gives additional insight into her role as a healer. Morrison writes in *Song of Solomon*, "Her house sat eighty feet from the sidewalk and was backed by four huge pine trees, from which she got the needles she stuck into her mattress" and "whose basement seemed to be rising from rather than settling onto the ground" (27).[16] In Pilate's world, materialism and modernity represent exoticisms. Occupying a liminal space, Pilate lives in her un-numbered house with no modern appliances such as a telephone. Guitar describes Pilate's house as "shiny," "shiny and brown. With a smell" (35).

Pilate's house in the Ki-Kongo language is a *kanda diamoyo dimbu yemba* (a house open to others) and a symbol of spiritual vitality (*African Cosmology* 104). Additionally, similar to the house situated between heaven and earth, *aye* and *orun*, Pilate has the ability to move between realms and shift-shape, demonstrated when she retrieves Milkman and Guitar at the police station.[17] Having been trained in the spiritual arts while in Virginia, her fluency in reading the spirit helps her to understand not only her life's mission, but also gives her the ability to assist Milkman through his cycle of rebirth/birth/rebirth. In the novel, various characters remark on her capacity to know things in the spiritual realm. Macon tells Milkman to stay away from her, saying, "Pilate can't teach you a thing to use in this world, maybe the next, but not this one" (55).

Pilate's insight is evident upon her arrival in Michigan to reunite with her brother and to supposedly heal their fractured relationship. Shortly after her arrival, Pilate's "real" mission is revealed. She returns to usher in the birth of Macon Dead III. According to Patrice Malidoma Somé, a birth is the arrival of someone, usually an ancestor that somebody already knows, who has important tasks to do here" (*Of Water and the Spirit* 20). Somé speaks of a prebirth ritual where a hearing with the fetus is convened to determine who the soul is, the nature of his or her life mission, and whether some object is needed to assist the "becoming" child. The living must know who is being reborn.

Pilate helps Ruth to become pregnant by giving her an herbal preparation to drink that not only increases her fertility, but also brings Macon to Ruth's bed as if under a spell. Next Pilate conducts a ritual as a prelude to the arrival of "a little bird." In the novel's first ceremony, Pilate sings a blues riff, opening the spaces for the call-and-response format necessary for group participation similar to an *oriki* praise chant. The particular type of oriki called *orile*, stresses the accomplishment of family members and lineage ancestors (183). She sings "Sugarman done fly away." Wearing "a pair of four button ladies' galoshes" (5), symbolic of the Kongo cosmogram, Ruth accompanies Pilate in this ceremony by spilling the red petals.[18] This is the first reference to Ruth, not by her name, but as the "dead doctor's daughter" (3). This appellation extends Ruth's identity beyond herself to ancestral relations.

Toni Morrison will develop Ruth's ancestral proclivity throughout the novel. Ruth's participation in Robert Smith's ritual flight prefigures his physical transition; her spilling of the red petals, corresponds to the blood offering or sacrifice in a propitiatory offering. In exchange for the life of the child she is preparing to deliver, she offers this *ebo* or physical sacrifice of an inauthentic flying man, who needs "wings" to execute his flight, for the life of her son, Milkman, who will not need wings to launch his own flight.[19] Mr. Smith reads the ritual sign, which signals his taking flight.

Soyinka discusses the connection between sacrifice and music from a Yoruba perspective, stating, "Music is the intensive language of transition and its communicant means, the catalyst and solvent of the regenerative hoard. The actor dares not venture into the world unprepared, without the symbolic sacrifices and the invocation of eudaemonic guardians of the abyss" (*Myth* 36). Additionally, using the device of repetition, which Drewal speaks of as critical to African performance, the songs advanced the "transformational" and "generative" processes directing their quests for liberation (xiii). Although Pilate has had only limited access to her spiritual charge after his birth, she is able to sing him a song.

In Kongo culture the individual's existence begins on the day of birth and moves from being the property of the parents to being a part of the community through a series of initiations into his new world. After being born the child is taken by the Nganga or the ceremonial priest who introduces the child to the community. This first initiation, which occurs when the child is about one month old, is accompanied by presentation of gifts and food. The community sings, "Seer show me the way. Seer show me the way. Seer help me see" (Bockie 32).

After Macon bans Pilate from the house, she is able to *fix* Milkman with a look, ensuring that he will eventually find his way to her door. Cut off from family, Milkman is caught in a spiritual crossroads represented by a clash of cultures. Because Milkman does not have a fully constructed African value system, he is not able to negotiate the in-between space and access spiritual power. In order for Milkman to be successful, Pilate must relocate him to a space of mythic consciousness to repair the cosmic ruptures in the material and ancestral realm. The stories Pilate tells Milkman take on a religious sensibility as spiritual revelations. Pilate helps to construct new *beliefs* as she helps him *believe* or imagine the possibilities of himself. Although Milkman does not understand Pilate's role in assisting him on his journey, her stories plant the seeds that ultimately assist him to distinguish authentic desires from the distractions of the material world.

∗   ∗   ∗

> I implore you Eshu
> to plant in my mouth
> your verbal ashe
> restoring to me the language
> that was mine
> and was stolen from me.
>
> —Abdias do Nascimento, "Pade de Exu Libertador"

Once delivered by Pilate, Milkman begins the next phase of his journey assisted by Guitar. A correlate of the Òrìsà Elegba, Guitar like the Òrìsà, represents a link between the past and the future. Because Milkman's deprivation lies in his disconnect not only from his family, but also from African people in a communal sense, his spiritual separation must be mediated by Guitar. Guitar first appears at the interstices between life and death when Robert Smith, who is at a spiritual crossroads, leaps from Mercy hospital. Elegba has the ability "to bring life and death into clear focus, thereby giving people a clear view of reality" (Mason and Edwards, *Black Gods* 13). Similar to Elegba, who is the lord of the in-between, the readers meet Guitar at the crossroads (the locus of departed spirits or water egress for departing spirits four ways), between Robert Smith's leap from the roof of (No) Mercy Hospital and Pilate's singing the death/life song.

In *Song of Solomon*, Guitar transports Milkman through American history as he documents a series of racial atrocities occurring over a broad sweep of time. His words convey more than the stories. He expresses the terror experienced by African people in an oppressive racist society. Given Milkman's sheltered and privileged life, these lessons were a revelation to him. The newly arrived southerner—now northerner—is indeterminately described as "a cat-eyed boy about five or six years old" (7). The dialectical direction of being partly up and partly down as well as the juxtaposition of cultivated farms and abandoned fields clearly establishes the identity of Elegba within the Yoruba spiritual frames.

Morrison provides the reader with numerous clues to establish Guitar's archetypal identity and affinity to Elegba. The first is his presence to witness Smith's sacrifice, since Elegba oversees all sacrifices, prescribes all ritual acts, and bears all sacrifices to Olofi—the Supreme God. Elegba's usual function and primary role is that of an intermediary between God and humanity: between the Òrìsà and God and between human beings and the Òrìsà. Originating in the Yoruba culture of Nigeria, Elegba is also found in the cultures of the Fon, the Ewe, and others throughout global Africa. For the Yoruba, Elegba is a paradox. Two of his names relate to his duality or dialectical contradiction. He is called Elegba—"the powerful one" or Eshu Odara—"Eshu is not good." According to the *apataki* or stories that make up the sacred literary corpus know as Ifa, he is the keeper of Asé—the essence of God. Asé has various meanings including ability, skill, power, and aptitude.

The second clue is Guitar's role as the first male character to speak in the novel. One of Elegba's strongest aptitudes is talking. Elegba owns speech, and his verbal attributes include the ability to talk with great innuendo, to carp, to cajole, to needle, and to reverse situations. His ability to speak all languages and act as the ultimate mediator is reflected in his names:

Alaroye (owner of talkativeness) and Oloofofo (bearer of tales). Yoruba devotees chant *Ago laroye* (make way for the owner of talkativeness) to induce spiritual possession by Elegba.

As the keeper of Asé, which also corresponds to the power of the spoken word that brings phenomena into existence, there is a clear correlation between him and Morrison's Guitar. For instance, Milkman meets Guitar when Guitar beats up four boys who were teasing him. Later, Guitar takes off his baseball cap and hands it to Milkman, telling him to wipe the blood from his nose. Milkman bloodies the cap and returns it, and Guitar slaps it back on his head. This action of sacrificial blood feeding the head of Guitar corresponds to the offering of a blood sacrifice to Elegba. While in Shalimar when Milkman thinks about that incident, "a black rooster strutted by, its blood-red comb draped forward like a wicked brow" (268). In describing elements of sacrificial rites, Awolalu refers to all sacrifices as *ebo*. In the category of birds, *oromadie* (roosters) are two-legged who are sacrificed to Elegba as propitiary sacrifices. Awolalu notes that Elegba (Esu) "is fond of black fowls" (163).

Anthony Ferreira remarks that Elegba also employs the power of the Iyami, the earth mothers who morph into the birds of the night. As they head to Pilate's house to get the "gold," Milkman "saw a white peacock." Morrison reiterates this connection with birds and sacrifice in the excursions at Feather's pool hall "in the middle of the Blood Bank area" (56). In addition, Guitar's revelation that he is "a natural-born hunter" (85) confirms the association of Elegba with Ogun and Ochossi—both hunter Òrìsà and spiritual forces in the triadic construction called the warriors. Guitar also provides Milkman with a link to his destiny by introducing him to his aunt, Pilate Dead "who had as much to do with his future as she did his past" (35).

Additionally, Elegba shapes culture, advances history and civilization, and reveals the sacredness of life. The actions of Guitar are compatible with these ideas. Through language, Guitar reveals the sacred passages to Milkman making him privy to the cultural and political history of African people, which Milkman considers "racial problems" (108). There is an *apataki* or spiritual parable that speaks to Elegba's ability to disrupt as well as cement human relationships. When Elegba heard that two friends never quarreled, he made a two-colored cap. One side was white and the other black. (In some stories, the colors are red and black.) He passed between two friends and later they quarreled about the color of his hat, since each of them had seen only the side closest to him. The spiritual lesson in the *apa-*

taki speaks to the duality of nature: that two things can be true at the same time. Throughout this novel, Morrison challenges the linear construction of either/or and posits a cyclical reality where, the concepts coexist.

Elegba also serves as the enforcer of the universe, as a type of cosmic police, ensuring that a person lives a moral life. Morrison draws Guitar as a person who keeps the balance when he confronts Milkman about causing Hagar's distress. Furthermore, Guitar directs him to give up the things that weigh him down in order to achieve spiritual transformation. Mason states, "Elegba was the idea that it was possible for man to fly, he ushered in this new ability and thereby set up new rules concerning flight" (Mason and Edwards, *Black Gods* 11). In trying to assist Milkman to understand some things concerning African people—of which Milkman at this point in time has been oblivious—he says, "Wanna fly, you got to give up the shit that weighs you down" (*Song* 180). Elegba is the Òrìsà who represents the concept of choice and freewill assisting a person in deciding his or her own destiny through the manipulation of forces and phenomena. Ferreira notes that Elegba "puts us in a state opposite to the one we are in until we discern the real purposes of life" and "to establish harmony between the visible and invisible worlds" (1-A).

Guitar's association with Elegba as being a protector is further substantiated when he reveals to Milkman that he is a "Sunday man." Explaining the meaning of his name, he states that if someone kills a black person on a Sunday he balances the death of a white person on Sunday. Guitar's day corresponds to the Akan day name of Kwesi. According to the Akan, each day has its own controlling spirit force or energy associated with it; the Sunday-born person is considered a protector.

When Milkman goes on his journey without including Guitar, he gains his ire, causing Guitar to conclude that Milkman has duplicitous intentions concerning the fortune of gold. Yoruba believe that one must propitiate Elegba at the beginning of all activities in order to ensure success of the endeavor. Additionally, if this placation does not occur, there will be obstacles. Guitar has been looking for Milkman since his arrival in Shalimar. The Yoruba proverb, *ko se I duro de, ko si se isa fun* (one neither flees from him nor waits for him), speaks of the slipperiness of this Òrìsà who cannot be constrained. When he least expects him, Milkman encounters Guitar leaning against a tree.

For the Yoruba, Elegba's mission on earth is to establish the foundation for human beings' perception of nature and reality. He negates existing conceptions of reality and forces the establishment of new ones. One of his praise songs illustrates this idea:

Bara suwa yo omo yalawa na
Keni irawo
Bara suwa yo omo yalawa na
Keni irawo bara wa yo Eke e Esu Odara
omo yalawa na keni irawo e

Vital force who far and wide appears;
Child that separates, splits and divides the road
Do not cut the initiate's mat of goodness; Vital force will come to deliver
    [us]
Forked stick,
Esu performer of wonders
Child that separates, splits and divides the road
Do not cut the initiates mat of goodness. (*Orin Òrìsà* 69)

Guitar helps Milkman to separate the two distinct halves of his one personality. After Milkman decides to rob Pilate's house, he feels "a self inside himself emerge, a clean-lined definite self—a self that could join the chorus at Railroad Tommy's with more than laughter" (184). The narrator describes how Guitar's persuasive words not only help to define Milkman, but also give the idea "a crisp concreteness" (184). Concrete is one of the components in the symbolic recreation of the Òrìsà Elegba. In fact, Mason notes that Elegba is the "cement that holds society together" (*Orin Òrìsà* 63). Through stories, Guitar, like Elegba, helps to gather the various indispensable elements necessary for the creation of an authentic spiritual culture, giving it credibility, validity, life, and creative power.

✳   ✳   ✳

This little light of mine, I'm going to let it shine.
    —Traditional Spiritual

Who was the first one to wear shiny clothes? That was me, Baby.
I started that. You remember that burgundy jacket I had with
the bolt of lightning on the back. The lightning was in glitter.
Glitter is shiny, Baby.
    —James "Thunder" Early, "Dream Girls"

Toni Morrison uses the Kongo concept of *vezima* (flash) as the major conceit in the novel to indicate spiritual presence. The idea of *vezima* relates to spiritual interaction between the material and spiritual realms. Manifestations of light assist one to recognize his or her destiny or to have a moment of spiritual remembrance from past incarnations. Robert Farris Thompson notes that the flash can arouse the spirit (*Face of the Gods* 57). In *Song of Solomon*, Toni Morrison employs a variety of words to represent this impulse of spirit such as shiny, glitter, gleam, and gold. For example, Milkman's quest for gold symbolizes his intense need for spiritual fulfillment, which he realizes through his reunion with his family and his connection with the land. A Ghanaian maxim describes Milkman's ultimate realization:

> It is the human being that counts;
> I call upon gold, it answers not;
> I call upon cloth it answers not;
> It is the human being that counts. (Gyekye 25)

The Kongo idea that human beings are representations bringing radiance in the form of light from the spirit world substantiates the symbolic significance of mirrors and iridescence. Thompson reports that before the importation of mirrors, Kongo ritual experts used wing-case charms constructed from the iridescent wings of a beetle. These charms were "something full of light, like water, that you can see through to the other world" (*Faces of the Gods* 175). He adds, "The idea of the glitter of the spirit fused with the notion of second sight through symbolized flight in order to expand the beyond—*vila mu bangula bweno a ku mpemba*" (174). Glittering objects and the embedding of spirit became fundamental to African cosmos since the shine "arrests the spirit with its light and hints of movement—to the other world" (175).

In an interview of the Georgia Federal Writers' Project recorded in *Drums and Shadows*, George Boddison of Tin City states that the copper wires strung with charms around his wrists and mirrors worn at his temples, which "flashed and glittered when he moved his head," were worn to keep evil forces from hurting him. He states, "Du debil caahn dwell on me. It hab tuh pass on." The interviewers state as they drive away, "The last glimpse we had was of the fragments of mirror bound to his head glittering in the sun" (22).

The terms *glitter* and *gleam* are used to describe a range of characters and their spiritual reactions and inclinations throughout the novel. Guitar describes Pilate as having "silvery-brown skin of her ankles" (38). Addition-ally, as Pilate relates the story of her father being shot "five feet into the air." Guitar's eyes are described as "too shiny" (42). His shiny eyes relate to his spiritual connection with the horror Pilate recounts as she tells the story of how and when white people murdered African people with impunity. Emblematic of his mission to balance the score, when asking about who shot her father, his eyes were "glittering with lights (41). Glitter can also represent Milkman's contentment with his evolved sense of "self" after the physical confrontation with Macon. He reconsiders its impact measuring it for his worthiness against "the kind of story that stirred the glitter up in the eyes of the old men in Tommy's" (85). Again as he relates his stories to Reverend Cooper in Danville, "He glittered in the light of their adoration and grew fierce with pride" (238).

Finally, the term *silvery* describes spiritual encounters and transforma-tions. Following Circe's direction to the cave's location, Milkman falls into the water and is submerged completely. He gets a glimpse of small "silvery translucent fish" (251). The silvery gleam of the fish according to Kongo belief is a reflection of the *simbi* (water spirits) who inhabit rivers and other freshwater estuaries. Thompson notes that, as such, "rivers mark the boundary between two realms" (*Face* 49); Milkman experiences a symbolic death having crossed the *kalunga* line into the world beyond. Fu-Kiau notes that fish and other amphibians deliver messages to the ancestors on behalf of their descendants (quoted in Thompson, "Kongo Influences" 152).

Milkman's ritual space for this preliminary ritual is in the woods, the realm where the demarcation between spirit and the physical are blurred. In Milkman's journey to the cave, he is able to connect with nature via the stream, the earth, trees, and elements typifying both the natural world and ritual spaces. This ritual that introduces Milkman to the shared rhythms of patterns of nature is an overture for his comprehension of future spiritual events. As in all ritual space, boundaries and thresholds are clearly delin-eated to mark the ingress and egress from ritual activity. Milkman's ingress was through the "parted bush." From there, he "wades in water," climbs "twenty feet of steep rock," and enters a cave (251–55). He egresses through the cave and walks across a bridge indicating his spiritual evolution.

Within an African frame, rituals culminate with a meal corresponding to the cool-down phase of spiritual performance. As Milkman emerges, he begins to shake with hunger. Milkman's intense hunger is a desire for an authentic life. Moreover, his feeling that he is going to pass out suggests that he is in a state of spiritual possession/transformation. His behaviors following his emergence from the cave are inconsistent with previous actions. Furthermore, his eating of leaves is what the Yoruba would refer to as a type of spiritual *osain* (herbal infusion) readying him for another phase of the ritual.

After Milkman leaves the bush and heads back to "civilization," he notes the time. He observes the position of the sun, which is "a quarter of the way down from what even he knew was high noon" (256). The time "quarter of the way down" corresponds to a position on the dikenga dia Kongo called *luvemba* (death) denoted by the color white prefigures Milkman's death.[20]

Maneno ya Melele

The people in Danville are also a key to the web of community for which Milkman is searching/not searching.[21] When Milkman first arrives in Shalimar, he walks past the men on the porch, enters the store, and asks for a drink without speaking or introducing himself. A major cultural breach of not speaking or bringing the good word identifies Milkman as someone who lacks the social values of African people. In this preliminary stage of the ritual, the men teach Milkman the power of language through a verbal ritual. One of the formulary insults referring to sexual inadequacy begins the round, which indicates the utmost disrespect and to what length the contest will escalate.

Milkman has no other option but to participate after the first challenge. Soundin' and signifyin' are both valued social behaviors among African males and considered a type of cultural initiation. After the verbal exchange, a physical fight ensues with a man wielding a "glittering" knife, and Milkman is cut with a broken bottle. In that fight, Milkman gets a cut on his face described as a slit. I read the mark as a cultural signifier, foreshadowing his acquisition of a new identity, as a flying African. Drewal and Mason note that certain incisions or *gbere* in Yoruba language are protective, signaling the "invisible transformations of persons" (Henry Drewal and Mason 332).

*   *   *

> I got a black cat bone I got a mojo too I got the John the Conqueror root I'm going to mess with you.
>
> —Willie Dixon, "I'm Your Hoochie Coochie Man"

After Milkman engages in these verbal and physical exchanges and holds his own, his provisional acceptance as a member of the community is signaled by his invitation to hunt. Attired in the ritual gear of the hunter and situated in the ritual space of the woods, his personality dissolves. In the woods—a space of social deprivation away from his father's money, his own clothes, and other material possessions—Milkman learns the power of language and is able to gain the information he needs to survive Guitar's attack against him.

The Zulu healer, Credo Mutwa, explains the significance of hunting a bobcat as a rite of passage. Called *Izilo ze Nkosi* (Beasts of the King), bobcats were often used to test the courage of men who were to be promoted to the next level (Mutwa 188). Milkman is able to begin his "new" life by performing a once imponderable activity: hunting. Doing so, he emerges from the woods with self-confidence and self-acceptance.

Similar to rites of passage, the ritual hunting advances Milkman to the next phase of his soul journey. Milkman's ability to be exhilarated by simply walking the earth is an indication of his new status. His walking is analogous to his being part of the earth, like a tree "his legs were stalks, tree trunks, a part of his body that extended down down down into the rock and soil, and were comfortable there" (284). Walking the earth, Milkman regains the spiritual balance indicated by being able to walk upright without a limp. This is similar to the *ese* or story of Babaluaiye, or Omolu, Lord of the earth, the curative Òrìsà who has dominion over illness and health. The *ese* explains how Babaluaiye developed a club foot after Nana Buruku cast him into an abyss. Milkman has also been in a cultural abyss and has now achieved the balance necessary to walk strong on the earth.

The Dogon describe the earth as the soil where man lives and walks (Griaule and Dieterlen, *Pale Fox* 64). In this stage of his life, Milkman heads toward his true self. Although he does not help the men catch the bobcat, the hearty joke they enjoy at his expense engenders an acceptance of Milkman, especially after he acquiesces to become the subject of the joke. After the sacrifice of the animal, the next phase of the ritual is the skinning of the animal. Milkman takes part in the ritual vivisection and pulls out the heart, which is symbolic of Hagar's impending death from a broken heart and in accordance with the theme of love consistent with all of Morison's novels.

As the men ritually skin the cat, Guitar's words mediate the incisions the men make. Using a call-and-response motif, Toni Morrison re-creates a litany or liturgical homily reminding the reader that a portion of all sacrifices is given to Elegba to make certain that the message is sent to Olofi. The textual description of the vivisection punctuated by Guitar's words signifies the presence of Elegba—the interlocutor who carries the message from the horizontal earth to the vertical heaven. The ritual meal following the sacrifice returns the men to a normal state of social interaction after their heightened state of excitement. Milkman finishes the ritual experience with a bath given to him by Sweet. In this act of washing, he learns the idea of reciprocity and the true exchange of love that he has not been able to share with Hagar. Through water imagery, an archetypal idea, Milkman is transported from his singular life and is initiated into his new status as a member of the African collective.

*   *   *

> This little light of mine, I'm going to let it shine. Let it shine, let it shine, let it shine.
>
> —Traditional African American Spiritual

Milkman also begins to feel linked through "some cord or pulse of information" (296). He begins to make other connections about his "people" after hearing the children sing a round game. Milkman tries to make the link concerning who begat whom and the nature of his kin relationships. Additionally, their singing reminds him of the cultural breaches in his own childhood where he never was allowed to join in any of these ring games. This round is what Olatunde O. Olatunji refers to as an *oriki* (praise poem) in the Yoruba oral tradition. Olatunji notes that the result of chanting this type of *oriki* is to create a sense of solidarity with one's ancestors and to gain pride and confidence in the self (183). Moreover, because he has no pen, Milkman has to tap into the oral tradition, the primary way in which culturally relevant information is exchanged intergenerationally. With his back against a tree, a sudden tiredness overcomes him, and Milkman curls into a fetal position. As his awareness of language heightens, he is able to understand his family heritage, which ushers in a rebirth of spirit. Overhearing the children singing he listens to the round. He commits the song—described as consisting of "some nonsense words"—to memory.

Toni Morrison's inscription of words derived from various African languages is taken from *Drums and Shadows*. White Bluff community member Prince Sneed recounts a story told to him by his grandfather:

Muh gran say ole an Waldburg down on St. Catherine own some slaves wut wuzn climatize an he wuk um hahd an one dey dey wuz hoein in duh fiel and duh dribuh come out an two ub em wuz unuh a tree in duh shade, an duh hoes wuz wukin by demself. Duh dribuh say "Wut dis?" An dey say, "Kum buba yali kum buba tambe, Kum kunka yali kum k'unka tambe," quick like. Den dey rise off duh ground an fly away. Nobody ebuh see um no mo. Some say dey fly back tuh Africa. Muh gran see dat wid he own eye. (*Drums and Shadow* 79)

Using Lorenzo Dow Turner's *Africanisms in the Gullah Dialect*, I translated these "nonsense words" and came up with the following phonetic variations and their accompanying semantic values. For the word *booba*, I found *bubu*, which in Mandingo means "to fly." Additionally, *booba* yielded the Yoruba *buba*, which means "to ambush" or "to hide." The same word in Ki-Kongo language means "to strike" and in Kimbundu from Angola "to run out." In the Vai language of Liberia and Sierra Leone, the word *bubu* is a term imitative of the noise made by a fowl when about to fly.[22] For the word *tambee*, I make the correlation with tambi or ntambi from Ki-Kongo meaning "footmark" (202). For *yalle* the closest equivalent is in Umbundu language of Angola, *yala*, which means "to spread" (184). In Yoruba *ya* is a verb meaning "to make way." Finally, *ka* means "to rise" in Vai (206). *Kan* also means "to be dropped" in Djerma of French West Africa (196).

The meanings of the words are consistent with the basis of the song and the stories narrated about Solomon flying away and dropping the baby in flight. Morrison's imaginative prose assumes a greater cultural legitimacy and links Milkman's heroic quest to the millions of other Africans who have fashioned their own heroic stories and maintained an unbroken circle of language and narratives refuting the erasure of culture in the Americas. Milkman's epiphany is twofold consisting of the reclamation of his name and the surrender of his self-centeredness.

Arrival

In this cautionary tale about balancing community interest with individual objectives, Toni Morrison reiterates the values of heritage, history, and heroism. Through Milkman's transformation and discovery and Pilate's selfless example of spiritual integrity, readers are challenged to reflect and reevaluate their own principles, reclaim their names and family stories, and challenge historic hegemony, cultural erasure, and spiritual stasis. At the novel's end, having returned with Pilate to bury the bones of his deceased grandfather, Pilate restates the power of love to sustain.[23] She says, "I would have loved 'em all. If I'd a knowed more, I would a loved more" (340).

Simon Bockie reports that before an important person dies, they address the community, saying: "I loved everybody. I am not troubled to join my ancestors" (98). Becoming a singer of the song in this inversion, Milkman sings Pilate's transition to the status of ancestor as she had sung him into his birth. Her death adds one more element to the story of the flying Africans, those who could fly "without ever leaving the ground" (340). Prior to his leap of flight/faith, Milkman achieves apotheosis. He shouts, "Guitar, Here I am." "You want my life?" (341). Afterwards, the hills respond, echoing tar, am, and life three times each (341). Milkman realizes that Tar am (is) Life—or he comes to an understanding of the tree of life—a metaphor for self-realization. At last, he realizes his relationship to all that is and all that will ever be. His connection to his ancestors is the source of power.

The power he now senses in that ancestral connection and with nature supplants the material wealth he once sought. Accordingly, he becomes a "mud father," the male correlate to Pilate's "mud motherliness." With this revelation, Milkman can finally relieve himself of the thing that has weighed him down—his singular, individual life. Leaping as "fleet and bright as a lodestar" Milkman's sun has "wheeled" toward completion and he has become eternal.[24] Now the round sung by the children in the circle/ring will expand, adding Milkman's name to the Song of Solomon.

4

Dancing with Trees and Dreaming of Yellow Dresses

The Dilemma of Jadine in *Tar Baby*

There is a spirit of nature, the spirit of the river, the spirit of the mountain. There is the spirit of the animals, of the water, the spirit of the ancestors.

—African Oral Tradition

They have a road they follow, and something called a god they worship—not the living spirit that is in everything but a creature separate raised above all surrounding things.

—Ayi Kwei Armah, *Two Thousand Seasons*

In her third novel, *Tar Baby* (1981), Toni Morrison inscribes indigenous knowledge, representing physical and cultural landscapes as sites of power to balance individuals and restore community cohesion.[1] Using patterns of African traditional beliefs where nature is revered and deified, Morrison enlarges the spiritual territory of the literary canon by linking her narrative with eco-critical considerations of the natural world. Morrison's choice of epigrams for *Tar Baby* reiterates the idea of spiritual contentions and contested identities. Quoting the Bible's book of 1 Corinthians, "For it hath been declared unto me of you, my brethren, by them which are of the house of Chloe, that here are contentions among you," Morrison argues throughout the novel that these conflicts are spiritual at the core. My analysis of *Tar Baby* concerns the ways in which the natural environment interacts with characters and reflects their respective values, spiritual ethics, or spiritual paucity.

I also consider the role and symbolic representation of the Yoruba spiritual force Iyami Osoronga or Ajé. Highlighting my analysis of the Iyami, or mothers of the earth, is an exploration of two Yoruba Òrìsà, Oshun and Shango as leitmotifs of beauty and sacred medicine and justice, respectively. As spiritual forces, Oshun and Shango, like the Ajé, represent the potential for self-realization as well as for ecological and spiritual balance. For that reason, an examination of the tensions between the un-natural and the natural will direct the discussion of transgression and reintegration, taking into consideration two of the characters: Jadine Childs and Son Green.

In *Tar Baby*, Morrison makes it apparent that she plans for her readers to walk away with knowledge of their true and "ancient properties"(305). For example, on her dedication page she affirms her allegiance to a circle of ancestral women, as well as concentric circles of Iyami, or other mothers, in the African American tradition of Ma Dear or Big Mommas, beginning with her maternal great-great-grandmother Mrs. Caroline Smith, her maternal great-grandmother Mrs. Millie McTyeire, her maternal grandmother Mrs. Ardelia Willis (for whom she is named), her mother Mrs. Ramah Wofford, her sister Lois Brooks, as well as all of their "sisters." Included in this sphere are other mud mothers who may not be related to her by blood, but are connected through shared spiritual inclinations. These qualities sacred and fluid are rooted in the creative imagination and are reflected in the natural realm.

Morrison's depiction of Isle des Chevaliers, the primary setting for the novel, illustrates an African-derived idea of the natural world as a primary dwelling for the divine. Under the canopy of the natural world, one has access to God and to the source of one's ancient properties. Consistent with Morrison's previous novelistic endeavors, when tradition is violated her didactic narrative opens up spiritual/cultural spaces to bring the world back to its equilibrium. Subverting the hegemonic attempt to separate African people from sacred communion with nature, Morrison's insistent prose reestablishes nature's prominence.

Formerly, as well as presently, hegemony has supported this partitioning as a prerequisite to being civilized and to being converted from African "heathenism." Laurenti Magesa advances the depth of this connection for African people:

> Sustaining the universe by maintaining harmony or balance between its two spheres and among all beings is the most important ethical responsibility for humanity and it forms the basis of any individual's moral character. Even more significantly, however, it determines the quality of the universe itself. It requires commitment in upholding the sanctity of the creation in everyday life, because as Sindima has

emphasized, "All life—that of people, plants and animals, and the earth—originates and therefore shares an intimate relationship of bondedness with divine life; all life is divine life" (73).

For the most part, African people have maintained this relationship with the land. Being in a place where they were not only physically different, but were also environmental and philosophical aliens, they have maintained many attitudes, customs, and cultural characteristics that can be traced indirectly to Africa (*Blues People* 7). These ecological ethics, intrinsic to African spiritual traditions, correspond to the Africans' need to live in harmonious ways with their environments and are intimately connected with the broader framework of worldviews concerning physical landscapes.

The prevailing practice of revering nature and understanding that people and land are never separate caused great tension between them and their white captors. From earliest contact with African people, Europeans posited that the African's closeness to nature meant distance from God. To tame, domesticate, civilize, de-nature, and de-spirit Africans became the mission of American plantation owners and the process to affect control over an African population, which in many southern states outnumbered European-American enslavers. Concomitant with these Christian teachings is a rejection of nature explained by Eve and Adam's expulsion from the Garden of Eden. Having access to the natural world is having access to the source of one's ancient properties and to God.

E. Bolaji Idowu explains that natural sites such as trees, rivers, hills, "primordial divinities and the deified ancestors," are places to petition God (45). In *Tar Baby* Morrison gives primacy to the power resident in trees. As a literary trope, trees must be considered in any exploration of nature owing to their special significance in African culture. Janheinz Jahn notes, "In them [trees] the water of the depths, the primal Nommo, the word of the ancestors, surges up spontaneously; they are the road traveled by the dead, the loas, to living men; they are the repository of the deified" (102).

As with her previous narrative figurations, Toni Morrison represents disruptions of nature as metaphors for the spiritual displacement of African people. Chronicling the characteristics of spiritual collapse—when the natural order is disrupted by those who do not know the language of nature, or its signs— Morrison writes:

> The men had already folded the earth where there has been no fold and hollowed her where there had been no hollow, which explains what happened to the river. It crested, then lost its course, and finally

its head. Evicted from the place where it had lived, and forced into unknown turf, it could not form pools or waterfalls and ran every which way. (9)

For instance, many African indigenous spiritual systems share a common corpus of knowledge and complex belief systems relative to river systems. The river's disappearance is significant given its location where communication takes place between human and spiritual worlds. As the essence of both spiritual and physical life, rivers are regarded as the ultimate source of such life-sustaining powers with potential to transform an individual from one spiritual state to another.

For the Yoruba, places where land and trees converge with water are thought to be sites of great spiritual energy, as is any place where two natural forces come together. This natural dilemma foreshadows the meeting between Jadine and Son as a cosmic attempt to restore the equilibrium of the natural world. Additionally, at the symbolic level, Mircea Eliade points out that a river, a stone, a star, an animal can be transformed into something greater than self. These images of God in nature are extensions of reality that go beyond representation and demonstrate the primary spiritual edict—of living in balance with the surrounding forces of nature as well as establishing sacred space in the natural environment (*Sacred and the Profane* 12).

The establishment of sacred space in the natural environment coincides with Yoruba thought as eco-spiritual emblems represent phenomena that humans can draw on to access *ASE* (vital life force) that leads to transformation. The river also connects the Iyami or Ajé with the manifestation of Oshun, whose name translates as spring or source (Mason, *Orin Òrìsà* 315). Oshun is the owner of all fresh waters in the Yoruba thought. Other names attributed to Oshun—Ololodi (the stream is the owner of fortification) and Oshun Ikolé (the stream that builds the house)—are double significations of Oshun and the Iyami. Mason notes that Oshun Ibukolé who drags herself through the mud at the bottom of the river is the friend of the Ajé (*Orin Òrìsà* 316). Even the diamondback snakes that are annoyed by the muttering trees are recodified pythons, associated with the Iyami as signs of immortality and transformation (T. Washington 43). On Isle de Chevaliers, an inverted world, nature has succumbed to the terror of men; houses grew instead of orchids and the "poor insulted, brokenhearted river," no longer having access to its source, became a swamp and "sat in one place like a grandmother" (*Tar Baby* 10).

Becoming a swamp because of its lost memory, the river, called Sein de Vielles or literally old women's breast by the Haitians, is now "a shriveled fogbound oval seeping with a thick black substance" (10). However grim the destiny of the river has become, Toni Morrison's prose opens up the space for renewal. All is not lost; the river's transformation becomes the sacred location for the *Ajé* or Great Mothers. Recovering its ancient properties or primordial rememory, the river turns into tar. As Henry John Drewal and Margaret Thompson Drewal describe, "Darkness is the natural abode of mothers and the creatures most associated with them, such as birds, bats, rats, and reptiles" (11). Transforming its identity, the river represents the power resident in old women to traverse both the physical and spiritual realms. Noting this spiritual capacity, Drewal and Drewal assert that "the mothers by definition, also have this ability; they are mortals who have access to the otherworld. It is in their supernatural capacity, reflected in the power of transformation, that women are considered 'owners of two bodies' (*abara meji*) and the 'owners of the world' (*oni l'oni aiye*)" (*Gelede* 11).

Situated against the backdrop of this spiritually charged environment— the domain of earth mothers and blind horsemen who ride the night—is Jadine Childs a potential mud mother, who drinks hot chocolate in the tropics and has knowledge enough of Paris to make reference to the Tuileries in casual conversation with her relatives. Although Jadine can boast about having knowledge of that neatly sculpted and controlled green space located in the middle of a city teeming with people, she is uncomfortable and dislocated amidst the natural beauty of the tropics. Valerian Street, the retired candy manufacturer who neglects the beauty remaining on the island to grow foreign species such as peonies, dahlias, anemones, and hydrangeas in a greenhouse, introduces Jadine (Jade) by invoking her name as someone "as honest as they come" (18). Margaret's description of her as "having the world" is consistent with the description of the Ajé, *oni l'oni aiye* (owners of the world).

In his interpretation of the Ifa *odu*, Osetua, David O. Ogunbile notes that Oshun has an expansive knowledge of the origins of the world and participates in its maintenance as the leader of the Ajé who manipulate human and divine endeavors (*Eerindilogun* 205). Finally, Ondine, Jadine's aunt, portrays her in terms of her physical beauty. Referring to her being "in every magazine in Paris" she boasts, "Prettiest thing I ever saw" (40). Considered the essence of female beauty and sexuality, Oshun is the touchstone for feminine charm and motherhood. These early descriptions foreshadow the challenges Jadine faces when she encounters the tar-black woman in Paris and later on the island when she meets the Ajé in the woods.

Haunted by the vision of the woman she encounters in a Paris supermarket "with skin like tar" in a "canary yellow dress" and "two upside-down V's" scored into each of her cheeks, Jadine retreats to the island to recover from the disquieting thoughts caused by the woman holding three eggs in "tar-black fingers" (45). By internalizing her discomfort, Jadine begins to engage in the type of introspection that could lead her to the knowledge of deeper things. Heading for Dominique, she confesses to herself that the "woman in the yellow dress who had run her out of Paris" had made her "feel lonely and inauthentic" (48). The source of the woman's power is symbolized, not only by the yellow of her dress, but in the description of the "two upside down V's" on her cheeks.

Bunseki K. Fu-Kiau calls the concept of V the "basis of all realities" and "the foundation of the Bantu system of thought as well their cosmologies" (*African Cosmology* 129). Because all things emanate from V, it is crucial to explore its meaning as a cosmological concept. Not only is V biological, but also it is ideological forming at the *musoni* level of the cosmological process. Fu-Kiau asserts, "It is the process [*dingo dingo*] to all changes, social and institutional; natural and unnatural, seen and unseen" (*African Cosmology* 139).

The dissonance in Jadine is connected to the idea that inside the V stands the master teacher, the Nganga, also a priest and emblem of spiritual power. If Jadine had walked in the direction of the discomfort she felt when encountering the woman, she would have *had* to evolve into a new person. For example, each of the woman's four V's etched on her tar-colored skin represents the four main demarcation points of the Kongo cosmogram, *dikenga dia Kongo*, which also represents the vitality of life inside the circle of community. The first level, V1 or Vangama, is the formation of the person; V1 is the "most fertile garden." The next level, V2 or Vaika, represents the existence stage: to be, to exist, to rise. The third level, V3 or Vanga, means to perform or do. And the last level, V4 or Vunda, represents death both natural and unnatural (*African Cosmology* 130).

Like her tar blackness, the eggs the woman carries are elemental to the understanding of life and the primordial reality undergirding its foundations relating to the Ba Kongo notion of the physical world, which comprises three basic forces "whose power lies in the balance between them" (*African Cosmology* 31). This upper world is widely known in the Kongo traditional symbolizing system as *makuku matatu* (three firestones). The three firestones, which uphold the social Kongo structural motor, *kinzu*, are linked with the Kongo worldview through its presence in the Kongo cosmogram. Traversing the doorway toward *ku mpemba* into the realm of the ancestors, a person is reborn at the *musoni* stage. Fu-Kiau explains that at this level a person should "become a true knower of what is marked on one's mind and body" (destiny) in order to become "a winged person, a flier" (129). Furthermore, the color yellow, symbolic of the *musoni* stage, is associated with knowledge that leads to the "deepest things." *Musoni* reminds the Nganga or spiritual officiate that things should be done in their natural order (*African Cosmology* 33).

Despite all of her perceived accomplishments, Jadine is powerless when confronted with the spiritual presence of the woman in yellow. Potentially, a representative of Oshun Ibukolé, whose only clothes are a yellow dress that has turned white from all the washing (Mason, *Orin Òrìsà* 316), Jadine is the yellow-skinned woman who has been white-washed and seduced by European cultural values. In her acculturation, she has become something other than herself, casting aside her own personality. However, Jadine is both attracted to and repulsed by the woman in the yellow dress who represents her spiritual double. The narrator's description of the woman's multireferential identity as "woman—that mother/sister/**she**; that unphotographable beauty" (*Tar Baby* 46) juxtaposes with Jadine's singular superficial reality. That is, Jadine had recently been selected to be on the cover of *Elle* magazine and had considered this to be one of the "happiest days of her life" (44). It is interesting to note that *elle* is the French word for the pronoun *she*. However, the woman in the canary-yellow dress with her unphotographable beauty displaced Jadine's photographed beauty. After seeing the woman, Jadine yearns for *real* power and authenticity, not the plastic world of advertising where a woman had to camouflage and pass herself off as a "nineteen-year-old face" (45) in order to be employable.

While still in Paris, Jadine takes stock of her inauthenticity and admits her comfort in being the type of black woman who does not like jazz, does not wear hoop earrings, and longs to be an individual free from racial burdens/boundaries. For example, her falling asleep listening to Charles Mingus signifies her inability to understand the cultural complexities of sound at the second level, V2. At this level one learns how to code and decode and to feed the ears with "our waves" (Fu-Kiau 139). These sounds, according to Fu-Kiau, are "genetically coded/printed [sonwa] inside one's inner darkroom" (139). The notion of sound corresponds to the demarcation of *kala* whose representative color is black. Jadine's failure to appreciate black sounds leaves her in a cultural void and cuts her off from the process of being and becoming within the circle.

Moreover, her dislike for hoop earrings indicates the linear contours of her worldview. The wearing of hoop earrings by African women is not just a fashion style, but also a cultural signifier glossing the power of the circle to be the central organizing principle of the world, an index of memory relating to the cyclical worldview that continues to inscribe the body as cosmological statement and a mnemonic reference. Jadine also expresses her willingness to step outside the circle of the blackness and the community and to be an individual. From a Kongo spiritual perspective, the closer a person is to the center of the community, the more powerful; conversely, the more distant the less powerful. Jadine's anxiety of not measuring up to the standards of blackness is motivated not by the circle of black people but by her need to be accepted by the white men who have proposed to her. Instead of accepting the woman in yellow as the Nganga to teach her, or as an opportunity for self-awareness, she moves away from the uncomfortable feelings and tries to put "the woman in yellow out of her mind" (49). Her individuality thwarts the creative objective of the Iyami realized through cooperation of women in the circle of community (T. Washington 68).

The dream/vision of the woman in the yellow dress represents Jadine's private mythology of who she can/ought to be in her deeper being. Eliade says the symbols that re-present themselves to a person's subconscious transmit a particular message linked to that person's destiny and are presented to awaken the person to a metaphysical understanding of that world and their relationship to it (*Sacred* 211). Key to this awakening is contemplation and ultimately acceptance of the spiritual information. Jadine's reticence about her spiritual inclinations resigns her to cable old relatives and head to the island of Dominique. Jadine's traversing of physical boundaries is insufficient for healing and transcendence. The threat of sacrilization keeps Jadine from heeding the message presented by the woman in yellow. That is to say she is content with the secular image of herself as the sole agent of her destiny and refuses to heed any information that could possibly liberate her. She must kill the god within to proceed on the worldly path she has chosen for herself (*Sacred* 203).

In order for Jadine to traverse the boundaries separating the imagined self from her real self, she would have to open up the possibilities of time to include a succession of eternities. Kongo spiritual culture iterates the notion of the human being as consisting of two selves: collective and private. Any breakdown between the two produces a personal and social crisis. By choosing flight from Europe to the Caribbean, she has not alleviated her discomfort with herself and her blackness.

Musing about her resignation to separate herself from the wider African American community, Jadine reveals that the Street's only child, Michael had accused her of abandoning her people. However, Michael's assessment of her has no effect on her consciousness to perhaps reconsider the direction in which she is heading. Additionally, the desire to become or behave like something else finds agency in her over-identification with white people. Even when Valerian makes an off-color remark in Jadine's presence about Michael's idea of racial progress being "All Voodoo to the People," Jadine agrees and replies, "I think he wanted me to string cowrie beads or sell Afro combs" (73). Not offended at all, by either Valerian's comment indicated by her own response, Jadine alerts Valerian of the cultural void in which she makes choices.

Jadine's rejection of African culture and her acceptance and valorization of the white aesthetic is uneven. Her insistence that Pablo Picasso, who duplicated and merely imitated African masks, has more value than the originator represents her shallow understanding of the trope of black creative genius and its allegiance to autonomous black values. For instance, in Africa, masking is a tradition that represents the spiritual and cultural worldview and the relationship African people have with different realms of experience and representation. For African people, spirituality forms the basis for all cultural representations. When the masks are prepared ceremonially, worn, and danced—celestial, ancestral human, and organic forces (wood) converge to provide a sense of well-being for the community. A mask is never danced alone without social interactions. Picasso's work does not signify the same things. His replication of the masks unattended by the culture that supports and breathes the ontological agency into their fashioning is insignificant from an African perspective.

Jadine asserts that the conversation with Michael was difficult but productive, since it forces her to consider his propositions. However, in the final analysis, she makes the choice to free herself from being bound by the cultural mores of black people. The choices Jadine makes are based on her desire to rise above her former life on Morgan Street in Baltimore and not for the spiritual transcendence that she will need to be whole and a productive member of a community. Prior to meeting Son, she has tried to think of other possibilities. She tries to visualize them, wave after wave of chevaliers, but somehow that makes her think of the woman in yellow who had run her out of Paris.

＊　＊　＊

> She does not sing, her body is a song. She is in the forest, dancing. Torches flare . . . juju men, gree gree, witch doctors . . . torches go out. . . . The Dixie Pike has grown from a goat path in Africa
>
> —Jean Toomer, *Cane*

Another indication of Jadine's spiritual personality and destiny occurs in her interaction with the Ajé in the woods. Instead of the panic that she has initially thought was an option, Jadine grabs the waist of the tree and the women looking down from the trees misread the sign and think that she wants to dance. The drawing pad with "Son's face badly sketched looked up at her and the women hanging in the trees looked down at her" (182). The trees communicate that Son is one of the horsemen and that Jadine is one of them. Their message also confirms that Son is her spirit partner. Moreover, the women advise her that Son is the one who can rescue her from the rot/rut of her life. This ritual act with the tree reveals Jadine's current condition and indicates the effort she will have to put forth to get in touch with herself, her spirit, and her ancestors. Jadine's communion with the trees opens up the possibilities that she *can* return to nature, partner with the trees, and whittle away false perceptions of her physical self that belie her spiritual personality. Her dance prefigures not only her potentiality, but also her relationship with Son.

The trees have claimed Jadine as a runaway child returning to them. Jadine is not their *runaway* daughter, but a *runway* model. The trees "wondered at the girl's desperate struggle down to be free, to be something other than they were" (183). Morrison writes, "The women hanging from the trees were quiet now, but arrogant—mindful as they were of their value, their exceptional femaleness, knowing as they did that the first world of the world had been built with their sacred properties" (183). Eliade remarks on the idea of the tree to remind a person of their deeper self and soul's inclination, available if they would only tap into their subconscious mind or to their dreams. For Eliade, trees have the potential to communicate that knowledge to humans (*Sacred* 212).

Trees represent a major trope in Morrison's other novels. In *Beloved*, for example, from the connection Sixo makes about going to the trees at night where he danced "to keep his bloodlines open" (25) to the chokecherry tree on Sethe's back carved from the lasher's whip, Morrison re-enshrines the tree's spiritual prominence, revealing this sacred connection between humans and trees. Paul D's testimony on the nature of trees iterates their status. Commenting on Sethe's scarred back; he refutes its identity as a tree contrasting the terror of her keloidal flesh with his tree, Brother. He says, "Trees were inviting; things you could trust and be near, talk to if you wanted to" (*Beloved* 21). In *Song of Solomon*, Milkman has his definitive moment of self-realization leaning on the back of a tree listening to the children repeatedly sing the song of Solomon, the flying African. In another encounter with a tree, Milkman feels the tree's roots cradle him "like the rough but maternal hands of a grandfather" (*Song* 282). Within a Bantu cosmological frame, trees are one element of the natural world that does not need the command of a Muntu (human being). This special status given to trees in African philosophy explains why they are given primacy as a motif in the fiction of African Americans. In some novels for instance, they are given status as minor characters; such is the case in *The Autobiography of Miss Jane Pittman*, written by Ernest J. Gaines, where the title character comments about how the indigenous people of America worshipped the river and shared her beliefs concerning talking to trees.

Jadine fails to understand the value of the communication from the Ajé who have selected her to join them, indicated by the earth that has marked the hem of her dress with "a deep dark and sticky" substance (*Tar Baby* 183). Later when Margaret sees her, she says it "Looked like pitch" (185). Jadine does not acknowledge or consider what has happened to her beyond getting her clothes soiled and being inconvenienced. But for spiritual people, nature is never only natural. Eliade notes, "Only the religious vision of life makes it possible to decipher other meanings in the rhythm of vegetation, first of all the ideas of regeneration, of eternal youth, of health, of immortality" (*Sacred* 149). Failing to see the connection, Jadine misses the opportunity to probe her relationship to the land, to other people, and herself. Among the Nguni people of South Africa, particularly, the Xhosa and the Zulu believe that future *sangomas* (female priests) receive their calling by being submerged under bodies of water or a river pool for many hours, days, or years. This indicates their "calling" to be a diviner and a traditional healer. This summoning can also occur in a dream state indicating their having been "called." After they accept this spiritual beckoning, they are trained in various healing capacities including knowledge of the sacred, psychic abilities and understanding concerning herbal pharmacopoeia.

Being marked in this river of concentrated tar signals Jadine's connection to her spiritual personality as a child of Oshun who controls the *ajé* and the rivers that bind the nation. This connection is extended to relationships with the ancestors. Kamalu Chukwunyere remarks that the concept of tar "is the complete world," which includes the body, soul, all temporal realities; it is also connected to the ancestors (164). Since the word *tar* is etymologically related to tree, the connection with the land and the capacity for endless regeneration, the significance of Jadine's inability to pay attention to her anointing by the earth and dancing with the trees must be underscored. This is not the first time that she has ignored the implication of tar, first revealed to her by the *tar-skinned* woman in the *yellow* dress. Now as a *yellow* woman with a *tar-stained* dress, Jadine fails to see the mirror pointing her toward self-realization. For Jadine the signs have ceased to signify. Prefiguring self-rejection, the rejection of Son and her family, her refusal to recognize the signs is analogous to her own cosmic death and the improbability of future offspring.

*   *   *

No power can stay the mojo
when the obi is purple
and the voodoo is green
and Shango is whispering,
Bathe me in Blood.
I am not clean

—Henry Dumas, "Rite"

Juxtaposed with Jadine's experience, Son's relationship with nature and the trees reveals his acceptance of his connection with Shango, the Òrìsà of lightning and redistributive justice. The description of his "beard hair," which "crackled like lightning," and his hair, which looked like "the crown of a deciduous tree" (132), are consistent with his symbolic representation as lightning and his royal office of kingship. As a correlate of the Òrìsà, whose earthly representation is wood, the trees interact with Son as he walks, taking on a human presence "muttering in their sleep" (134), "parting their wide leaves," and "touching his cheek" (135). Like Shango, one of the exalted sons of Olodumare, Son, the figurative representation of the natural world, has multiple names and multiple identities. But Son "was the name that called forth the true him. The him that he never lied to, to the one he tucked in at night and the one he did not want to die. The other selves were like the words he spoke—fabrications of the moment, misinformation required to protect Son from harm and to secure that one reality at least" (39). Because Shango represents the power of truth to transform a person, one of the mandates of Shango is to never lie.

Magesa discusses the significance of names to represent destiny:

> More than merely symbolic or for the purposes of identification, real re-presentation (making present again) takes place in the act of naming. Naming involves the incarnation or actualization of a person (ancestor); certain desired moral quality or value, a physical trait or power, or an occasion or event. To confer a name is therefore to confer personality status, destiny, or express a wish or circumstances in which the bearer of the name was born. (89)

Son's name integrates him with his personality. Like his solar correlate that remains unchangeable, the name "gives expression to the religious values of autonomy and power, of sovereignty, of intelligence consistent with the solarization of the supreme beings in various cultures" (*Sacred* 157). When Son visits the island where Thérèse and Gideon live, they parade him through the "streets of town like a king" (*Tar Baby* 149). The comfort with which Son wears his name is consistent with a devotee of Shango. Shango is at once literal, mystical, archetypal, and historical. Benjamin C. Ray asserts, "The Òrìsà is thus a magnified symbol of his or her own personality. It enables the devotee to express certain unconscious aspects of the self and to channel and integrate his or her total personality" (38).

Toni Morrison's inscription of Shango and his accompanying thematic idea of redistributive justice is an appropriate novelistic figuration: simultaneously semiotic and political representing the ideology and the values recognized by the group. Shango, a deified warrior-king is considered a moral force and a champion of justice. As a human being, he is the fourth alaafin (king) of the Oyo Empire, the former political capital of the Yoruba. As the most recognized Òrìsà of African people in the western hemisphere, Shango makes a smooth transition across the Atlantic Ocean.

Shango's sense of justice is evident in Son's thoughts in response to Thérèse and Gideon being fired for stealing apples. Son is incensed that the people who have been summarily dismissed are the denizens of the very land that has yielded the raw materials for people like the Streets to create wealth and privilege. Son judges those who tear up the land and exploit it

(*Tar Baby* 203). Besides, he reflects on the idea that the sole purpose of the exploiter is "to make waste," and he surmises that Valerian Street was one of the "killers of the world" (204).

Valerian recognizes Son's spiritual identity when Son challenges him for having fired Gideon and Thérèse for allegedly stealing apples. In Valerian's mind his actions are correct, and he contemplates vindication for his decision represented by the cavalry coming to his defense. The horses that Valerian envisions do not belong to the French chevaliers; the evocation of equestrian soldiers is the presence of the African riders invoked by Son's bold actions. What is interesting to note is Son's assessment of the signs: "Somewhere in the back of Son's mind one hundred black men on one hundred unshod horses rode blind and naked through the hills and had done so for a hundred years" (206).

Son's version is consistent with his destiny objective and explains his being positioned on this island when he has no conscious intention of being there. Morrison repeats the phrase, "He had not followed the women" (133–37), along with its variants—"for he was not following the women" (135) and "because he was not following the women" (138)—a total of eight times to reiterate his trancelike arrival on the island. What follows are the circumstances that precipitate Son's advent to the island as well as the sense of destiny relative to Jadine as an analogue of Oshun.

In the opening pages of the novel, the reader meets the yet unnamed man, Son Green, on the railing of a boat named Stor Konigsgaarten, which literally translates into star king's garden. The naming of the ship corresponds to one of Shango's accolades: "King of the earth." Also, the concept of star and a "heart pounding in sweet expectation" represents the Òrìsà of the sweet waters, Oshun, one of Shango's three "wives," whose physical correlate is the heart and one of whose cosmic emblems is the five-pointed star.[2] Additionally, Oshun's description of being a coquette who uses her wiles to gain the power needed to save the world is revealed in Morrison's careful prose personifying the schooner *Queen of France* as a flirt that "blushed a little in the lessening light and lowered her lashes before his gaze" (3). Furthermore, this same reference represents Jadine, who is on the Isle des Chevaliers vacationing from Paris, and foreshadows Son's subsequent relationship with her.

Other descriptions of Oshun substantiating her literary presence are Morrison's cataloguing of Oshun's symbols: the butterfly, the heart, blood, and teardrops. The narrator reports, "When he'd rested he decided to swim *butterfly* and protect his feet. . . . All he saw was water, *blood*-tinted by a sun sliding into it like a fresh *heart. . . . Queen of France* was already showing lights like *teardrops* from a sky pierced to *weeping* by the blade tip of an early *star*" (4–5; emphasis added). For the Yoruba, Oshun represents the blood that flows through the veins and speaks of relationships both familial and amorous. Moreover, in this one passage Toni Morrison condenses Oshun's key symbols related to her exclusively from a Yoruba traditional perspective, such as the butterfly, the heart (*okan*), teardrops (crying), and the star (*irawo*). During his relationship with Jadine, Son tries to instruct her about her identity and destiny as a star.

Son's initiating ritual occurs when he leaves the ship and swims toward an unknown shore. Like Sula's Shadrack, Son's lack of material possessions indicates his status as a spiritual individual, a man with "no book of postage stamps, no razor blades, or keys to any door" (3). This enumeration of items tells the reader he exists in a liminal space, "A man without human rites: unbaptized, uncircumcised, minus puberty rites or the formal rites of manhood. Unmarried and undivorced. He had attended no funeral, married in no church, raised no child. Propertyless, homeless, sought for but not after. There were no grades given in his school, so how could he know when he had passed?" (166). The school to which Morrison is referring has to do with a type of spiritual training for a person "who wanted another way to be in the world" (167).

With the inclusion of this brief list, Morrison primes the reader to anticipate his spiritual mission. With his "knees to his chest," his assumption of a fetal position symbolizes his re-birth in the primordial ocean—represented by Yemonja the mother of Òrìsà, the mother of humankind and the mother of all things on earth. Son's leaving the ship is a way for him to reconnect to himself after years of running away after committing a crime due to his "hot-headedness," which is one of Shango's principal flaws. He swam in the "soft" and "warm" water "where a bracelet of water circled" him and "yanked him in a wide empty tunnel" (4). In this rebirthing in the ocean, Yemonja, the mother of life allows Son access to a new life and identity. Yemonja represents the tendency of all things in nature to regenerate with the determination to survive, to nurture their own kind and to promote growth. As the Mother of all she is the idea of growth and fertility and her principal stories are of the raising of Shango (Weaver and Egbelade xvi).[3]

As Son gives himself to the water, "whirling in a vortex" . . . he thought of nothing except, "I am going counterclockwise" (4). This directional orientation signals his journey toward the recovery of self. Moreover, the tugging underwater indicates a ritual cleansing by the Yoruba Òrìsà Olokun representing the bottom of the ocean, described in his going "down." In the western hemisphere, Olokun becomes an Òrìsà of salvation for Africans helping to restore spiritual unity breached by the Middle Passage and the emotional and physical brutality experienced in the crossing into American captivity. Lloyd Weaver notes Olokun is "the dark and unknowable bottom of the sea" and "collective unconsciousness of mankind" (xxviii). Weaver says that because of the millions of bones lying at the bottom of the ocean as a result of the Middle Passage, Olokun becomes a sympathetic messenger on behalf of the "spiritual collective" interred in his domain (xxviii). Son's being pulled down expiates him from the mistakes of the past and situates him to reenter life restored.

Once ashore and discovered, Son's presence as an authentic black man appears to rescue Jadine from spiritual nihilism. The first question she asks him about having been in Sein de Vielles is, "Did you see any ghosts while you were there?" His reply informs Jadine—and all in the room—that he believes in the ideas associated with the spiritual realm. In her question, Jadine probes the prospects of him leading her to an authentic life replete with the powers available in the invisible world. His presence stirs up both nature and Jadine. Both have a heightened awareness of Son's presence: "The heavy clouds grouped themselves behind the hills as though for a parade. You could almost see the herd assemble, but the man swinging in the hammock was not aware of them. He was dwelling on his solitude, rocking in the wind, adrift" (165). Even with her emotional constraints, Jadine's imagination is also charged with ideas of spiritual subjugation denoted by the presence of the *gleam* and *shine* of his presence.

The recognition of his spiritual connection to her is revealed in the image in the mirror, which seizes her attention. She has to struggle "to pull herself away from his image in the mirror" and resist drowning in the "riverbed darkness of his face" (114). Oshun, the queen of sweet waters and rivers, represents the first mirror where human beings meet images and imagination. Oshun is the Òrìsà of beauty allure: the appeal, the attraction, and ultimately, the burning love between man and woman that makes for procreation. Son is equally invested in his estimation of her identity. Using imagery emblematic of Oshun, such as the mirror, Morrison points out Jadine's link to the Òrìsà with the description of the dress she is wearing in the fashion magazine, "Natural raw silk . . . honey-colored. . ." and her adornment with "heaps of gold necklaces above the honey-colored silk" that cost "$32,000" (117). Honey, gold, and the number five (3+2) are all designations for Oshun.

Similar to the Yoruba stories where Shango is obsessed with Oshun, Son is obsessed with the idea of Jadine revealed in his first encounters with her. By breathing the smell of tar into Jadine, he attempts to re-fashion Jadine to be one of the earthy women of Eloe, his all-black hometown, and the "tar black" woman lingering in Jadine's conscious and subconscious memory. He also tries to activate her suppressed earthiness preparing her to be his spiritual counterpart. Apataki testify to Shango's unrelenting pursuit of Oshun. Son will remark later in the novel "She crowned me, that girl did. No matter what went wrong or how tired I was, she was my crown" (193).

When the narrative setting shifts to New York, Jadine easily exchanges the island for islands in the middle of Broadway: Isle des Chevalier's "avocado trees" for the "smart thin trees on Fifty-Third Street, juxtaposed with Son's sense of being abandoned by his memory, which recalled that there "used to be trees" (221). With competition in the "wilds" of the metropolis, Son "thought he would have to stamp the ground, paw it and butt horns with every male they came in contact with, but he didn't" (223). All of the aforementioned verbs are references to zoomorphic representations of Shango. For example, "stamping the ground" refers to a horse, a primary association with Shango, while "pawing" relates to a leopard, another familiar, and "butting horns" conveys the idea of a ram, the primary animal used in propitiary offerings to the thunder deity.

Similar to Milkman's comment in *Song of Solomon* about the security of being in the company of all black people, Son wants to return to Eloe, where "segregation was honest" and where "no white people live" (172). Eloe is a Garden of Eden, where African people can practice African culture, live close to the earth, and maintain earthy values and their own spiritual ethos. If New York is a test for Son's ability to adapt to Jadine's world, Eloe poses a more difficult challenge for Jadine's city sensibilities. Going through the formalities, Jadine is introduced to an assemblage of down-home folks. While at Aunt Rosa's house, which is rich in spirits and *egun* (ancestors), Jadine experiences her haunting denoted by being confronted with the "blackest nothing she had ever seen" (252). Jadine encounters this formless blackness, which allows neither "shadows," "outlines," nor a "line between earth and sky." In fact, the "place where the sky ought to be, was starless" (252). The erased boundaries between heaven and earth represent the state of spiritual activity where a convergence or an exchange of energies could result in Jadine's transformation, while the absence of stars in the celestial realm is a metaphor for her dispossessed self, her spiritual paucity and failed destiny.

Characteristic of her spiritual bereftness, Toni Morrison replicates the scene in the woods where Jadine first encounters the tree mothers with a few variations. Jadine's going out the *back* door and her encounter with an airless darkness is a metaphor for the abode of the ancestors and an opportunity to participate in a type of rebirth in order to cultivate a spiritual personality worthy of Son. In the Yoruba divination system of Ifa, the pattern known as *oyeku meji* concerns the relationship of dark spaces and individual actions and their ultimate connection to spiritual elevation. Instead of going down into a hole, this time Jadine experiences a glimpse of the darkness, emblematic of the spiritual void in which she dwells. Realized in her mind as a "cave," a "grave," the "dark womb of the earth, suffocating with the sound of plant life moving, but deprived of its sight" (252), this fleeting glimpse at darkness juxtaposes the notion of the flash of the spirit, apprehended as light and indicates the type of internal spiritual work that Jadine will have to do to acquire the necessary power to envision her authentic spiritual self.

In that darkness, the novel's African women, including her deceased mother and even the woman in the yellow dress, reveal their breasts (258), reminding her that to be female is to be able to mature, propagate life, die, regenerate, and continue. However, Jadine's sense of being competitive, a value learned in the worlds of fashion and white folks, thwart her understanding of their intentions. Similar to when she first encounters the woman in yellow, the apparition reiterates the importance of nature and the idea of the human life cycle. Jadine decides that she can no longer endure the possibility of more "plant sounds in the cave and the certainty of the night women" (259). Instead of moving in the direction of her ancestors, she backs away from them, going in the opposite direction toward regression, claiming it to be progress.

The *Ajé* intervene one last time. When asking herself what went wrong, Jadine says that she got "the same sixteen answers" (290). This reference to the merindilogun or sixteen cowries used to divine in the Yoruba spiritual tradition signifies the Ajé. Teresa N. Washington notes that the "crossroads sixteen or sixteen roads" is one of the spiritual locations of the Ajé. Additionally, this crossroads is situated at the interstices where spirit and material meet (*Our Mothers, Our Powers* 19). Jadine heads for Paris to her past (the material realm) that she thinks is her future, not to the domain of spirit. Accompanied by her material possessions, five pieces of luggage and her seal coat, Jadine returns to a life where there is no time for dreaming. Unable to answer the call of destiny, she flies, not like the Ajé who are associated with their spirit familiars, birds, but in first-class accommodations on an airplane, back to the material world to be an individual.

Son has tried to persuade Jadine to tap into the spiritual side of her personality. He has taught her how to see/be a star when she closes her eyes, as a way to get in touch with her inner self. The omniscient narrator describes Jadine using avian imagery; "she was like a bird in the crook of his arm" (210), and later Son remembers the "bird-like defenselessness" he had loved (220). At the core of their spiritual union is his recognition of her as a star. In the Dogon spiritual system, stars are considered to be in-spirited components of a dynamic whole, among which there is a constant exchange of energies representing the metaphysical and physical realities of the universe (Griaule and Dieterlen 15) Furthermore, he endeavors to show her that *she* is the lady in the yellow dress. Both of these attempts, if successful, would have empowered her spiritually. Failing to see the con-nection, Jadine misses the opportunity to explore her relationship to the land, to other people, and to herself. At this point, Son has no other re-course but to engender his own spiritual destiny indicated by his return to Isle des Chevaliers.

*   *   *

Remember this: against all that destruction some yet remained among us unforgetful of origins, dreaming secret dreams, see-ing secret visions, hearing secret voices of our purpose.

—Ayi Kwei Armah, *Two Thousand Seasons*

In *Tar Baby*, Toni Morrison crafts Marie Thérèse Foucault as the female healer who demonstrates the power of interacting with the natural, non-human world and the necessity of spiritual return. Described as a member of the "blind race" (152), "Thérèse had her own views of understanding that had nothing to do with the world's views" (151). Subverting the role of the colonizer to be the "source of all value judgment, "beauty, manhood, good, evil, justice, her value does not come from the interlopers to the is-land who "elevate themselves to God-like stature to be revered, awed and feared by the colonized people" (Memmi 149), Thérèse's identity comes from a deep reverence and connection to the land and not from aspiring to be like her employers, who, like others before, have historically exploited her people. Using the aesthetic strategy of masking, Morrison blurs the value of the sign, ensuring that in order to apprehend the core message her readers will have to work diligently to understand the culturally nuanced information—similar to an initiation. This act of containment symbolized by Thérèse's mask also encodes knowledge such as family histories, myths, and morality to those who practice the culture.

Since masks are the mediators between God and humans, masking is the medium by which the human and the spiritual world may interact. In the traditional sense masks are birthed, ritually fed, and activated to become powerful spiritual sites of power. As such, masquerading is not only evocative, but also invocative to spiritually teach/learn, reveal/conceal/, instruct/learn. Purifying the community and chasing away evil, some masks chase away souls who have overstayed their welcome in the living world. Additionally, masks honor the deities and spirits of nature, thereby spiritually renewing communities and ensuring prosperity and fertility. Half-blind, but able to see spiritually, she wears the disguise as one of the many "Marys" who come to L'Arbre de la Croix to wash clothes for Valerian and Margaret Street and the assemblage of black folk in their employment and under their patronage. Marie Thérèse Foucault is an Ajé. And like the Ajé, Thérèse is powerful and has the ability to transform. Wearing the mask of an ignorant washwoman, one of the many "Marys," Thérèse is situated to meet Son—William Green—and lead him to his destiny as one of the blind galloping horsemen, just as the washwoman from Valerian's childhood, the "birdlike colored woman" (140) made Valerian feel "limitless" and helped him "tread the black water in the bucket that had no bottom" (141).

Thérèse, a woman with "magic breasts" who has the ability to read signs, is akin to the epistemic sensibilities of other women who know things in Morrison's other novels. For example, she has known of Son's presence twelve days before any other residents of L'Arbre de la Croix and before he leaves the trail of chocolate papers. In the Yoruba divination system of the *merindilogun*, the number twelve represents the *odu, ejila shebora*, whose refrain is "the soldier never sleeps," referring to an attribute of Shango, the owner of cosmic justice. Morrison reiterates this idea of *ejila* as the narrator reports: "She caught the scent twelve days ago: the smell of a fasting, or starving man, as the case might be, human" (105). Moreover, the occupants of the house hear "no tramp of soldier ants marching toward the greenhouse" (103), but Thérèse has "seen him in a dream smiling at her as he rode away wet and naked on a stallion" (104).

Thérèse's deep reverence for the land—the primordial *ayé*—connects her to the Ajé who are the spirit guardians of the earth. Equally she is connected to the waters, and, like the Ajé, "knows the water just like the fishermen" (153).[4] When Son returns to the island in search of Jadine, Thérèse consents to ferry Son across the ocean to Isle des Chevaliers—but not for the reason he thinks. She is not accommodating him, but obeying the spiritual mandates as one of the blind race. She tells him, "I see better in the dark and I know the crossing too well" (302). "I'll take you when it's time" (302). The time to which Thérèse is referring is not the chronological time, but the cosmic moment when Son can meet his true self, consistent with his destiny. She navigates across the foggy expanse of water feeling the current. His eyes begin to change and his vision begins to fade, limited to shadows and outlines (303–4). This diminished physical vision prepares him to regain his "in" sight. Consulting with the fish for directions, Thérèse appears as a faint outline of herself to Son's eyes as he disengages from the material world heading to his spiritual destiny.

Son's passage across the water is a birthing ritual "rocking on baby waves," comparable to when he first arrives to the island. But this time he is on top of the water instead of being in the water; this time he arrives to the back of the island contrasting his first arrival to the front of the island, indicating the completion of his journey. When they reach the *back* of the island, emblematic for the ancestors who stand behind their descendants and support their activities in the world of the living, Thérèse teaches Son to use his spiritual eyes. She says, "Don't see feel." She delivers him to the far side of the island, where he can make the choice to be free and whole, juxtaposing the fragmented Jadine whom Thérèse admonishes him to forget. Thérèse says, "There is nothing in her parts for you. She has forgotten her ancient properties" (305).

Thérèse's commentary concerning Jadine's spiritual fragmentation is emphasized by her loss of those traditional spiritual values that can lead to her resurrected spiritual personality. Bereft of spiritual *form* and the ability to spiritually *perform*, Jadine is not a fitting companion for Son. Shapeshifting from the personality of Son to one of the riders, he "felt the sister rock at his fingertips. According to Dogon tradition, for reasons of ritual and initiation, raised stones or stacked boulders near water or on steep slopes represent the idea of spiritual challenge, transcendence and reenactments of mythical events (Griaule and Dieterlen 65). Thérèse informs Son that he has a choice; he can get free from Jadine. The narrator describes Son's rebirthing after crossing the water "rocking on baby waves":

> Then he grabbed with both hands the surface of the rock and heaved himself onto it. He lay there for a bit, then stretched his arm again

and like a *baby*, "First he *crawled* the rocks one by one, one by one, till his hands touched shore and the *nursing* sound of the sea was behind him. He then took a few tentative steps" like a *toddler walking* for the first time. Then he *ran*. (306; emphasis added)[5]

After being ferried across the primordial waters, Son goes through the developmental stages of crawling, taking tentative steps, and then running, which allow him to transcend from Son Green to one of the galloping horsemen of Isle des Chevaliers. Unlike Jadine, Son makes the choice to be true to his destiny, thereby creating a divine and enduring existence for himself. His return as one of the horsemen intimates that another solution, a spiritual one, can deliver nature from the incursions of those who fail to see a connection with the land. In making his decision, Son creates an opportunity for the rivers to return and reflect his true and ancient properties.

5

In(*her*)iting the Divine

(Consola)tions, Sacred (Convent)ions, and Mediations of the Spiritual In-between in *Paradise*

> We hammer wood for a house, but it is the inner space that
> makes it livable.
>
> —Lao Tzu

> Receiving, giving, giving, receiving,
> all that lives is twin. Who would cast the spell of death, let him
> separate the two.
>
> —Ayi Kwei Armah, *Two Thousand Seasons*

Invocation

Morrison structures her seventh novel, *Paradise* (1999), beyond the literary doppelganger or a re-fashioning of the oft-cited Duboisian concept of "Double Consciousness."[1] Instead, as I argue, she inscribes the negotiation of spiritual tensions in her use of spiritual amplification represented by the Yoruba Òrìsà known as Ibeji and the Dogon concept of twinning referred to as Nommo.[2] The main goal of this chapter is to examine the distinguishing elements in this conceptual paradigm. Drawing upon the shared intersections of ecology and spiritual traditions, I explore the notion of spiritual balance, the re-construction/resurrection of the matriarch, and the nature of spiritual transcendence. A fundamental query guiding my eco-critical investigation is the nature of female spiritual traditions and the manner in which African women have redefined, restored, reclaimed, and recovered identity through a symbiotic relationship between themselves and the land. Additionally, I examine the ways in which women healers engage in African spiritual practices to engender those relationships to extend and regenerate life.

Advancing the novel's theme of complementarity, Morrison relies on assemblages of dialectical unities in her consideration of the spiritual and material, male and female, heaven and earth, propriety and impropriety. Moreover, Morrison insists that in order to be whole, African people need to know their story through inquiry and contemplation iterated by Connie's comment to Mavis, "Scary things not always outside. Most scary things inside" (*Paradise* 39). To achieve a similar sense of this interiority, Morrison acquaints her readers with those spiritual principles that have endured despite disruptions along the way.

Re-enacting beliefs and spiritual values over geographical space and time, African people have picked up new items correlating to those left behind and discarded excessive items. Moving beyond the pattern of bifurcation and "missing contents" attributed to modernism and postmodernism by Jean-Francois Lyotard, Africans have supplemented missing contents and recovered meanings in those spaces or breaches (244). The tensions created by missing information and other caesura along with dislocations, distortions, ambiguities, and unreliable information, challenges both characters and readers. From the beginning line, "They shoot the white girl first," readers are lured into a world where nothing is what it seems either on the surface or at the core. Immediately, readers are engaged; they have to keep a keen eye open to be able to identify the "white girl" with limited clues. If they have read anything that Morrison has written, there is much work ahead; and they must actively participate to gain any meaning they hope to create.[3]

Exemplified in the next paragraph after the opening statement, Morrison's omniscient narrator gives misleading information in the form of a miscalculation revealing that there are nine members in the posse, "over twice the number of the women they are obliged to stampede or kill" (3). However, there are five women in the convent—the math is wrong. This aporia or logical disjunction will not be the last to occur. For example, the narrator recalls the "one hundred fifty-eight freedmen who left Louisiana and Mississippi" (13). But Deacon Morgan and his twin brother Steward, who are recognized as having "powerful memories" (13), who "between them they (could) remember the details of everything that ever happened—things they witnessed and things they have not," and who "have never forgotten the message or the specifics of any story" (13), offer a different account. The number 158 is *twice* the number reported by Steward in the chapter titled "Seneca"—he reports the number of ancestors as being "seventy-nine" (95). This is not the last time the truth will reside in *two* distinct domains. There will be many versions of the story regarding what happened to the Convent women and about how the "raid" went down.

Perhaps, multiple examples of doubling prepare readers to rely not on the assigned value of words—but to look beyond words to the mythic layers, which render the words as feeble approximations. What I am suggesting here is that in order to enter the literary experience of Toni Morrison's *Paradise*, readers must not suspend disbelief; they must have the willingness to suspend their beliefs and to freely imagine. Additionally, readers must be capable of encountering meaning in the indeterminate space between the realms and consider alternate ways of believing and being. Ritual provides the space to expand meaning and time and helps to deliver characters and readers alike to spaces of renewal.

As Catherine Bell notes, ritual space creates eternity through an endless stream of signifiers (104–5). Moreover, examining these presumed variances from the vantage point of African spiritual culture also helps to diminish these ambiguities. Accordingly, ritual enactment helps us come to terms with these perceived discrepancies. In these performances, the experience of coherence generates opposites affording the experience of order as well as the fit, harmonizing into what Jacques Derrida would call the space of "difference" or "free play." For instance, a common denominator in African spiritual systems, the concept of twinning presents the world as a balanced whole where opposition is seen as one of the twinned elements. Here core meaning resides in the interstices between complementary opposites. Consideration of interstitial realities is an important critical approach to extend meaning. As Nkira Nzegwu argues, this idea of transspatiality allows us to know things in different ways and suggests that a new framework needs to be developed to allow these formerly "pre-theoretical" and "primitive" ideas to become a new heuristic technology, an innovative way to conceptualize reality (182).

Corresponding with Morrison's imaginative bricolage, with no absolutes, no fixed meaning, I utilize the concept of doubling to interrogate the spaces in-between the usual binaries investigated by literary critics. In *Nation and Narration*, Homi Bhabha suggests a similar methodological approach, which I refer to as conscious indeterminacy "generating other sites of meaning" (3). Bhabha's idea of the center or between is the nucleus of meaning, which shares information between the binaries, can be applied to the concept of the Middle Passage. Employing this view, one can argue that nothing was lost, just altered, suggesting the possibility of return and the idea of an enduring memory. For this study, I consider the idea of passage as situating or passing information at the middle to create triadic structures of emancipation from the two given ideas.[4] This biodynamic process imparts new life at the intersection where oppression and resistance interact in order to strengthen sacred functioning. The Yoruba express this tripartite structure in their concept of Ibeji illustrated in the proverb, "two who are one who cannot walk alone who needs another to walk with them." Idowu, the oldest of them and a triplet in the twin structure consisting of Taiwo and Kehinde, comes to cool the house and restore balance between the two.

In the same way, twinning relates to the various realms as it is said that twins exist in three worlds at one time: the bush, the spirit world, and the world of human beings. African identity in North America reiterates this premise. In America, bolstered by deep-core values and cosmological structures, the African's insistent practice of culture in the forms of spiritual traditions has produced a dynamic range of expressions in language, myth, music, dance, and material representations that continue to inspire survival amidst the soul-extinguishing effects of racism and its attending spiritual paucity. Thus Africans have taken the experience in North America and have created the third new identity as Africans in America or African Americans.

The Yoruba concept of Ibeji, based on the idea of one spirit residing in two identical bodies, emphasizes the dualism of life described as being constructive and destructive— representative of both divinity and heritage. John Mason describes them as:

Thunder children, wonder made visible
Divine twins, male and female
Left and right, up and down
Hard and Soft
Day and night
Fire and wood
The governing principle of existence (*Idana Fun Òrìsà* 105).

Furthermore, Ibeji symbolize the spirits that connect all things, conceived as different, but which in reality are the same things—such as life and death (existence), man and woman (human life), et cetera. By inscribing twin histories (the history of Haven and the history of Ruby), literal twins (Deacon and Steward, [Zechariah] Coffee and Tea, Merle and Pearl), two stories (one story of the inhabitants of Ruby and the other story of the women in the convent), two ovens, two mottos (that become three), and a host of other doubles or twins (including literary tropes, figurative language, situational juxtapositions, and symbols such as mirrors), Morrison prepares the reader to imagine a world where the dualities of spirit connect. Here, in the in-between, a space of exchange and mediation, healing and regeneration occur. Like her literary and spiritual foremothers who encoded sacred knowledge in culturally resolute ways, Morrison re-establishes these traditions accessible to those who stand within the circle of culture.

The Hunt

The women of the convent live and die in a space whose geographical location is one of alterity described as being, "seventeen miles from a town which has ninety miles between it and any other" (3). That is, they reside in an indeterminate, unnamed space, a place in-between another: positioned and un-positioned at the same time. At the outset, Toni Morrison establishes a paradox—a type of linguistic twinning that offers two realities that are logically exclusive of each other. The double entendre located in the phrase "God at their side, the men take aim for Ruby" (18), is one of the novel's many instances of doubling. This suggests two things that are actually the same thing. First, the men have hunted the women of the convent to preserve the notion of African womanhood exemplified by Ruby. Second, this action has been carried out to preserve Ruby, the "all-black town worth the pain" (5).

Similar to the idea of hunting down a defenseless female, a taboo that Morrison introduces in *Jazz*, Morrison begins her novel, *Paradise*, with the men from Ruby night-hunting women accompanied by the "nocturnal odor of righteousness" (18). Preceding the slaughter of the women, the men have worked their tongues against the women for over a year, accumulating "outrages" that have taken "shape as evidence" (11) about "abandoned women with no belongings" (14), "slack . . . members of some other cult" (11), and "un-natural" women without men. Also, analogous to the scapegoating in *Sula*, the convent women are blamed when "a mother was knocked down the stairs by her cold-eyed daughter," when "four damaged infants were born in one family," and when "Two brothers shot each other on New Year's day" (11).[5] Moreover, the nature of the women's character is also castigated as they are judged as "bodacious black Eves, unredeemed by Mary" (18).

The convent's inhabitants and the space described as "out there," situated seventeen miles away are both condemned for being unconventionally free from male-defined authority and domination. In *The Bluest Eye*, Morrison initiated the discussion of the concept of outdoors as synonymous with being in the open, away from home, in a transient state. Being "out there" was a predicament to be avoided at any cost. Morrison writes: "Outdoors, we knew, was the real terror of life. The threat of being outdoors surfaced frequently in those days. Outdoors was the end of something, an irrevocable, physical fact, defining and complementing our metaphysical condition" (*Bluest Eye* 17–18). It does not have to be this way. When the women enter Ruby days before the hunt, their presence could have been liberating for all the inhabitants of Ruby.

Prefigured by a variety of signs—including the appearance of the deceased Scout and Easter to Soane, feathers lying in the sink, and the "pairs and pairs of buzzards" that flew over town—the women arrive in Ruby. Manifestations of the feathers and buzzards confirm the power of the women as bird women or Iyami Osoronga. Their presence represents their potential to save the townspeople from the hubris, which not only isolates them from other black people, but also threatens their physical extinction through inbreeding and sterility, the results of endogamy. Unlike the Yoruba *apataki* where Oshun Ibukole, symbolized by the buzzard, saves everyone in the city of Ile Ife from death, this highly ritualized behavior of hunting reflects the learned exclusivity of their insular society and encompasses their idea of normative behaviors, religious beliefs, concepts of virtue, and mirrors European aggression and violence acted out on African people.

What follows in the novel is a description of the hunt. The men arrive "Out there where the entrance to hell is wide" (114). The hunt first begins with the idea of blackness as a trope of barbarism and illogicality, supplanting "whiteness" as a marker of racial superiority. Next the women are metonymically displaced; their difference is so peculiar the men refer to them in zoomorphic terms, calling them "panicked does" (18). Just as Pat Best thought earlier—or at another point in the cyclical narrative—"everything that worries them must come from women" (217). Arriving at the convent prepared to participate in the ritual murder of the women, the men are armed with a variety of weapons: "a rope, a palm leaf cross, handcuffs, Mace and sunglasses, along with clean handsome guns" (3). The inclusion of the rope and handcuffs intimates that either capture and or torture are both possibilities, while the mace matches their imaginative musings on the wild nature of the women. The palm-leaf cross suggests a type of spiritual implement to wield in case the guns do not work. The addition of the sunglasses implies that their dark deeds will meet abundant light as spiritual counterpoint.

Descendants of former enslaved Africans who sought to negotiate "safe spaces" away from the terror of the Klan and other anxieties associated with the South, they established a heaven/haven where they as African people could be free to be themselves. Ironically, they are driven by the need to judge and destroy. This mirrors the cult of human sacrifice and mob violence committed against black people by the Ku Klux Klan. For the members of the Klan, the ultimate form of blood sacrifice is the sacrifice of a human being. In his anaylsis of Ku Klux Klan behavior, Orlando Patterson reframes the formulaic analysis of ritual described by Marcel Maus and Henri Hubert acknowledging, "There were always certain ideas about the victim(s). That is the victim(s) mediated against the sacred and the profane, symbolic of good or evil" (182).

The violence perpetrated on the convent women protects the men from the perceived horrors of external influences considered a threat to their imagination. For example, after the Disallowing, consistent with their patriarchal orientation, the men build an iron stove as a site to commemorate the shared experience of the journey, leading them to Haven.[6] Here they sacrifice roasted animals, bake their bread, gather to disseminate information, hold meetings, and perform other collective ceremonies. The oven marks the town's sacred space, even before a church was built. Situated in the middle of the town, this symbol of maleness takes on the religious significance of a shrine, an iron shrine. The oven's motto, "Beware the Furrow of his Brow" serves as a statement of God's judgment and a guiding principle to inspire the men to assume a vaulted moral stance.[7]

Before moving again to the place they will eventually name Ruby, the men dismantle the town's symbol of maleness even before they attend to packing their own possessions. When they move in 1950 and establish the town of Ruby, their second settlement, the oven is re-installed. This oven re-codifies the Yoruba deity of iron, Ogun, who represents both creative and destructive forces of metal. Harper Jury's appearance after the women's massacre as a "bloodied but unbowed warrior against evil" (299), is similar to the description narrated in a Yoruba *apataki*, where the Òrìsà Ogun comes out of the woods covered with blood after a slaughter.

Unlike the story following Big Papa's proclamation, "This is our place" (98), where the group sacrifices a male guinea, this desacralized murder of the women does not ensure the group's well-being. In the former story, the appearance of the male guinea and its subsequent sacrifice establishes their new beginning by symbolically cleaning the group from the epistemic violence experienced prior to arriving to this place they would name Haven. For instance, after the *matanza*, the ritual sacrifice of four-legged animals and an assortment of birds, performed to initiate a priest in the Lukumi Yoruba tradition, a *fifeto* ritual is performed to spiritually clean and cool down the energy engendered from the bloodshed of the sacrifices. Passing a guinea over the head of the participants in the ritual space, the fluttering feathers clear the hot energy from the person's aura and prepare the ritual participants to rejoin the normal realm of human interaction free from aggression. Moving from the denunciation of enslavement, through the duplicity of reconstruction, and beyond the intragroup hostility of the "Disallowing" to the "safety of brutal work," the violence perpetrated on the women is enacted to protect the residents of Ruby from the imagined horrors of external influences considered a threat to their survival.

Relocated from Haven to Ruby, the original families continue their self-imposed isolation. A Yoruba song lyric about twins corresponds to the historical mission of the founding fathers: "*Famo beji. Beji so ndo. Beji so ndo*" (Cling as twins. Twins produce the building of settlements; twins produce the building of settlements) (Mason and Edwards, *Orin Òrìsà* 183). According to the Dogon, a twin pair of heavenly agents of creation called Nommo created the earth. The Dogon predecessors were four pairs of human ancestors representing each of the four cardinal directions. Similarly, the Dogon people have a noncontradictory holistic cosmology, whose ideas are mirrored in the social order, in the building of a house, and the design of everyday reality. Instead of the twins bridging the gap between the world of the gods and the world of humans consistent with the Dogon cosmology, Deacon and Steward deviate from this purpose through their participation in the slaughter.

For the Dogon, twinship dominates Dogon thinking, and in their architecture the physical arrangement of each Dogon village consists of two sections: an upper and a lower area.[8] Morrison's imaginative layout of the town of Ruby organized as a cross recalls the cosmic principle of Amma's egg, called "the womb of all world signs" (Griaule and Dieterlen 84). For example, the town of Ruby consists of four streets to the east named after the gospels, Saint Matthew, Saint Mark, Saint Luke, and Saint John, flanked Central Avenue. And four streets were laid on the west side of Central, where they acquired secondary names Cross Matthew, Cross Mark, Cross Luke, and Cross John (*Paradise* 114). This relates to the Dogon idea of two axes or collateral directions, North and South, which create the number eight and intersect the four points. When multiplied 8 {x} 8 {x} 4 yields two hundred and fifty-six outlines or signs referred to as the complete "signs of the world" (Griaule and Dieterlen 84). These signs give all things color, form, and substance or an understanding of everything that exists in the world. An interesting correlation, the number 256 also corresponds to the sacred number of Yoruba *odu*, which also defines and cosmologically structures the narrative of phenomena.

The town's layout also characterizes the myths held by the "8-rocks," such as the number of original ancestors or families that in turn are reinforced by the strategic positioning of landmarks just as the oven occupies the place where the Hogon or spiritual head of the Dogon village would reside.[9] Where they live and walk in the world represents where they reside spiritually in the narrow inscription of the four Christian gospels—where there is no space for any other belief system to reside without being thought of as evil. Within this framework of intolerance, the people of Ruby establish their settlement and include land regulations where one can neither buy nor sell land where an ancestor of the tribe or clan lineage has settled, similar to the Dogon system of systematic unity that ensures the insular ideas of the group (Griaule and Dieterlen 39).

Paradise has the potential to become an etiological tale, complete with an accompanying morality to assign blame and explain the disastrous results of evil in the midst after the norm of womanhood is breached. Save-Marie's death was Ruby's first: a "town full of immortals" where now the "reaper was no longer barred entry" (296). This was accompanied by "Two editions of the official story of what happened to the convent women" (296). One story was that the nine men requested them "to leave or mend their ways; there had been a fight; the women took other shapes and disappeared into thin air" (297). The other story was that five men had gone to evict the women; that four others—the authors—had gone to restrain them. These four were attacked by the women but succeeded in driving them out, and they took off in their Cadillac; but unfortunately had lost their heads and killed the old woman. There is an in-between story as well: "that nine 8-rocks murdered five harmless women (a) because the women were impure (not 8-rock); (b) because the women were unholy (fornicators at the least, abortionists at most); and (c) because they could—which was what being an 8-rock meant and what the 'deal' required" (296–97).

At this point one has to ask, what deal? The deal made with whom? The deal they struck with each other in each generation subsequent to the Disallowing? The deal was actually struck when "Ruby was buried, without benefit of a mortuary" (113). Another contradiction in this slippery narrative is that Ruby was not a town where death was a stranger. In fact, despite the dynamic abundance associated with twins, there are significant deaths in the novel that threaten the continuation of Ruby. From an African perspective both Deacon and Steward are *abiku* destined to die, without offspring to call their names into the future.[10] By the novel's end, K.D. is the only one left to ensure continuation of the Morgan family line. Even at that, K.D. is not a Morgan; that is, his seed would call forth a resurrection of the matrilineal heritage of the twins' deceased sister, Ruby.

It seems as if the deal is for them to have life on the material plane and thereby forego future perpetuity in the form of offspring, which ensures eternal life from an African spiritual perspective. The Yoruba idea of *abiku* works well with the concept of twins, because like the Ibeji, who have the ability to move in-between realms, the abiku are timeless, ageless, and are not limited by boundaries. Additionally, the correlate idea of *ogbanje*, an Igbo spiritual reality as a transitory being relates to the men of Ruby. Chikwenye Okonjo Ogunyemi writes:

> As a mobile site, the *ogbanje* is the trope of migrations, thereby disquietingly scrutinizing the lack of social mobility of her constituency in the living world. She is the bridge between the call and its response, the prayer and the fulfillment of desire. As a people's nostalgia reinforces their resentment at being displaced, the promiscuous transmigrations and fugitive status of *ogbanje* become a given. Itinerancy, with its perennial search for another place for security, is the destiny of ogbanje, as it is of black peoples, if West African restlessness and the makings of a diaspora are proof of the desire for survival. (666)

The men of Ruby are still in a transitory space: between the stable residences where they will have the security they need to no longer fear the threat of the other to displace them from their uncertain security, and the place where they have previously been disallowed. A metaphor for the continued unease of exile characteristic of the African American experiences in America, this netherworld of Ruby becomes a space to act out the violence on each other, instead of confronting the seed of dread, white supremacy.

Let us Prey/Pray

Toni Morrison also employs the leitmotif of twinning in her inclusion of the women in the Convent. For example, after the Mother Superior's death and at the time of their own death, there are five women living in the convent: Consolata (called Connie), Mavis, Grace (called Gigi), Pallas (called Divine), and Seneca. This number corresponds to the definitive delineation of the Yoruba Ibeji. Although they are only two beings—the Ibeji concept consists of five beings comprising the original two twins and the three children born to the mother after the birth of twins. The names of the Ibeji are Taiwo (taste the world); Kehinde (the last to come or second child); Idowu (the third child); Alaba (the fourth child) comes after Idowu; and Idogbe (the next child) comes after Alaba. The women—injured physically and emotionally—appear at the door of the convent as if summoned by a cosmic force. Connie receives and accepts them all. The women have come to the convent by coincidence and have stayed seeking consoling. First, Mavis appears—the mother of twins accidentally smothered when she left them in a car unattended. Then there are Gigi, a promiscuous woman looking for love, Seneca who carves crosses all over her body, and Pallas who has been betrayed. The identities of the convent women are characterized as being between the women of Ruby and the women of the Brazilian Candomblé.

Morrison employs situational irony, another type of twinning, to bring the two communities together. For instance, when the families move to Ruby, they no longer use the oven to make bread; instead they begin buying bread from the women in the convent. Marcel Griaule notes in *Conversations with Ogotemmeli* that trade and commerce began with twins (199). However, the people of Ruby compromise some of their independence and become reliant on the produce grown by the women of the convent. Their actions invert the opening line of the Lord's Prayer, which requests, "Our Father who art in heaven, give us this day our daily bread and forgive us our trespasses as we forgive those who trespass against us" and instead becomes, "Our Mother, who art on earth, sell us today our daily bread." Additionally, there is not a plea for forgiving trespasses—only judgments and betrayals. Moreover, Morrison uses the subterfuge of buying food— "man does not live by bread alone"—to represent the spiritual nurturance available at the convent, "a big stone house in the middle of nothing," an environment where elements of nature are constructed as sites of power attracting the people of Ruby for healing. Potentially a place to restore community cohesion, the convent is instead seen as the abode of the resident evil.

The convent and the women who live there are parallel to the Brazilian Candomblé structure.[11] In *The City of Women*, based on her experiences with female ritual specialists, Ruth Landes records her observations of spiritual practices, rites, and ceremonies in Rio de Janeiro. In her ethnographic research, she notes that in the Yoruba Candomblé of Bahia, these spiritual leaders are individuals who have inherited their title and who are highly trained in African religious knowledge and ritual. Like the *terreiro* or Ile structure of Brazil, the convent is presided over by a Yalorixa or Iyalorisa, Mother Mary Magna. While Mary Magna was living, Consolata acts in the role of little mother—Mae pequena or Iya Kekere (Yoruba). Landes explains the role of the Mae pequena, the next in authority to inherit the authority of the terreiro, as being responsible for the initiates to carry out their ritual obligations. She also makes the food for the propitiary offerings (*City of Women* xi). Another responsibility of the Iya Kekere (Mae pequena) is the supervision of the initiations, which last six months or a year. As a part of the initiation preparation there are restrictions in food and drink, sex taboos, hair cutting, and instruction in the rituals and songs of the *orixa* (Òrìsà), usually in the Yoruba language (xi).

The women of the Candomblé and their children who live in the terreiros operate as a collective mutual aid society providing a basis for female solidarity. The women have ritual autonomy; their social and economic lives are female-centered and autonomous as well (Landes xii). Correspondingly, the Ba Kongo have a community structure where women come together to share and learn from one another called the Kikombe womanhood school. Young women come right after menstruation to begin their training as women. Interesting to note is the similarity between the words *Kikombe* and *Candomblé*. In Ki-Kongo and Kimbundu, the languages spoken in the kingdoms of Kongo and Angola respectively, the word Candomblé means house of initiation, from *ka*, a diminutive, *ndumbe* (initiate) and *mbele* (house).[12] In Morrison's narrative, however, the women are of various ages, but connected through the common experience of emotional or spiritual distress. Ultimately, as a result of living in the convent and receiving spiritual instruction, each of the women will transform herself through an initiation process.

The Change

In one of the *apataki* or Yoruba narratives, Oshun, the mother of the Ibeji, delivered the twins to Yemonja in order to protect them from Sango, who could potentially send them off to war. She keeps Idowu with her, but dresses him up as a girl to ensure his not going off to war with Sango.[13] The notion of Yemonja having protective custody over the children of another woman is consistent with the role of supreme mother and speaks to the correlative role of "other mother" in African American culture. Accordingly, Connie as Iya Kekere or Mae pequena takes in the women who come to the convent, provides them with a home environment, and facilitates their ultimate healing.

In her transformation, Consolata Sosa achieves another state of consciousness, which reconnects her twinned self/body and spirit—the template for soul evolution. There are twin stories of how Connie came to be in Mary Magna's custody. One story is that she was kidnapped; the other is that Sister Mary rescues Consolata from Brazil, where her nine-year-old body had been a victim of sexual abuse.[14] Then the instruction begins: "body is nothing . . . spirit is everything" (263). After having been indoctrinated into the Catholic idea of being a bride only to Christ, but ravenous for earthly desires and hungry for male companionship, Connie turns to the living man, and thus begins her womanhood and the unity of the two discrete aspects of her existence. Morrison writes, "Those thirty years cracked like a pullet's egg when she met the living man" (225), who caused "the wing of a feathered thing, undead, fluttered in her stomach" (226). By presenting spirit and body as separate ideas, Morrison intimates that some balance of the two will have to be restored in order for Connie to evolve into Consolata. Through the use of egg imagery, Morrison signifies the Dogon concept of the egg of creation that brings forth life.

Moreover, the concept of twinning associated with Dogon cosmology is depicted in language emblematic of the relationship between Deacon and Connie. Henry John Drewal notes that the paired male and female are venerated as one existence (*Nine Centuries of African Art and Thought* 39). The metaphor of the "two fig trees growing into each other" (230) evokes the idea of two mirrors placed opposite each other, which keep reiterating the image. Morrison's use of mirror imagery deals with the representations of consciousness and reflection. Moreover, Connie's subsequent spiritual contemplation is enhanced after perceiving the notion of the self through an acquaintance with her own face in the reflection of Deacon. In his face, she glimpses the destiny that she will ultimately face. To explain, mirrors clearly connect us with our own consciousness reflecting both reality and illusion. They are a significant idea of duality since, as reflective surfaces, they have no meaning without an observer. When Deacon asks Connie, "Do you know how beautiful you are? Have you looked at yourself?" (231) she responds, "I'm looking now" (231). Like two mirrors placed opposite each other, which keep repeating the image, the two are able to visualize the potential of eternity realized as completion. Additionally, the trope of mirrors is analogous to Connie's eyes, which will become mirrors to visualize ideas in spiritual proximity as well as to forecast future events as sites of potential truth. Her eyes are like the mirrors in fairy tales—places where one may go and ask questions and make assessments.

Mirrors also provide multilayered visual information. Connie thinks, "He and I are the same" (241). Even the sound that Deacon's spirit speaks to Connie is doubled as "Sha sha sha, Sha sha sha" (241). For Deacon, Connie's mirrored reflection provides an opportunity for imaginative musings and narcissistic predilections. It is also helps him to distinguish himself from his twin brother, Steward. When Deacon tells Connie that he has a twin, Connie asks, "There are two of you?" To which he replies, "No . . . there's just one of me" (232). He has begun the process of differentiation, forging an identity separate from Steward in order to pursue his relationship with Connie, which will eventually lead him to feel "Exotic to a twin—an incompleteness" (300). This inversion is notable, because Steward has told Anna that being a twin makes him feel "more complete" (116). Later in the narrative, this fracture between the twins causes him to expose his feet, like his grandfather "who walked barefoot two hundred miles" (301). His naked feet become the distinctive feature needed to separate himself from his twin in order to walk in the direction of his own forgiveness. Connie, on the other hand, begins after the split with Deacon to fuse her identity, even though one of the things that she discovers is that Deacon is her twinned soul.[15] When he breaks off the relationship, the mirror is shattered, he can no longer see Connie again, and she becomes an illusion of something fleeting and transitory that threatens to fix his gaze beyond the commitment he intends to make. Like A. Jacks/Ajax in *Sula*, Deacon takes flight.

Ultimately, Connie's eyes will become mirrors to "fix" or forecast future events. After the affair is over, Connie begins the next phase of her journey: "Consolata had been spoken to." The sign that marks the change is the sun shot that seared her right eye "announcing the beginning of her bat vision." The idea of "bat vision" glosses the notion of the Iyami Osoronga, who are also affiliated with bats and other nocturnal birds. Ironically, Connie now as Consolata begins to see using her inner vision; her symbolic sight connects her with *nyama* or vital energy and allows her access to the spiritual life—not the dogma-filled life prescribed by Mother Mary Magna. Her soul is now opened to the realization of itself and others allowing her to see "what took place in the minds of others" (248). Consolata's glasses function like the *mamoni* lines painted around the eyes of the Nganga, which help her to see the hidden and dangerous things of the world such as sickness and evil (MacGaffey, *Kongo Political Culture* 53). Moreover, the flash of light that sears her eyes does not leave her totally in the dark; instead it illuminates the internal space where spiritual light resides.

When the change comes, Lone Du Pres initiates her into a new consciousness: one of balance and connectedness. Nzegwu argues that the various chapters in the narrative of life do not "subvert the unitary character of the self or personal identity" (177). Instead, she asserts that people only re-arrange and organize the meaningful and relevant values and inject new stories to frame the narrative of self (177). Lone tells Consolata, "You need what we all need: earth, air water. Don't separate God from his elements. He created it all. You stuck on dividing him from his works. Don't unbalance His world" (244). Morrison advances that skills in healing, knowledge of the sacred, psychic abilities, and knowledge concerning herbal medicine are constructed by aligning oneself to the rhythms of nature. In nature one has the potential to learn that the universe is sacred and that divine forces merge and interact with terrestrial forces.

The ritual of "stepping in" that Lone teaches Consolata—which Consolata calls "seeing in" or "in sight"—causes dissonance in her personality. However, when she is able to keep Mary Magna alive by entering her body, this helps her to reconcile practicing what felt "like evil craft" (246). Consolata learns to accept the different modes of traversing reality—different ways to perceive the power of the self as she expands the *nyama* or vital force to sustain and continue life. Nzegwu describes the process of "stepping in" and "stepping out" as an invocation of "the manner in which at the transfiguring moment of death, we permanently step out of the conditions of the everyday three dimensional reality, and into the pneumatic mmuo conditions of spirit-space and time" (176). Movement from one space to another, or transspatiality, can occur during spirit possession or other spiritually charged states where one accesses other realms of existence. These epistemic constructions are culturally defined and expand time beyond the European delineation of a three-dimensional structure.

Nommo

> With speech, man receives the life force, shares it with other
> beings, and thereby achieves direction for living.
>
> —Dogon Oral Tradition

Not until the chapter titled "Consolata" has Toni Morrison divulged Consolata's twinned name. Called Connie by the novel's other characters, Consolata now tells the women as though introducing herself for the first time, "I
call myself Consolata Sosa" (262). As Connie, Consolata employed a mask
of concealment. The visit from the man with eyes "round and green as new
apples" (252), her deceased grandfather, Tea, the twin of Coffee, speaks
the language that wakes up the remembrance of her suppressed linguistic
code. As Consolata, she recovers her language and reconnects to a series
of ontological relationships including a recovered concept of God, her family, and her former land. The Nummo or Nommo twins, whose number is
eight, represent the Dogon idea of speech, *dogo so*.[16] This recovery of *dogo
so* ferries Consolata to a memory of self before the cultural impositions
perpetrated by Mary Magna.

The Dogon have terms to describe the process of language occurring in
four stages. Beginning with *giri so* (front speech), the person proceeds to
grasp concepts at the next level, *bene so* (side speech), then to *bolo so* (back
speech), and on to the final stage of a profound mastery of the ideas of the
world called *so dayi* (clear speech). *So dayi* is reserved for initiates and is
not available or accessible to all. Regaining her language helps to relocate
Consolata's true voice. Benjamin C. Ray notes that one's primary language
leads to the real nature of things (101).

In *Paradise*, Morrison reminds us of the process of Consolata's cultural
assimilation. She writes, "The first to go were the rudiments of her first
language. Every now and then she found herself speaking and thinking
in that in-between place, the valley between the regulations of the first
language and the vocabulary of the second" (242). The former process of
linguistic embezzlement occurs as a matter of practice and the process of
the religious indoctrination of "forgetting." Just as the students Arapahoe
or Algonquin have to whisper "to each other in a language the sisters had
forbidden them to use" (233), Consolata's reclamation of her primal language liberates her from the hegemony characterized by linguistic imposition. Like her diminished sight, her restored language gives her insight and

mastery to preside more efficaciously over the rituals of transformation. By removing the linguistic constraints, Consolata reintegrates and renews her connection with those African women who "know things" and the rituals that bind them in sisterhood. The medium of language transfigures her, extends her senses and functions, modifies the codes, and creates an injunctive form of language consistent with her spiritual identity.

As ritual leader, Consolata employs *so dayi* (the language of knowing). Using this new language, she prepares each of the women to meet her particular spirit twin. The name Consolata is a derivative of the Spanish infinitive, consolar, which means to console. Having spent her life forgetting, she now vows to teach the women what they are hungry for (262). One of the songs sung in praise of the Ibeji states, *"Olomo, beji mo (a) kara wa (a) kara wa bo (i) ya re"* (owners, parents of children born in twos know bean cakes are prepared to feed mothers to console them) (Mason and Edwards, *Orin Orisa*, 183). While another song says, *"B'eji la Omo edun b'eji. B 'eji la O be Kun Iya re"* (Give birth to two and be rich, Give birth to two and be rich. They cut off the weeping and console mothers) (182). Also significant about the lyrics is that each verse is sung twice, in keeping with the concept of twinning.

The Ritual of Transformation

The nexus between real and imaginative is imperceptible through the metaphor of ritual. African ideas of the divine and the significance in ritual determine the success or failure of characters. Moreover, ritual incorporation serves Toni Morrison's narrative purposes and sheds light on the ways in which African people rely on corporate behavior to engender their healing. Through the ritual of transformation, Consolata reestablishes the concept of the matriarch and the female notion of divinity linking ritual power to act in response to the particular aims of the individual women. This spiritual nurturance provided at the novel's end by Consolata, allows the convent women to find the spiritual in-between and discover their spiritual selves. Drawing sacred ideograms representative of their spiritual selves, the women express their sacred selves in silhouettes characteristic of Kongo Pembas or Vodun Vévés. Using white, the color associated with the ancestors and the color of kaolin or *mpemba* found at the bottom of rivers, the women refashion *minkisi* to heal and help them realize their potential (MacGaffey, *Kongo Political Culture* 91).

These iconographic representations help the women mediate the space between their scarred physical selves and their spiritual identity. Morrison writes in *Paradise*, "They altered. They had to be reminded of the moving bodies they wore, so seductive were the alive ones below" (265). These outlines juxtapose the silhouettes of decay to that against which the people of Ruby were always on guard, related in the stories of how other towns had merged with white towns. These towns "had shriveled into *tracery*: foundation *outlines* marked by the way grass grew there, wallpaper turned *negative* behind missing windows, schoolhouse floors moved aside by elder trees growing toward the bell housing" (6; emphasis added). The ritual the women performed is not for material considerations, but for spiritual uplift and renewal. As individuals, the convent women shift their identities through space and time in the physical world, body space, mental world or ideational space, and the pneumatic or spiritual world. Nzegwu notes that these spaces are mutually permeable and interpenetrable and ontological spaces. For example, spirit time (oge mmuo) and human time (oge madu) are interconnected at the ideational level. Additionally, she asserts that these spheres constantly shift and change and allow a person to access these spirit spaces in the same way as one does objects in the physical world (Nzegwu 172).

First, Consolata paints each woman's silhouette, representing a sacred cocoon to enclose each individual self, delineating it from the profane, externalized self. Since the body is the transgressive text employed to judge the women, it is apropos that the marking of the body becomes the site of ritual regeneration strengthening each individual woman as well as filling the gaps in the circle or protective ring that surrounds the soul according to Kongo belief. To that end, each of the women's hair is shaved as a symbolic act of releasing the old and preparing the head for a new life—one unencumbered by the accumulated pain of the past.

The preliminary activity of the women's spiritual "make over" is to have the women position themselves on the floor in order to trace their life's story, choosing the positions for themselves in any way they feel comfortable. The omniscient narrator describes the shapes and directions their bodies assume:

> They tried arms at the sides, outstretched above the head, crossed over breasts or stomach. Seneca lay on her stomach at first, then changed to her back, hands clasping her shoulders. Pallas lay on her side, knees drawn up. Gigi flung her legs and arms apart, while Mavis struck a floater's pose, arms angled pointed in. (263)

The configuration of these poses are visually represented with Gigi in the *center* as a cross, Pallas in a *fetal* position as the center at midpoint of the cross, and Seneca on her *back* and Mavis on her *stomach* as the intersecting lines creating the four-quadrant cross with the two intersections yielding the sign of eight, the Dogon sign of the world. The templates that Consolata draws of the women invoke repressed memories that they will ultimately embellish to illustrate their journeys.

Consolata then initiates the women into the healing power of narratives by telling them the story of her life's journey from Brazil, starting with a description of a place where "fish the color of plums swam alongside children," where fruit tasted "the way sapphires look," where "gods and goddesses sat in the pews with the congregation." She also describes "Piedade, who sang but never said a word" (263–64). The women recycle themselves as divine mothers.

The Yoruba lineage has conserved the concept of the ancestral mother, one of the oldest and most persistent within the African spiritual universe. These ancestral mothers are represented by the Iyami Osoronga, also refered to as Iya Won, the mother of all people. Moreover, like the divine mother Òrìsà, Yemonja, Pieta or Piedade represents the mother and child serving as the foundation of African families, communities, and society.[17] In Brazil, one of the hymns sung at an "intraculturated" mass, defined as combining elements of Catholicism with African cultural practices, praises the women as mothers. An important prayer states, "We believe in a Mother God, who is alive, fecund, of great fertility, a God Who, as a woman, knows what it means to bleed in order to give life" (104).[18]

After the preliminary drawings, the women begin to dream loudly, which in turn calls to mind stories. Once recovered, the stories serve as conduits, to release buried memories. Subsequently, each woman adorns her respective outline. Incorporating pictographic representations of unresolved issues, unrealized hopes, fears, disappointments, and a wealth of distress, in the forms of dots, etchings, flowers ("a majestic penis pierced with a Cupid's bow"), the women integrate themselves with their unscathed spirit doubles. These drawings invoke the earth's participation as a portal to transport the ritual participants to dimensions beyond the physical realm. There is also a correlation to the inscriptions on the earth illustrated by the following Dogon cosmological event:

> The fiber skirt absorbed the moisture and became language. Nommo are the guardians of the natural order. After the earth was defiled by incest by the jackal, and the Nommo saw that twin births were in

danger of disappearing, they drew a male and female outline on the ground on top of each other. This led to each human being having two souls: one male, one female. Man's female self is removed by circumcision, as is a woman's male soul at initiation (Griaule, *Conversations With Ogotemmeli* 156).

The experiential captions the women create become personal altars to alter their pockmarked souls. Sites of tremendous transition, the outlines mark the beginnings, middles, and endings of individual narratives. In this embodiment ritual, the women prepare to resurrect themselves. Griaule remarks that as part of the creative process, the Dogon Supreme deity, Amma, "traced within himself the design of the world and of its extension" (*The Pale Fox* 83). The drawing of signs creates the meaningful images or symbolic icons—*yala*, expressing the beliefs. All of the signs convey an idea, and although not considered a writing system, they communicate meaning in the same way writing does. Since the term *yala* also means reflection and expresses the future form of the thing being represented (*The Pale Fox* 96), this supports the spiritual transformation that the women will experience and ties in with the mirror imagery used throughout the novel. This is not the first time this motif of graphic invocation would appear in twentieth-century literature. In Ishmael Reed's *Mumbo Jumbo* artists use cornmeal and water to draw vevés to invite "loas for New Art" (49). The vevés are the portals for divinities to enter the physical realm.

The Return

> *Ibejire, omo Ibejire, omo edun kere kere yan.*
> Behold twins, children of the monkey. They do not die.

At the novel's end, Billy Delia, who had been taken in by Consolata, hopes that the women will return. Consistent with the African cyclical view of the human experience, life is a release from death and death is an entrance for life. For the Bantu Kongo, dying is not the end, as the proverb *tufwanga mu soba* explains: "We die in order to undergo change as a process or as a 'dam of time' it permits life to flow and regenerate to create a new state of being freeing the spirit" (Fu-Kiau, *African Cosmology* 27). In the same fashion, the Dogon believe that the power to continue life is within rather than without. When the spirit of community or tradition is violated, something ancient rises to restore equilibrium. The Nommo's resurrection is performed by Amma five "periods" or stages after the sacrifice, which is five days (Griaule and Dieterlen 333).

Compelled toward the possibility of return, Misner's sermon at Save-Marie's funeral captures the principle of Toni Morrison's theme of spiritual dualism. He says, "it is our own misfortune if we do not know in our long life what she knew every day of her short one: that although life is terminal, life after life is everlasting. He is with us always, in life, after it and especially in-between, lying in wait for us to know the splendor" (307). The idea that life continues beyond the physical body in an alternate realm is corroborated in the resurrection of the women at the end of the novel and their appearance to relatives and friends. When Reverend Misner and Anna go to view the convent after the massacre, Anna collects five fresh eggs (304), symbolic of the five Convent women and the Dogon concept of completion and unity representative of Amma, the Dogon supreme deity. Additionally, Anna gathers some of the "purple peppers from the bushes in full flower" (303) amidst the lost garden. Harvey Birenbaum explains that transformation is represented as "stages of life, phases, emotion, aspects of personal relationships—all pass and alter, often in predictable rhythms, but also in ways that provide continuity in difference, complementarity in unity, self-transcendence, and self-exhaustion" (31–32).

This complementarity is illustrated in the description of the garden:

> Beyond was blossom and death. Shriveled tomato plants alongside crops of leafy green reseeding themselves with golden flowers, pink hollyhocks so tall the heads leaned all the way over a trail of bright squash blossoms, lacy tops of carrots browned and lifeless next to straight green spikes of onion. Melons split their readiness showing gums of juicy red . . . a mix of neglect and unconquerable growth. (304–5)

Like the garden, the women have conquered death. Although changed, the women still exist indicated by the fresh eggs and uninterrupted flowering of the bush. Morrison establishes the relationship of women with the land in her depiction of the convent women as Ajé. Fundamentally the power of the earth is connected to those women who have the ability to wield spiritual power.[19] Streams, springs, rivers, oceans, trees, stumps, bushes, twigs, berries, barks, mountains, hills, valleys, caves, sun, moon dirt, earth, pharmacopoeia belong to women in the same way the hunt belongs to the domain of men.

Bunseki K. Fu-Kiau speaks of the Bantu concept of the first eternal seed *ngina* informing the *tambukusu* or genetic code as a memory of creation. The cultivation of soil and the planting of seeds put one in direct contact with that process, and sacred rites and ceremonies have evolved after observing and creating meaning to accompany those spiritual considerations. Agriculture rites foster an idea of the sacred and the idea of memory. Fu-Kiau notes that the game called "hopscotch" is actually a mnemonic device used by the Ba Kongo to remember one's genealogical lineage. Each box on the grid represents the following narrative: I am the seed of a seed of a seed of a seed of a seed, ad continuum.

Agriculture in itself is an act of solidarity with the earth and access to power that now the women of Ruby only deal with as "gardening" to showcase plants competitively. Removed from the camaraderie engendered by the convent women tilling the soil corporately, the women of Ruby are powerless. The twinned ideas of death/rebirth, fertility/barrenness, nature/culture, and order/disorder find its parallel in Dogon agricultural activity, as planting/harvesting is a central metaphor for life among agriculturalists. Additionally, the women tend to the fluids of life: water, wine, fruit (semen), in the form of the peppers (a fruit), which have all the qualities needed to bear life. The women's agricultural activities represent the symbolic landscape of power raising the ire of the men incensed about the nature of women who do not need men and prefigure their demise.

Home Is Not a Small Thing

Another key idea that Toni Morrison presents about passages or means of access occurs when Anna and Misner are at the convent. While collecting the peppers, one sees a door, the other a window. They ask: "What did a door mean? what a window?" (305). In the Kongo spiritual system, doors and windows are considered *mwela*, or portals between the material and spirit realms. These doors revolve and spirits can egress and ingress at will, evident by the women who visit with the living. Consolata is reunited with the mother God, Piedade, "black as firewood," whose "black face is framed in cerulean blue," who sings to her and strokes her "tea brown hair." Consolata has gone "home to be at home" (318). Morrison intimates that Consolata has crossed the watery depths, journeyed to the other realm and is resting in the arms of Mother God. The enslavement lyrics, "Sometimes I feel like a motherless child, a long way from home" and "Deep river my home is over Jordan" are revised as Consolata rests in the arms of the Blessed Mother.

In a conversation between Patricia Best and Reverend Misner, they consider the notion of home as a *third* place, Africa. Even though distanced by time and experience, "One, three centuries removed" as the poet Countee Cullen muses, Misner tells Pat Best, "Africa is our home, Pat, whether you like it or not" (210). Not willing to be resigned to a place where being an outsider or an enemy means the same thing, Misner's explanation of home warrants our attention.[20] Misner's statement also establishes the idea of paradise being here on earth. Additionally, he asserts that this heavenly place (Africa) was given to African people, not taken by conquest suggesting that instead of fighting over this small piece of physical or ideological territory of the west, African people need to consider some other options. Finally, he asserts that nothing good can come out of repressing other black people. In this narrative of doubling, Toni Morrison informs her readers that it is possible to move from destruction to construction, from removal to restoration, and that the real power for the continuation of life exists in the journey within and between the passages.

III

❋

Remembrance Has Not Left Us:
What the Record Shows

6

Living with the Dead

Memory and Ancestral Presence in *Beloved*

I was made to touch my past at an early age. I found it on my
mother's tiddies. In her milk.

—Gayl Jones, *Corregidora*

Now women forget all those things they don't want to remember and remember everything they don't want to forget.

—Zora Neale Hurston, *Their Eyes Were Watching God*

The ax forgets the tree remembers.

—African American proverb

Using the conceit of memory as the central organizing principle, Toni Morrison lays the necessary mythic foundations to invoke ancestral presence
in the novel *Beloved* (1987).[1] The focus of this chapter is an examination of
the heroic character, Sethe, and the ways in which the ancestor, as memory,
works in consonance with Yoruba Òrìsà, African iconography, and ritual
to engender psychic wholeness. Examining memory is an important place
to begin, because it is only when characters regain a sense of the past that
they can begin to imagine a future.

Ironically, the novel ends with the sentence, "It was not a story to pass
on." Repeated three times, this sentence frames the last five paragraphs of
Beloved. In these concluding lines, the eponymous character, Beloved, is
described as "disremembered and unaccounted for" as well as irretrievable
and "unclaimed" because they "don't know her name" (274). Perhaps, the
reason they do not know her name is because Sethe's deceased child, did
not have a name while living. From an African perspective, this innominate
status would leave her nameless in the spirit world. Even though Sethe had
"bought" her name by trading sex for a headstone with the seven-lettered
inscription "beloved" shortly after her death (204), by not having been so-

cially incorporated into the community with that name, she would remain nameless to them.

How then can Beloved be remembered? Beyond the spiritual dilemma created by postmortem considerations of naming, this tension of remembrance is complicated further by the historical disjuncture of enslavement and the anonymity corequisite with African people's status as chattel. Morrison attempts to retrieve the lost contents of culture and to mitigate the trespass caused by un-naming in the dedication to the novel by connecting the character Beloved to the *unnamed* "sixty million or more." Morrison also raises a few philosophical questions: is it possible to know on another level? Are there other epistemological approaches to gain access to the past? Throughout the novel, Morrison highlights the characters' reluctance to delve into memory, while coterminously invoking that remembrance in her literary figurations. Using conservative estimates, sixty million ancestors not only lost their names, but also their lives during the Middle Passage from the west coast of Africa to the Americas.[2] Countless others would be renamed consistent with their predicament of being enslaved. In *Beloved*, this presence/absence manifests itself by the omniscient narrator's seemingly paradoxical ending of the story mandating a mass forgetting, which constitutes memory, albeit, in a different way than remembering does. It is as if forgetting and memory are twin activities; one has to forget something to remember something else. Mary and Allen Roberts note among the Luba of Southeastern Congo the concept of forgetting, like memory is complex and signifies a purposeful action of concealment. That is a person "may not have forgotten at all, but is purposefully withholding information as a secret" (*Memory* 33). In this construction, forgetting is a conscious disruption, yet still a remembrance.

Signifying on Frederick Douglass's recollection of his first remembered trauma and the dialectical idea, "I shall never forget it whilst I remember one thing," the characters in *Beloved* intimate that the process of memory is complex and highly nuanced. It can work in reverse, deleting items rather than storing them. In any case, memory acknowledges that some conscious decision has been made, some selection process has occurred. "They forgot her like a bad dream," "quickly and deliberately forgot her," "couldn't remember or repeat a single thing she said," "Remembering seemed unwise" (274), are word masks that disguise the deliberate recollection of Beloved.

In the deep structure where compelling meaning abides, the narrator fortifies the remembrance of the story events. Invoked by the twists and turns of historical deletion, these memories resemble Pierre Nora's notion of *lieux de mémoire*, since the environments of memory have been suppressed and silenced by trauma (284). Geneviève Fabre discusses the dissonance created by forgetting and remembrance and suggests that the tension between these two ideas find synthesis in the creation of an organizing principle to forge a strategy for collective remembrance (*History and Memory* 88). That is, the detailed listing of items to "disremember" and the trope of repetition reinforce memory. Ralph Ellison describes this ontological consciousness not as "historical forgetfulness" but as a product of memory (*Shadow and Act* 124).

One thing that is not negotiable for African people is a loss of memory. Concerning the agency of memory, Cornell West explains "African Americans have been the ones who could not forget. They have been the Americans who could not not know" (3). The subject of this present study, African spiritual traditions, necessitates an exploration of the nature of history and memory. Memory and history are connected but differ in their function. Mary and Allen Roberts explain that memory represents the process of evolution and is a cultural construction, while history concerns reconstruction or a reproduction (*Memory* 29). Furthermore, Roberts and Roberts define memory as "A dynamic social process of recuperation, reconfiguration, and outright invention" (*Memory* 17). Residing in the border "between self and other," memory is a social and cultural construct, rather than a biological or a mental activity (*Memory* 41). Thus memory contributes to the sense of historical consciousness, which provides a people with identity, is created in a variety of ways. The considerations in this chapter are memory's perpetuation through narrative and the reinvention and recodification of sacred ideas over time in language, dance, song, and gesture. Specifically, I want to explore the ways in which memory is at once a symbolic, sacred, and cultural conception.

As an active process of connecting and creating relationships, Nora advances that "memory installs remembrance within the sacred" ("Between Memory and History" 286). For instance among the Luba the word *lutê*, derived from *kuta* is defined as mémoire. However, more illustrative of the spiritual connection is the phrase, "kuta ku mushina" meaning "to fix in the spirit." Kuta, "to remember" is also related to words, such as *kitê* and *mitê*. Kitê translates as a little mound of packed earth where *minkisi* are placed for protection, to honor the birth of twins, and to *mark* death. Mitê represents sun rays, which allow one to perceive place and time (*Memory* 32). Moreover, for the Luba, memory consists of repetition; indicating continuity with the past, alongside the triadic structure of space, time, and the sacred implying that memory is a function of a particular cosmology. This sacred imperative of memory coexists in African American culture and is realized in *Beloved* in the concentric circles of plot, characterization, narrative structure, and ritual. Mircea Eliade explains that through ritual cosmogonic time is retrieved and brought to the present moment (*The Sacred and the Profane* 30).

A way to resolve this conundrum presented by "disrememory" (forgetting) and "rememory" (remembering) is to consider the dualism presented by spiritual considerations. This idea of spiritual lineage through invocation constitutes memory and engenders community cohesion severed in that historical breach. For example, in the Lukumi tradition the *mojuba* (invocational prayers) are recited before any ritual including divination. Calling the names of deities, community ancestors, lineage ancestors, and individual ancestors from the past into the present ensures the future of time. This invocation creates presence while simultaneously acknowledging absence in order to renew the community. These oral and performed traditions are fundamental ways of representing the past and maintaining a continuity with the present. Although these ancestors are unnamed, it is possible to create a commemorative space to bridge the gap created by the Middle Passage and the missing names. Previously, Toni Morrison began her inquiry into the recovery of names in *Song of Solomon*, ferrying her character to Africa, for this reflection. Macon Dead muses that he and Pilate had "some ancestor, some lithe young man with onyx skin and legs as straight as cane stalks, who had a name that was real" A name given to him at birth with love and seriousness" (17).

Besides a consideration of irretrievable names that could hinder memory and narrative integrity, in "The Telling of *Beloved*," Eusebio L. Rodrigues attributes the difficulty in recounting the story to the nature of the "unspeakable" and exceptional horrors of the memorates. He writes, "The past, racial and personal, seared into the being of her past, racial and personal, seared into the being of her characters, has to be exorcised by 'rememory'" (153). Shortly after winning the Pulitzer Prize for *Beloved*, Morrison remarks in a *Time* magazine interview that the enslavement of African people is something that no one wants to remember. She states:

> I thought this is got to be the least read of all the books I'd written because it is about something that the characters don't want to remember, black people don't want to remember, white people don't want to remember. I mean it's national amnesia. (120)

Sethe who consistently fights back the painful events of the past in her "rememory" confirms her attraction to amnesia. This struggle with the brain keeps her "not interested in the future," because it refused nothing (*Beloved* 70). The recollection of these dreadful memories forms the necessary bridge leading to healing—the central point of the novel. Insisting on recognition, memory signifies that life and is situated as much in the present as it is in the past (Nora 285).

Memory, a phenomenon of primary importance in an oral tradition, becomes a political, spiritual, and cultural statement in *Beloved*—evidenced by Toni Morrison's combination of myth and remembered history. This collective remembering is defined as the conscious historical and cultural knowledge common to a group of people. Transmitted from generation to generation through the use of traditional oral forms, this shared knowledge assures spiritual and cultural continuity. The reformation and relocation of memory through scenarios that conjure up ancestral images are accomplished by linking characters' recollections of past events with re-enactments of African ritual behavior and eulogistic tributes to the memory of Baby Suggs. Working in concert with language, these mythologies are foundational to the memories and their accompanying narratives that lead Sethe toward healing.

Moreover, characters in *Beloved* embody the African idea of community since they provide the primary support for the individual. Offering different accounts of events, each provides what is significant and poignant for them and omits details that do not inform their personal mythic realities. What some characters leave out, others furnish; the result of which is the creation of a complete story. Morrison inscribes the noun memory as a verb to emphasize its dynamism. For example, Sethe remarks, "Funny how you lose sight of some things and *memory* others" (201, emphasis added). Memory performs and "rememory" names; together they help to elide the past into the present.

These stories rooted in the pain-filled past are not easily told. Rodrigues says that all the characters "have to tear the terrible past, bit by painful bit out of their beings in order to be healed" (153). The result of their collective account is a view of captivity from a sweeping perspective in this circular narrative. Constructing the story in nonsequential order, using Baby Suggs as the central focus for relating major story elements from the characters and omniscient narrator, this circularity, akin to the African tradition of call and response, allows for the affirmation of the ancestral ontological experience.

Circularity is the antithesis of lineality, which Marimba Ani describes as "the interpretation of phenomena" constructed of "unidimensional, separate entities arranged in sequential order" (xxvii–xxviii). Since linear conceptions are necessarily secular and result in de-sacrilization, besides denying circularity and the spiral of organic development, they prevent transcendence of ordinary time and space. Morrison elucidates this circularity saying that she prefers to "develop parts out of piece . . . preferred them unconnected—to be related but not to touch, to circle, not line up" ("Memory" 388). Like memory, this circularity serves as structure, theme, narrative device, and ancestral characterization.

The ancestor's dual signification of rebirth and the principle of circularity finds agency in Toni Morrison's circular language, "I am Beloved's and she is mine" (214); language rich in oxymoron, "drove him crazy so he would not lose his mind" (41); paradoxical statements, "I'll protect her while I'm alive and I'll protect her when I ain't" (45). In this passage, Morrison reveals Sethe's beliefs about the continuity of life beyond the physical realm. In this passage, Sethe affirms the idea of the dead being able to interact with the living and influence outcomes for them. Morrison also encodes the notion of information available at the interstices where meaning is intensified.[3] She writes, "Ella listened for the holes—the things the fugitives did not say; the questions they did not ask" (92). Establishing the frame for remembrance by her deliberate recording of those insufferable events that define both the community highlighted in the novel and those in the realm of the ancestors, their historical experiences of captivity and enslavement make strong spiritual and historical statements.

Time distinguished by spiritual emphasis is one of the decisive elements that shape both narrative structure as well as content. The concept of history, posited to be linear and serialized, is razed as Morrison replaces it and offers a definition of African-centered history harmonizing with African notions of time. In addition to circularity, her narratives focus on embellished personal accounts of individual lives in ways that the enslavement narratives could not. Barbara Christian says that nineteenth-century writers were "constrained by the socio-political biases of their time," which restricted the expression of traditional beliefs because of the "detrimental effects that such 'superstitious,' or non-Christian concepts would have had on their own people" ("Somebody Forgot" 330). These narrators were also restrained from the illustration of overt acts of resistance considered outside the mainstream of abolitionist-approved behavior. These self-determining acts were avoided as they would "muddy the already murky waters of sentiment" toward African people by "presenting characters that might terrify their readers" ("Somebody Forgot" 330).

In "The Site of Memory," Morrison describes some of the conventions used by these nineteenth-century writers to avoid the unholy details of some of their most harrowing experiences. She notes: "Whenever there was an unusually violent incident, or a scatological one, or something 'excessive,' one finds the writer taking refuge in the literary conventions of the day" (301). The effect of this type of stricture was to make the reporting of the brutal conditions of bondage acceptable to the abolitionists who were in a position to influence its end. In this way, an authentic view of the African's suffering was veiled, the interior life of the captives was obfuscated, and a realistic picture of their actual existence denied.

In her unrestrained narrative, Morrison's omniscient narrator reveals Sethe's desperation at the thought of being remanded into captivity: "Inside, two boys bled in the sawdust and dirt at the feet of a nigger woman holding a blood-soaked child to her chest with one hand and an infant by the heels in the other" (149). Morrison also depicts the brutal practices of enslavement, "It was a place where bits were put on human mouths to prevent them from eating the food they were harvesting. She remembered the bottom teeth she had lost to the brake and the scars from the bell were thick as rope around her waist" (258). It was a place where kneeling men were sexually abused and women were raped. "She had delivered, but would not nurse, a hairy white thing, fathered by the 'lowest yet'" (258–59). These memorates are not individual components of memory, but represent the shared, collective experience of African people who suffered these abuses over time through the practices of enslavement, including the traumatic forced migration and transportation from Africa and the subsequent psychological seasoning on the plantations.

In her reconstruction of the enslavement period, Morrison employs a recursive narrative structure that takes the various personal accounts of "facts" recorded by characters and recounts a story of enslavement and its repercussions. Morrison remarks, "The exercise is also critical for any person who is black, or who belongs to any marginalized category, for, historically, we were seldom invited to participate in the discourse even when we were its topic" ("Site of Memory" 302). Valerie Smith writes in *Self-Discovery and Authority in Afro-American Narrative* that the extent of the control people have on their lives depends upon his or her capacity to tell his or her own story (4). Morrison is clear about the empowerment in telling one's own truth and reveals that significance by including the disquieting horrors of enslavement usually obliterated in historical accounts.

Additionally, absent from this novel is the determinism seen in some of her other novels, especially *The Bluest Eye*, where characters are presented with a dearth of possibilities and a limited capacity to work through their difficulties. Toni Morrison endows characters in *Beloved* with the ability to reverse the apocalyptic contours of their lives and emerge with a modicum of hope. In this reversed apocalypse, the past, not the present, is where future rewards are to be found.[4] This achievement may be considered attributable to the power of memory. The characters are empowered by telling their stories, which are composites of significant features of their experiences. In this manner the interior lives are shared and the story is enriched.

For example, in an episode where Denver, the surviving daughter of Sethe, chronicles what she misses, she remembers "Baby Suggs telling her things in the keeping room. She smelled like bark in the day and leaves at night" (19). As the novel opens, Baby Suggs is dead. However, Morrison inscribes her as the living dead cohering to John S. Mbiti's explanation where he expands the classification of ancestors, dividing them into "long dead," "recently dead," or "living dead" (70). Those classified as being "long dead" are so codified because they are "spirits" of forgotten people who are no longer within the personal memory of the people (76). The living dead are spirits for whom the family has a conscious memory. Mbiti suggests that as long as the departed spirit has not lost its personal name and identity it more or less leads a personal continuation of life (125).

Throughout the novel, the characters will invoke Baby Suggs's memory to ask for assistance. This is consistent with Morrison's dictum, "If we don't keep in touch with the ancestor we are, in fact, lost" ("Rootedness" 344). This sense of being lost or detached from the ancestors results from the absence of guidance from the other realm. Janheinz Jahn defines the *magara* principle as, "the force of intelligence which flows in to the living man from his ancestors (or Òrìsà) without whose help there is little he can do" (116). In addition to offering guidance, the ancestors are also "the guardians of morals." In the life of the community each person has his place and each has his right to *magara,* to well-being and happiness (116). This adherence to community morals engenders well-being. Morrison expresses this sentiment saying, "If anything I do, in the way of writing novels (or whatever

I write) isn't about the village or community or about you, then it is not about anything" ("Rootedness" 344).

Denver's memories of the earthy Baby Suggs connect Baby Suggs to an ancient source, which supplants her enslavement origins Like M'Dear in *The Bluest Eye* and other elderly women that inhabit Morrison's novels, Baby Suggs is spiritual roots worker. The individual memorates form the collective memory of political, ideological, and cultural themes particular to African peoples. These pieces of memory are delivered primarily through the narrative devices of an omniscient or implied narrator who shapes these memorates and shares them with the readers through interior monologues. In this way, the narrator contributes to both content and structure. The narration also consists of direct exposition through dialogue, alternating flashbacks, and flash-forwards that create a sense of circularity, which resembles the African epic and signifies the cyclical idea of the ancestor. For example, in *Beloved* there is a nonadherence to the delineations of past, present, and future, indicative of the notion of *hantu*, the construction of time from a Bantu cultural perspective.[5] In epic fashion, Sethe, having upset the balance associated with maternity, must restore harmony.

The structure of the novel is divided into three major sections. Part 1 consists of eighteen chapters (163 pages), Part 2 has seven chapters (70 pages), and Part 3 has three chapters (38 pages). These structural delineations also roughly correlate in content to ideas of past, present, and future and are also specific foci for each one of the trio of women inhabiting the house. The house at 124 Bluestone Road also indicates this triadic structure. The house number indicates displacement of order consistent with the disruption of family, dislocation from Africa, and the ruptured psyche resulting from being captives. The missing number three, however, is not an actual omission since the mind insists upon making closure and inserts it anyway, symbolizing the adjustments African people have made in order to survive in America. They have had to continually supply the missing pieces—family members, memories, and other crucial elements—in order to remain whole.

This multivoiced intergenerational story begins in medias res.[6] The first paragraph of Part 1, Chapter 1, informs the reader that Baby Suggs is dead, that Sethe's sons Howard and Buglar have run away, and that Sethe and Denver are the only two left in a spiteful house possessed by a mischievous baby spirit (4). In this synopsis of some of the salient plot elements there is the omission of Sethe having committed infanticide. By the end of Part 1, a clear cycle of abuse has been established, and it becomes clear that the goal of the heroic quest is to terminate this cycle and circle of pain.

At the beginning of the novel, Sethe's spiritual strength and courage as a potential heroic figure are demonstrated. She states, "I got a tree on my back and a haint in my house, and nothing in between but the daughter I am holding in my arms. No more running—from nothing. I will never run from another thing on this earth" (15).

In an epic sense, bold affirmations of this nature usually prefigure a test to assess the character's dauntlessness and tenacity. This passage signifies Sethe's demonstration of personal commitment and sacrifice and shows her willingness to face whatever is ahead of her in contrast to her unwillingness to examine the past. The keloidal skin on her back represents an overhealing of the skin and is a type of external memory juxtaposing the emotional or internal healing that has yet to occur.

As she begins to journey through memory, Sethe recalls her physical violation when the white boys on the plantation steal her milk. Using the trope of repetition, Morrison underscores its significance: "I had milk. . . . All I know was that I had to get my milk to my baby girl. . . . Nobody knew but me and nobody had her milk but me. . . . those boys came and took my milk . . . held me down and took it." When Paul D tries to get the facts from Sethe through questioning, Sethe repeatedly responds, "And they took my milk" (16–17). This chanting of the word *milk* stills her mind and temporarily helps her transcend the horror of this memory. Moreover, the remembrance of the past activates the *asé* or vital forces necessary for her healing and inspires recall of the past, which has previously kept Sethe from reaching her potential. Having been violated by the boys taking her breast milk, Sethe is robbed of the vital life forces resident in white fluids such as breast milk and semen considered in spiritual traditions to be white blood. Sethe reveals another damaging memory when she recounts giving birth to Denver in the woods. Through her reflection on this incident, Sethe revisits the distant past. When Sethe refers to her baby in vitro as an antelope, she calls forth images from a remote time. The image of the antelope has surfaced from the deep recesses of a memory long restrained by the twin sensations of pain and fear. Not remembering even where she was born "Carolina, maybe? Or was it Louisiana?" she does, however, remember song and dance.

Ronald L. Grimes asserts that performative, nonverbal elements of action are important to interpret meaning (xii). This one recollection jump-starts her stalled memory and connects her to a remembrance of a mother signified by a "cloth hat" to distinguish her from her other mothers, all of whom "were also called Ma'am" (30). Similar to the indeterminate memories of vital statistics and parental separation documented in the enslavement-era narratives, Sethe's memories are fragmented, but present. The power of the song and dance memorates dominate her mind, and after a brief digression to another resurrected thought, Sethe and the narrator jointly recall the liberating effect of the song and dancing the antelope until they shape-shifted. In *The Myth of the Eternal Return*, Eliade notes that all dances were originally sacred rooted in a mythical moment informed by an ancestor (28). Conflating the present with the past, Sethe's recall of the dance is an example of memory's ability to transcend time and space.

It is significant that the narrator sees Sethe as one of the dancers, further reinforcing the continuity between the multitiered past and present symbolized by the image of the antelope. Among the Bambara people of Mali this antelope is called *tji wara*, or *chi wara*, and is said to have introduced agriculture to them. *Tji* means work and *wara* means animal, thus, working animal. The dancers appear in pairs, a man and a woman, an association with fertility, and spiritually prepare the ground for planting. Wearing masks, aided by song and drum, the dancers become the spirit symbolized by the antelope as they dance. The prime purpose for the masks is to serve as a temporary dwelling place for the deity. Functioning at its highest level, the mask expresses the myths of a society or even an element of those myths. Its image is used in ritualistic dances to ensure germination of the seed and a good harvest. *Tji wara* is also the name for the goddess of fertility as well as the name of an earth goddess (Segy 148).

Sethe's exercise of memory forces her to listen to her own voice and to recall her own mother, her ma'am, with the special mark on her body, along with her mother's native language, songs, and dances. The remembrance of dance is noteworthy as a memorate since dance makes a smooth transition in religious worship in America and represents a primary vehicle to store sacred information. As a consequence of memory lapses dance is an apt medium for the safe keeping of memory, which can be performed again and again. That is, dance is a way to both mask and preserve culture. Morrison emphasizes the indispensability of dance in her depiction of Sixo's resistance. She writes, "Sixo went among the trees at night. For dancing, he said, to keep his bloodlines open, he said" (25). Similarly, singing "too loud" songs helps Paul D. and Sixo keep to recover their challenged manhood and to keep them going. The songs also helped to preserve memory as the men "sang the women they knew; the children they had been" to control the discourse of their lives(108). Referred to by Bob Marley as "Redemption Songs," these songs helped them smash "Mr. Death" (109) as they combined sounds, garbled and tricked the words to yield up other meanings (108). At the novel's end, the women in Cincinnati sing a song "wide enough to sound deep water and knock the pods off chestnut trees" as they exorcise Beloved's unruly spirit (261).

Contributing to what Sethe refers to as her "homeless" mind (204) is her physical and psychological separation from her mother at an early age. One of Sethe's most vivid memories of her mother occurs when her mother tutors her on how to recognize her (mother) from the other women in the field by the circle and cross burnt on her skin. Being instructed to recognize her mother by the *dikenga dia Kongo,* not only connects her to her mother, it is also a spiritual memorate that connects her mother to an African past. Sethe's mother reminds her that most of the people who had this mark are now dead. Readers can infer that those African bodies were not only branded with marks from their oppressors as the identifying marks of bondage, but they were also inscribed with cicatrizations and other descriptive markers referencing distinct African nations and identities. Fu-Kiau notes, "To be a true knower is to know what is marked on one's own mind and body" (*African Cosmology* 33). The mark, emblematic of the Kongo cosmogram, *dikenga dia Kongo*, and the Yoruba sign *orita meta*, continues to connect the un-named displaced Africans to origin and subverts the enslaver's intention to signify the body as property and subsequent racial stigmatizations. Roberts and Roberts note that the body becomes a text to be written and read (*Memory* 41). Commenting on the body as a visual representation of memory they assert that marks on the body perpetually reify "the embodiment of memory to be enacted in the present" (41). Sethe's recollection of the mark provides the necessary memory to invoke the ritual petitioning of Baby Suggs—the idea of mother that Sethe can comfortably remember.

The telling of this story also unites Sethe with transplanted African ancestors who "used different words" (*Beloved* 62). This explains to Sethe why she has forgotten almost everything except singing and dancing. Paradoxically, even through the remembrance of Nan, her other mother, she was able to translate the code that was in the "same language that her mother spoke and which would never come back" (62). Somehow, Sethe transcends the present and journeys to a place where she "was picking meaning out of a code she no longer understood" (62). This reminiscence brings to the fore much of what has been haunting Sethe's unconscious mind: that her mother had in some way abandoned her.

After this "rememory" session Sethe yearns for Baby Suggs: "A mighty wish for Baby Suggs broke over her like surf . . . in the quiet following its splash" (62). Water is a metaphor for remembrance, and Sethe's remembrance of Baby Suggs invoked in water imagery also encodes the idea of *bakulu* or venerated ancestors who dwell under the surface of living waters as manifestation as well as memory. After Sethe arrives at 124 Bluestone Road "all mashed up and slit open" (135), Baby Suggs provides her both physical and spiritual nurturing. As Sethe is the substitute for Baby Suggs on the Garner's Sweet Home plantation, Baby Suggs is the surrogate for the mother who was hanged and is one who can teach Sethe knowledge of traditional practices and provide a sense of spiritual and cultural continuity.

Additionally, this memory of Baby Suggs, ushered in with the recurring image of water, emphasizes the value of water associated with cleansing, healing, and regeneration. The river to which Sethe alludes is also a major metaphor in African and African American culture that provides a symbolic paradigm for ritual as a place of transition, locations of memory, and locus for spiritual initiations. Judith Gleason writes in *Oya: In Praise of an African Goddess*, "The river is a matrix of memory" (55). This statement's profundity pertains to its analogous relationship to the novel's dominant motifs: memory, motherhood, and the ancestor as the river resembles the circularity Toni Morrison employs in narration, diction, and plot elements.

Additionally, the symbols of dancing, water, and the number nine are so intricately related that it is difficult to comment on one without examining the other. For example, when Sethe calls for Baby Suggs in the passage cited above, she longs to hear the echo of her voice. Deciding that she is in need in some fixing ceremony, Sethe goes to the Clearing where Baby Suggs had performed the ring dance in the sunlight. Dance and river suggest each other because as Gleason says, "The river remembers transmitting sacred information through its dances" (56). Since they are a part of each other, they cannot be separated. In much the same way, the number nine also signifies both memory and river. In the Yoruba religion the number nine is associated with Oya, the Òrìsà of the Joliba (Niger) river, who is also identified with the ancestral maskers whom the Yoruba call the *egungun.* This secret society is charged with the task of bringing the ancestor back to life in masquerade form—a reiteration of memory.

Oya is the female warrior, owner of the ancestral cult, and a river Òrìsà. One of the praises chanted for Oya is "Se Oya l'o ni Egun" (Oya owner of the *egungun*). Additionally her name means "she tore," a verb form that signifies an event with "disastrous consequences" (Gleason 5). The myth that explains the event says, "A big tree was uprooted, literally and figuratively: the head of the household the one in whose shade we felt secure suddenly perished. She tore, and a river overflowed its banks. Whole cloth was ripped into shreds. Barriers were broken down" (Gleason 5). The major elements in Oya's myth are analogous to those related to Baby Suggs who was the big tree that was uprooted.

Baby Suggs was once the head of the household and the spiritual leader of the community. As its "unchurched preacher" she led "every black man, woman and child" to the "Clearing—a wide-open place cut deep in the woods" (87). The woods, a metaphor for a place dense with spirits, are an abode for the invisible powers in West and Central African spiritual traditions. Ras M. Brown notes, besides its location as being rich with spirits, wooded areas or *feenda* provide Africans with the organic materials for healing and for the production of *minkisi* or charms (308). Similar to experiences in Africa where sacred groves are dwelling places of individual deities and the loci of other supernatural beings, the Clearing represents the space for Africans to repair the ruptures of the past using dance movements to free their bodies from the trauma imposed by enslavement's limited opportunity for mobility. "In the heat of every Saturday afternoon she sat in the Clearing while the people waited among the trees" (87).

Paul Cloke and Owain Jones argue that trees are landscapes of memory that are significant from a cultural perspective as "deep currents of meaning swirl around our culture(s) and brush the branches of any tree place which is being encountered, experienced, narrated, or imagined at any given time" (19). It is her message of love, the power of dance, and the transcending nature of song that Sethe yearns for, even just to "listen for the spaces that the long ago singing had left behind" (89). The idea of absences—that things that are missing are as noteworthy as those that are present—relates to the power of memory to close the gaps and continually invoke meaning. Baby Suggs also represents the barriers that are removed or broken as she leads the people to deliverance in the wilderness. This place is defined not only by Christian sentiments, but also by African rituals. African spiritual sensibilities direct and sacralize the space accompanied by the invocation of self-affirming statements. Through her supplications in the Clearing, the members of the community are able to break through the barriers that keep them from loving and living. Baby Suggs's gatherings are acts of subversion and self-definition helping to restore her village's psychic equilibrium.

Baby Suggs, according to Morrison, was born in Africa. "Baby Suggs came here out of one of those ships" armed with proverbs, songs, folktales, and religious beliefs (Clemons 75). However, Baby Suggs becomes meditative and silent because she cannot deal with the "nastiness of life." Her detachment from speaking is symbolic of the denial of the word, which is necessary to sustain life. Resolved to the idea that "there is no bad luck in the world but white folks" (89), Baby Suggs dies contemplating color to augment a life where white things took all she ever had or dreamed (89). Dying nine years after the death of Sethe's baby, she leaves behind a legacy of remembered words as touchstones for the characters to measure morality, good character, as well as contradiction. Sethe's psychological duress is heightened by the death of Baby Suggs and finds a temporary respite some nine years later with the appearance of a woman called Beloved.

The first course of action in the examination of the complex nature of the title character must be a focus on her identity. This is not, however, a modest undertaking, as Beloved represents different things to different people in her multivoiced, multiple identified presence. For Sethe, Beloved is the murdered daughter returned from the grave. Deborah Horvitz sees Beloved's identity as follows: "She is Sethe's mother, She is Sethe herself; she is her daughter" (163). Explaining these "blurred boundaries," Horvitz continues, "Beloved exists in both the realm of the particular and the universal. She is a member of Sethe's family and a representative spirit of all the woman dragged onto slave ships in Africa" as well as the African women in America descended from the women on those ships (157). I concur and consider Beloved as representative of all the children who were transported into enslavement, not by the waters of the Middle Passage alone, but by the wombs of African women—the primary route that delivered enslaved Africans to their principal roles as plantation laborers.

Also significant in the formulation of Beloved's identity is the fourth chapter of Part 2 where the omniscient narrator's presence is effaced. The section begins with Sethe saying, "I AM BELOVED and she is mine" (210). Although this is the only sentence punctuated in the section, the spaces are left where the punctuation would have appeared. This focus on the interstices is significant on two levels. First, it suggests a remembrance of unseen things by providing a place for them anyway. And second, it reveals Morrison's willingness to suspend mechanical conventions and opens up

spaces for cyclical and temporal/spatial realities that do not separate phenomena in such severe frames. In addition, the capitalization of the first
three words suggests authority and deliverance. The word *AM* indicates a
state of existence that takes into account an inclusive and combined past,
present, and future (eternity), in short, a space of memory.

In the paragraph following this sentence, Beloved speaks, confirming
this cyclical overlay of temporal realities. She says, "All of it is now it is
always now" (210). This section also marks a turning point in the novel,
positing Beloved's multifaceted identity and prefiguring Sethe's fragmentation and reintegration. She recalls knowing that Beloved is the returned
daughter when her "water broke" after seeing her on the tree stump (202).
Like Eva in Sula, Sethe chides herself for not remembering the signs—
"fingernail prints"—that she purposely marks on Beloved's forehead when
she immolates her in the shed (202). The markings on the body are *lieux dé
memoires* or sites of memory confirming Beloved's identity as her daughter. Like the *abiku* child born again to the same mother, Beloved bears the
mark that Sethe should have recognized. For example, Mobolade notes
that these children who don't come to earth to stay very long are usually
given a mark, so that when they are reborn, their mothers can recognize
them as their *abiku* child. Sethe remarks that if Paul D had not distracted
her, she would have seen the fingernail prints on her "forehead for all the
world to see" (202–3). Also, instead of referring to urination, Sethe's choice
of language connects the domain of prepartum, postpartum, and postmortem and blurs the margins between the living and the dead consistent with
African spiritual sensibilities and in particular the *abiku*.

Bridging the gap between North America and Africa, the past and the
present, the dead and the living, the flesh and the spirit, the other person
to whom Beloved is significant is Denver. The exchange of blood between
them solidifies these relationships and connects Denver and Beloved spiritually, matching the way that a blood offering would connect a devotée
to the Òrìsà to whom the offering was made. In this section of the novel,
Sethe and Denver, two living members of this family of women, have made
the crucial connection to Beloved and her multireferential identity.

In an interview with Walter Clemons, Toni Morrison remarks that she
did the bulk of the research for *Beloved* in Brazil because that country
archived historical information not available in North America—such as
archival displays of mouth bits, brakes, and other metalwork used by the
captors to humiliate and break the captive Africans (75). Highlighting Mor-

rison's research in Brazil was her examination of Candomblé and Oya, an Òrìsà of primary importance. Morrison's depiction of characteristics and images associated with the character Beloved include a plethora of symbols that link Beloved to this Òrìsà. For instance, Beloved is the personification of Oya or Yansan, the other name by which she is known, which means mother of nine. This number consistently recurs in the novel. The feast that prefigures the killing of the baby fed *ninety* people; Part 1 of the novel where Beloved is introduced is divided into *eighteen* chapters (nine times two); Beloved appears eighteen years after the baby's death and *nine* after Baby Sugg's death.

Still another of Oya's powerful associations is with wind. She is described as the wind that precedes a storm, the wind made by sweeping (the broom is another of her symbols), and the wind energy manifested in the lungs. When Beloved first arrives at 124 her breathing is labored. "She was breathing like a steam engine" (63). Furthermore, one of Oya's praise names describes her as determined—someone who "when she's got her eye on something she never changes her intention" (Gleason 8). This is clear in the attention Beloved gives Sethe, walking her to and from work and always studying her [Sethe's] face and asking her questions. After being at 124 for five weeks, Paul D tries to find the underlying cause of this mystery called Beloved. He queries her about what she wants, "How'd you come? Who brought you?" (65). Other inquiries concerned her familial relationships of which their were none. Paul D asks, "Ain't you got no brothers or sisters" (65)? The narrator refers to her as "homeless and without people" (66). Gleason reminds us, "Oya has no home, no special road she guards the road into the world, and guards the road to heaven" (9). Paul D's perception of Beloved's nature is a shining he cannot place, "silver fish," "dark water," and "glistening" (65). This "water-drinking woman" (*Beloved* 66) who glistens correlates with Oya who represents the transition between life and death.

As the guardian of the cemetery gate, Oya provides access for the egressing of departed souls across the river. This is consistent with Beloved's appearance in the novel on the day of carnival, which is accompanied by decaying dying roses. On that carnival day, which literally translates into a day of death, or day of flesh, "A fully dressed [*sic*] woman walked out of the water" attired in black cloth (50). The motif of the black dress recurs in Chapter 8 of Part 1, "her black skirt swayed from side to side (74). And finally, "Beloved dropped the folds of her skirt. It spread around her. The hem darkened in the water" (105). The origin of the Joliba (Niger) River is explained in the myth of Oya's tearing the black cloth that formed the river making the kingdom of Nupe the land where Oya originates.

In addition, Beloved's appearance signifies the notion of *bakulu*, the realm of the dead and a site of memory located under the surface of water from a Kongo perspective. The BaKongo have generally thought of the universe as divided into two worlds of the living and the dead, separated by water. Any real body of water serves as the passage between the two, which may be affected at certain other boundaries. Both the Yoruba and the BaKongo understand death as life continued in another place. The Òrìsà Oya's, presence is indicative of the reconciliation of death crucial to Sethe's healing. Emblematic of the Òrìsà Oya Beloved assists Sethe by unveiling memories, enabling her to confront her accumulated pain. And, finally, as a primordial image, she provides a sense of release of the hidden stresses not readily accessible to Sethe's conscious mind.

Now that the ancestor, Baby Suggs, has been invoked and Beloved has appeared what remains the proper rituals to engender Sethe's are healing. The next element to be considered in this chapter is the use of rituals employed in the novel. The following discussion concerns the three rituals that assist Sethe to overcome her sense of desecration. These rituals are categorized as initiating, mediating, and culminating.

*   *   *

Congo, the hoodoo man, haunts these cabins, words mesh into night. He works spells; his spirit runs in deep rivers and sings in shadow trees runs deep rivers and sings in shadow trees.

—Larry Neal, "Fragments from the Narrative of the Black Magicians"

Stamp Paid performs the first ritual. The implied narrator says: "It was Stamp Paid who started it" (135). As a ferryman, he personifies the Òrìsà Aganju, who spiritually ferries people across great obstacles toward their destiny. As a deity, Aganju helps his initiates to confront the internalized pain and anger that left unresolved will thwart their future destinies. Aganju hurdles physical obstacles and opens both unchartered geographical and psychological frontiers. Morrison's description of Stamp Paid's familiarity with the Ohio River suggests knowledge of the river beyond the mundane: "He knew the secrets of the Ohio river and its banks" (170). Also matching his identity as the Òrìsà of the wilderness, Stamp Paid goes "off with two buckets to a place near the river's edge that only he knew about where blackberries grew" (136). The fruit he brings back is described as being consecrated: "To eat them was like being in church. . . .[Eating] just one of the berries and you felt anointed" (136).

This gathering of fruit is the ritual preparation for the community's full moon feast. This ritual performed by Stamp Paid is complete with blood sacrifice. Because of the inaccessibility of the berries, he only reaches them by going through "brambles lined with blood-drawing thorns thick as knives that cut through his skirts and trousers" (136). Also cadres of insects, "mosquitoes, bees, hornets, wasps, and the meanest lady spider in the state" contribute their life essences to the sacrifice in the form of stings (136).

It was after Stamp Paid brought the berries on a full moon day (a time of abundance) just twenty-eight days (136) after Sethe's arrival that the ritual stage is set. Both the new moon and full moon represent times of heightened spirituality. As such, rituals are performed to ensure the success of the community. Also, moon phases are thought to have chemical effects on food, people, tides (both river and ocean), and are therefore propitiated by ritual sacrifice.

When the moon is full, the next phase represents a dying or waning, a foreboding of imminent death. Baby Suggs escalates the ritual action with her decision to do something for the man who has demonstrated his love going through such an ordeal to get berries. Morrison writes, "That's how it began" (136). Like the female spider's poison, venomous resentment fills the air in the form of envious whispers disguised as concerns for the excesses they all knew to fend off, even on the north shore of the river. The community begins to stir, railing against the excess of eating, singing, and dancing. Instead of providing a release for the community, they register their collective disapproval and demand a sacrifice. Their displeasure becomes evident when they fail to warn the Suggs family that white folks are heading toward 124. Therefore, the feast is the necessary event that leads to one of the primary conflicts to be resolved in the novel: Sethe's sacrifice of the Crawling Already? baby.

The mediating ritual conducted by Paul D, a singing man, who has "experienced life on a plantation, a chain gang, and traveling around" (41), occurs when he takes Sethe and Denver to the carnival—reconnecting Sethe to the community. A spiritual truce is affected by her presence and is reciprocated by the community members who nod heads in affirmation.

Moreover, by sharing his pain with Sethe, Paul D helps her to reconcile some of her pain. Described as a man who has dealt with so much pain that his heart has hardened, Paul D brings a view of his past to Sethe that allows her to confront some of the horror from her own locked up past. Ironically, the breaking of her heart is a pivotal aspect of her healing. Paul D, who wants to put his story next to hers, represents more than a stopover halfway through the journey; he provides a way for her to continue on her journey.

The culminating ritual or last rites establish the conditions for rebirth and regeneration. They occur when Denver, recognizing that her mother is being consumed by Beloved's greedy "love," signals for help by leaving the safety of the front porch with ancestral guidance from Baby Suggs, who tells Denver, "Go on out the yard. Go on" (244). Like the ancestral presence, the eponymous character invoked in Ralph Ellison's *Invisible Man*, the ancestor is invisible, a disembodied voice speaking on the lower frequencies (503). According to Ellison's definition of the ancestor, one may draw the following conclusions from this series of propositions: The ancestor is not visible; knows things that need to be told to the living; is able to communicate with the living; and speaks on the lower frequencies to those who listen. Denver heeds Baby Suggs's advice and steps out of 124.

Leaving the liminal space of the porch, which is neither in the house nor out of the house, she embarks upon a personal healing, which ultimately leads to a communal cleansing. Denver, the daughter of Halle, described as an "angel man" has the gift of spiritual diagnosis and is referred to as "charmed" (209). When Denver tells Lady Jones of her family's physical hunger, she paves the way for the woman to make peace with the house and its inhabitants through food offerings, a ritualized way of reconnecting to the ancestor for the community's behalf with "sacks of white beans," "plates of cold rabbit meat," and "baskets of eggs," (249). The food accompanied with names—even when there were no plates or bowls to return—meets the pressing need to diminish hunger. By placing their names on the offerings, the women make peace with the ancestor, Baby Suggs. Their names replicate speech, and the re-introduction of their names to 124 Bluestone Road ultimately repairs their relationship with Baby Suggs's spirit. I argue that the spite in 124 described as being "full of a baby's venom" belongs to the Crawling Already? baby and Baby Suggs, Holy.

Following their propitiary food offerings (*adimu*), the women respond by tapping into the power of the oral tradition using the power of the tongue, which formerly castigated the inhabitants of 124. Now they raise their voices rallying the community to protect the occupants of 124. After the "story is properly blown up and they are sufficiently agitated," Ella leads the women "who convinced the others that rescue was in order" (256). The community invokes Baby Suggs through remembrance of the help she has provided to each of them along the way. Disarmed by the memories of 124 and Baby Suggs, the women move from "rememory" to redemption.

Equally important is their individual recollections of their own personal damage as a result of enslavement. These traumatic remembrances allow them to forgive themselves. As a result they forgive 124 and the people in it for their sins of pride and excess, as well as themselves for excessive pride and for failing the inhabitants of 124. The final ritual resembles a burial, a culminating ritual with which most people have a familiarity. Albert J. Raboteau notes the powerful position of the ancestors and the importance of burial rites. Improper or incomplete funeral rites may interfere or delay the entrance of the deceased into the spiritual world and may cause his soul to linger about, as a restless and malevolent ghost (13).

The women's mission is twofold: they come to exorcise the malevolent spirit incorporated as Beloved, and to heal the rift with the spirit of Baby Suggs that has kept the community from being united. In this symbolic reburial, they come to observe the proper rites, which they had not observed the first time. If they had been carried out properly, the spirit of the deceased child and/or woman would not have troubled the living. The concern for the spirit is coupled with concern for a proper burial. Without a proper burial, the spirit is certain to be restless—and that restlessness may lead to problems for those responsible for the interment. This time the women come together in the spirit of cooperation and unity, armed with the talismans (*minkisi*), roots, crosses, and an assemblage of items remembered from belief systems anterior to their Christian conversions. Marimba Ani notes the importance and power of rituals:

> Our rituals, our songs, our music our dance, became vehicles through which to contact the divine, media through which we reached the spiritual source and so received sustenance and energy from the knowledge of our specialness. (218)

This ritual reenactment, according to Ani, restates the solidarity of the community and allows regeneration of space and expansion of time to achieve eternity. Ritual allows imagination to bend time and, like memory, points toward evolution.

The group, assembled in the manner of an African council around the village tree, substantiates the idea that issues of morality are a communal concern that warrants input and consideration from all members. Ella, inspired by her own haunting memories, "set her jaws working" and "hollered." The women follow in suit. Through their unified effort, these women who collectively understood sound testify to its preeminence over words. With its "heat of simmering leaves," "right combinations" of keys, codes, and sounds that "broke the back of words" (261), the power of sound extends and expands the space beyond the individual body. The collective sound is liberating, releasing both Sethe and the members of the community from the web of grief and shame, similar to the therapeutic sounds made in the Clearing, which were intensified by the dance. In *Song of Solomon*, Morrison refers to these sounds as language and nonlanguage. She writes, "It was what there was before language. Before things were written down" (281).

Wole Soyinka interprets this dynamic:

> Language reverts in religious rites to its pristine existence, eschewing the sterile limits of particularization. In cult funerals, the circle of initiate mourners, an ageless swaying grove of dark pines, raises a chant around a mortar of fire, and words are taken back to their roots, to their original poetic sources when fusion was total and the movement of words was the very passage of music and the dance of images. (*Myth* 148)

Morrison gives a clue to the composite nature and the dimension of the kind of sound emitted by the women. In her article "Rediscovering Black History," she writes:

> A sound, very special sound. A sound made up of all the elements that distinguished black life (its peculiar brand of irony, oppression, versatility, madness, joy, strength, shame, honor, triumph, grace and stillness) as well as those qualities that identified it with all of mankind (compassion, anger, foolishness, courage, self-deception and vision). (16)

As a result of tapping into the power of the cosmic sound and remembrances of the past, both Sethe and the community emerge from the ritual experience charged with new strength. Being reunited with the community of women allows Sethe a return to herself and to properly situate the ancestor, the goal of ritual drama. Appeasement of the spirit of Baby Suggs and the exorcising of the demanding spirit of Beloved restores the equilibrium of the damaged community.

At the novel's end Paul D's return to 124 is inscribed as "his coming is the reverse route of his going" (263) and alternately "his coming is the reverse of his going" (270), a metaphor, which describes the process of memory. Here, Morrison suggests that entry and exit occur not only in the physical world, but also in the world of spirit. This fluidity is chiefly represented by the ancestors who occupy both realms of present and past—chiefly through the invocation of memory. In between the narrator's two statements, Paul D recalls Beloved's escorting him to the "ocean-deep place" where he once belonged (264). The "ocean-deep place: to which Paul D refers represents the realm of the *bakulu* and connects his relationship with Beloved beyond trespass to a cosmic return.

Furthermore, Morrison's inscription physically re-creates the tight packing of bodies in the holds of ships that brought Africans as captives to America, with their arms crossed, knees drawn up. These re-significations of Middle Passage memory and Paul D's survival of subsequent of inhumane acts realized in a scarred neck "collared like a beast," furnish readers with the expunged memorates to assist them in reconstructing their own painful memories. Morrison suggests that readers may also be healed. These memories and connections, ingressing and egressing not only in the "stream in back of 124," but also in the continuous stream of ancestral consciousness, are available if readers listen at the lower frequencies. This reconciliation with the pain too terrible to confront allows Denver and Paul D to face the repressed memory of their painful pasts. While managing his own recovery, Paul D is able to reach Sethe and help to release her from her "too thick love" and its attending guilt through the intersection of shared remembrance. Furthermore, through ritual re-enactment, Sethe has begun the process of revision, rememory, and remembrance of the ancestor. It is now possible for her to be "her own best thing."

Tracing Wild's Child Joe and
Tracking the Hunter

An Examination of the Òrìsà Ochossi in *Jazz*

> Once when I was tree
> Flesh came and worshipped at my roots.
> My ancestors slept in my outstretched
> Limbs and listened to flesh
> Praying and entreating on his knees
>
> —Henry Dumas, "Root Song"

Jazz (1992), Toni Morrison's sixth novel, employs a set of distinctive epic characteristics and constructs the concept of spirituality as the matrix for text, context, and ritual performance.[1] My analysis of this novel focuses on the heroic quest of Joe Trace, a character representing the Yoruba Òrìsà, Ochossi. Reading *Jazz* outside the frame of the migration novel, I focus, instead, on the transmigration of soul and spirit as I chronicle Joe Trace's quest for fulfillment. Key to this observation is a consideration of rituals such as the sacrifice of Dorcas and other spiritual intercessions subsequent to her spiritual transition.[2] These ritual performances, not only reintegrate Joe's fragmented psyche, but also heal the community at large.

Using syncopated, improvisational language, mimetic of jazz music, Morrison recodifies spiritual knowledge from various African traditions. These spiritual riffs allow characters and readers to gain meaning in their respective literary environments. My consideration of narrative modes includes a description of the Yoruba Òrìsà of the hunt, Ochossi, and the manner in which Morrison inscribes specific attributes to him. Moreover, an analysis of ceremonial acts of propitiation honoring the phenomenon of pursuit will serve as the basis for this interpretation. To facilitate this critical undertaking, I will consider Ochossi's major attributes as well as his connection with the Òrìsà Oshun and other spiritual ideas to advance Morrison's thematic trajectory of memory.

Jazz Impulses and Syncopated Rhythms of Time

Of the many essential characteristics of Kongo culture that have survived among African Americans, the concept of time and the person's relationship to it remains significant. For the Ba Kongo time is cyclical, which means it has no beginning or end. At the abstract level it is like a river, it flows. At the concrete level events or *dunga* give time its value of perception. Even at the concrete level, time is unending; it just keeps recycling (Adjaye 20). When a person's energy diminishes, they perish and begin a new cycle of existence.

Morrison inscribes this idea of time in her description of Rose Dear's emotional state prior to her jumping into the well. She writes, "Rose Dear was free of time that no longer flowed, but stood stock-still when they tipped her from her kitchen chair" (102).[3] After Rose Dear's death, her mother, True Belle, arrives from Baltimore to take care of Violet and her four siblings. True Belle expresses the concept of life as an adjunct of time within the Kongo cosmological frame when she says, "Thank God for life . . . and thank God for death" (101). Her statement underscores the idea that just as life begins the journey, death, too, is part of that journey—the return of the soul to itself and to the beginning. When a person dies he or she undergoes change; life flows to create a new state of being.

This change or invigoration of the spirit may also take place through interpersonal relationships, which refresh a person. After Dorcas's death Joe Trace remarks, "With her I was fresh, new again. Before I met her, I'd changed into new seven times" (123). Fu-Kiau notes that seven concentric circles situate human beings in the center of the circle defining the universe, according to the Kongo (*African Cosmology* 41).[4] When a person heads toward the seventh direction, he or she heads toward the self for soul-realization.

Joe's changes not only represent significant events, they "renew" time.[5] His changes are as follows:

When he names himself;
When he is picked out and trained to be a hunter;
When Vienna burns to the ground;
In 1906 when he takes his wife to Rome;

When they leave the apartment on Mulberry Street and little Africa
    and move uptown;
When the white men almost kill him in the white mob violence in
    the summer of 1917;
In 1919 when he walks every step of the way with the three six nine.
    (*Jazz* 123–29)

Joe's changes suggest a kind of spiritual metaphysics going beyond Western epistemic notions of migrations and suggest a type of shape-shifting or transmogrification in order to survive "white folks." In his recollection, Joe explains how he and others knew how to survive down and up South by following the example of the old people. Here, dissimulation can be read as an earnest attempt to remain culturally whole.

Some of the examples of culture that continue in the up South environment of New York City are the associations, lodges, and benevolent societies that African people maintained to demonstrate the axiological imperative of community cohesion. Moreover, the old people represent the concept of the ancestor, which in turn represents timelessness on an African continuum— another distinctive feature of African American writing as well as an African spiritual remembrance. After considering the extent to which his life has had its ups and downs, Joe muses that he is not prepared for the changes that Dorcas will bring. Each of his changes is an attempt to keep time flowing—giving him the emotional vitality to survive. Joe states that change is necessary given the contours of oppression: "In order to survive being colored, you had to be new and stay the same every day the sun rose and every night it dropped" (135). His explanation of changes reinforces the African idea of time being a social idea—the point of occurrence between one social event and the next.

Conveying the primacy of history and records, the narrator begins her oral recitation of the novel with the culturally nuanced sound of sucking her teeth, and then speaks in a familiar gossip tone: "Sth, I know that woman" (3). Unquestionably, the narrative voice is female with an attitude confirmed by her remarking "I don't hate him much anymore," when referring to Golden Gray's knocking the mud off his boots before entering Henry Lestroy's cabin (151). That is about all we, as readers, can rely on throughout the narrative. As if hunted, the narrator throws us off the track saying, "and that's how that scandalizing threesome on Lenox Avenue began. What turned out different was who shot whom" (6). As we find out in chapter 9, mostly narrated by Felice (who also narrates the final chapter), there is no corroboration for this alleged shooting. The narrator's unpredictability is illustrated in the first chapter of the novel when she gives readers a glimpse of Felice's visit to the house, which actually occurs in one of the final chapters. The narrator continues to reroute readers when speaking of the bright future to which black people should look forward: "Forget that. History is over, you all, and everything's ahead at last" (7).

Actually, the narrator's statement dismisses the validity of the present and undermines the novel's major conceits—recording, tracking, and tracing—which are all metaphors for situating time, history, memory, and the ancestor. One has to both regard and disregard most of the information supplied by the narrator, who implies that once in the city, this woodsman cannot find the necessary correlates to sustain his nature personality. The reader must, instead, follow the trails made by the characters if they are going to hunt-down meaning for themselves. Like the characters in the novel who "looked to the signs, the weather, the numbers and their own dreams" to draw conclusions about what is really going on, the reader must stay alert (18). For example, the narrator says, "In no time at all he forgets little pebbly creeks and apple trees so old they lay their little branches along the ground and you have to reach down or stoop to pick up the fruit" (35). She tries to throw the reader off the track; he does not forget. Later in the novel she notes that his voice retains the timbre of that former place and time, a "woodsy voice" (181) that "had a pitch, a note they heard only when they visited southern old folks" (71). He does not fool her, this nature man who feeds small animals in a city teeming with people.

Despite the narrator's sense of ambiguity and ahistoricity, the novel bears witness to persistent racial discrimination demonstrating that history is not over.[6] For example, Alice Manfred reports that she did not like to venture south of 110th Street, where a black woman "had no surname," could not try on a hat, where women who were not black could be dismissive of her presence and speak to her anyway they wanted. In such places, white men could "push dollar-wrapped fingers toward her" (54). Joe, as well as other black people, knew what was possible then and now. The riots in East St. Louis exemplify the anything-at-all type of violence evidenced in Alice Manfred's recollection of her brother-in-law and sister's deaths: he was stomped to death and she was burned after her house was torched. Adding to the historic cataloguing, Morrison's narrator volleys back and forth from past and present events with various characters providing different parts to recollect and therefore resurrect the unseen but known spiritual forces.

Morrison's reconfiguration of the epic is consistent with what John R. Roberts contends is the function of the African American folk heroic creation—that is, a normative cultural activity relating to building a distinct culture and the creation of a self (1). Not only is the subject matter of *Jazz* compatible with epic sensibilities, the narrator's ambivalent stories correspond with the general propositions of epics, which create a history complete with overlaying structures of past, present, and future fashioning fully realized heroic characters sanctioned by ancestral ordination. Similar to the epic, narration focus on genealogies, migrations, places, battles, and group histories. For example, we know the genealogical information for most of the characters in the novels, including minor characters. Redmond says that epic is "mytharchival, mythopoetic, mytharkic, and mythotestifying, framing, exchanging, and making strong statements about the ability of African people to adapt to the "change-up."[7] This double consciousness is rooted in a tradition that is intergenerational, ethnic in the fullest connotation, grounded in struggle—the day-to-day great family saga that has to have death and depth.

As with all epics, identity is a key concept, indispensable to the integrated cultural and spiritual personalities and tied intimately to knowing one's name. Similar to *Song of Solomon*, naming becomes an important consideration for the hero. When Joe changes his name, his reclamation of identity begins. Joe changes his name to "Trace" and initiates his quest as a hunter. Shortly after that, he is chosen to go hunting with the best hunter in Vesper County, reiterating the importance of Joe's action to his ultimate destiny and search for this familial past.

In this narrative, Toni Morrison warns about stepping out of the tradition represented by Africa and by extension southern values such as connection with nature. Joe's tryst with Dorcas and his shooting her are extreme examples of his displacement attributed to his nostalgia for the old country. Another way to read his shooting of Dorcas is his attempt to recapture the authority of his office as a hunter. Ras M. Brown notes that the hunter's ability to spill blood gives him the power associated with chiefs ("Walk in the Feenda" 3).

In this tale of people losing themselves in the city, Joe Trace represents the Yoruba archetypal hunter, the Òrìsà Ochossi, one of the primary deities of the Ketu group of the Yoruba of Nigeria. Described as a double-eyed man who loved the woods, loved them who fished, sold skins, and game, he is a devotee of the hunter god exemplified by his being a professional hunter who has the ability to kill from a distance with deadly accuracy.[8] Furthermore, Trace is a name that affirms his association with a hunter whose primary orientation for finding game is to rely on tracks and traces—all metaphors for memory. In the Yoruba pantheon, *Ochossi* is the son of the Òrìsà *Oshun*, who is associated with rivers and streams. The third time Joe tries to find his mother, he tracks her to a river called Treason where she lives above the surface of the water. Joe's killing of Dorcas for treason or betrayal mirrors the *apataki* (archetypal story) where Ochossi accidentally kills his mother with his arrow of truth. What follows are characteristics that reinforce his identity as the hunter Òrìsà.

Violet remembers him with respect to the place where she meets him, Virginia, as someone full of light, and a person with "razor sharp" shoulders and "two-color eyes" (96). The significance of his eyes relates to the folkloric idea of being double-eyed, like the conjure man or two-headed snake doctor, who uses one eye for spiritual vision and one for physical vision. Moreover, Violet's reference to the light identifies Joe as being more related to Ochossi than with Ogun, since Ochossi is connected to the moral light associated with Obatala, the supreme deity of ethical righteousness. Ochossi is an Òrìsà regarded as being exemplary in character as such; he is often thought to possess similar moral authority to Obatala, chief in the hierarchical arrangement of Òrìsà. Some of the attributes that represent Ochossi are absolute justice, truth, correctness, and innocence. Additionally, he is considered as the ultimate judge, the keeper of traditions, and the maintainer of customs. His impartiality and commitment to honor truth, no matter the consequences, testifies to his moral character. Morrison blurs the distinction between the hunter Òrìsà Ochossi and Ogun as she collapses their distinct identities.

This overlay is not problematic, because of the close affiliation of the two hunter Òrìsà. Using a variety of symbolic descriptions, Morrison invokes their textual presence using multiple references to iron. One of the references is to railroad tracks. A recodified spiritual idea, railroad tracks are emblematic of Ogun; in fact, the Yoruba say wherever two pieces of iron come together—there is Ogun. Other descriptions recall the style of Ijala praise poetry unfolding Ogun's characteristics.[9] Hunters predominate among the worshippers of the Òrìsà Ogun. In fact, it is often believed that Ogun actually lived and was a hunter and a deity. As such, he controls all metal implements as well as guns, machetes, and swords. Additionally, his number of attributes is seven as indicated in the phrase *Ogun meje l'Ogun-un mi* (The Ogun that I know are seven in number) (Babalola 147), which also corresponds with Ochossi's numerical delineation.

Toni Morrison begins *Jazz* with alternating invocations for the two hunter Gods. Morrison's re-signification of the razor denotes a primary odu or *merindilogun* divinatory pattern where Ochossi speaks in the *omo odu*, Ejioco Ogunda, which is described as sitting on the razor's edge; the *odu* Ejioco is associated with Ochossi, while Ogunda is emblematic of Ogun. She writes, "A poisoned silence floated through the rooms like a big fishnet" (5) and "Daylight slants like a razor" (7), and "just as wonderful to know that back in one's own building there are lists drawn up by the wives or the husband hunting an open market" (11). An additional attribute that confirm Ochossi's inscription is the idea of poison; as a hunter, he is considered a master of medicines and herbs and poisons.[10] The job that Joe takes to make extra money in the city is as a cosmetic salesman, an occupation that signifies a correspondence with Ochossi, a camouflage master. As a devotee of the Òrìsà of the earth and forest, the preparations that Joe carries in his sample case, which promise to beautify the women, are analogous to the herbal potions that Ochossi carries in his shoulder bag made of leopard skin.

Another connection with Ochossi is Joe's association with birds, especially trapping them. He traps birds and puts them in cages. Birds, the parrot or *odidé*, in particular, characterize sacrifices made to Ochossi. Additionally, Ochossi accepts all types of birds as his sacrificial food including roosters, guineas, doves, pigeons, chickens, hens, and especially parrots. At the beginning of the novel, the narrator describes Violet as a woman who used to "live with a flock of birds" (3). Even though they live in New York City, they still reside in a type of wilderness characterized by living with a "flock." After she marks Dorcas's face at the funeral, Violet sacrifices the parrots to mend the cosmic ruptures caused by Joe's shooting of Dorcas; freeing the birds is an *ebo* or sacrifice to heal the breach.

Throughout the novel, Morrison employs avian imagery in a variety of descriptions such as observations of "white plumes on the helmets of the UNIA men" (8), or hunting signs like "the signal Hunter relied on most—redwings, those blue-black birds with the bolt of red on their wings" (176). Violet is a woman who speaks mainly to her birds as Joe remarks, "Violet takes better care of her parrot than she does me" (188). It seems that the parrot who answers back "I love you," is the spiritual cohort and twin of Joe Trace or spirit double who reassures Violet when she is feeling unloved. When she releases the birds, including the one who says "I love you," a breach has occurred and she can no longer trust the birds to give her the information she needs. Functioning as a double sign, the release of the birds puts an end to Joe's hunting, since *odidé* (the parrot) assists Ochossi in being an effective hunter.

Additionally, the symbolism of hunters concerns itself with migration or society's constant movement. Ochossi keeps tracks of the seasons and the migratory patterns of animals. Likewise, Joe is the migrant who follows game and knows how to survive in the wild. This is an interesting concept, since Joe Trace is the child of Wild—and he is a wild child who inhabits trees. Violet who knew that trees could "be full of spirits" (103) meets Joe when he falls out of a tree. Their first conversation consists of Violet's insisting that "Nobody sleeps in trees" to which he replies, "I sleep in them" (103). Brown notes that the forest represents at once the primary path to manhood, abundant with invisible forces and a sacred "transitory realm in contact with the Other World" ("Walk in the Feenda" 306–7).

Having lived in the city for twenty years, Joe becomes nostalgic for the country as well as for family, especially for the mother of whom he has no traces of memory. Joe is on a quest to find his mother, Wild, and track her down. He has remembered his objective, and this time he will be careful not to be thrown off the track by time or location—aware that neither temporal concerns nor geography can impede his destiny. Existing in symbolic patterns, meaning can be recognized, even though distorted.

Because Joe cannot find his mother, whom he believes to be Wild, he looks for her in "Somebody called Dorcas with hooves tracing her cheekbones and who knew better than people his own age what the inside of nothing was like" (38). Further descriptions that relate Dorcas to a deer occur in passages such as "She rears up and, taking his face in her hands, kisses the lids of each of his two-color eyes" (39) and a reference to her eyes as being like those of a deer. Dorcas's spiritual familiar as a deer is significant and connects her with this woodsman. Addiitonally, this connection is coalescent with the Yoruba's worship of deer. For example, Yoruba hunters venerate the duiker—a type of deer— associated with the *Oduduwa* creation myth (Babalola 20). Furthermore, the sable antelope is another sacred animal that the Bantu "associate with the human soul" (Mutwa 191). Joe associates Dorcas with Wild. And as a result, the things he wants to share with Dorcas are things he never was able to communicate with his mother, who had abandoned him at birth. He wants to tell Dorcas things he never has told Violet. The part of himself that he wants to share with Dorcas is his missing part, the unconfirmed acknowledgment from a mother who never mothered him.

Reminiscent of one of the 256 Odu Ifa in the Yoruba spiritual tradition, *odi meji* represents the shells having been thrown twice with each throw having yielded seven cowries facing upwards. This *odu* speaks about the deleterious effects of maternal abandonment. If left unresolved the emotionality caused by this desertion can thwart the accomplishments of the person and lead her or him into great depression. In Joe's case, Wild's absence becomes the emptiness that defines his life. In short, Wild is also the sole/soul aim of Joe's unrelenting hunt, the maternal experience that he continues to track and trace; "Wild was always on his mind" (176). The elusive Wild could be anywhere, as she was difficult to track even for the most experienced hunter.

Victory and Hunter find traces of Wild in the "ruined honeycombs," as well as the sign of the blue-black birds with the "bolt of red on their wings" (176). The descriptions of her vary. When the reader first sees Wild through the eyes of Golden Gray, she is a "black liquid female" with "leafy hair" who lives in the woods where "wild women grow" (171). Hunter names the woman "Wild" when she bites him while tending to her after the birth of her child. She is hard to locate even for the Hunter's Hunter who has a great reputation for reading trails. While tracking her, "Hunter's Hunter got tapped on the shoulder by fingertips that couldn't be anybody's but hers"(166). The narrator emphasizes her stealthful approach saying, "he didn't hear a single crack" (166).

Wild's inability to leave a trail of sound indicates her bond with the spiritual realm. This otherworldliness is communicated to the reader by various characters in their response to her. When Patty's boy, Honor, encounters her, he tells his mother that the "whole cabin was rainbowed" (68). This correlation with the rainbow connects her to the Òrìsà Oshumare and one of the Vodun Loa, Damballah Wedo (*Ouido*) in the Fon tradition. Both of those deities connote expanded consciousness and the idea of the bridge connecting heaven and earth, since the rainbow arcs from the sky to the earth. For the Yoruba, the cosmic realms of the earth or *aye* and heaven or *orun* are distinct domains, but not separate. They connect and influence each other depending on the level or quality of communication between the person, other Òrìsà, and the ancestors.

Even though, Joe considers her abandonment of him incidental, once resigned to the idea of Wild being his mother, he sets out to find her. Joe's three attempts to find Wild represent a three-stage ritual. Toni Morrison uses an interesting narrative device in this chapter consisting of alternating memories of tracking Wild and Dorcas indicated by space between paragraphs. The first time he tries to find her, he has been fishing and thinks he hears what sounds like "some combination of running water and wind in high trees" (176). Hearing "the scrap of a song" from a "woman's throat," he rushes to find the opening in the rock formation. Morrison writes, "The song stopped, and a snap like the breaking of a twig took its place" (177). The second time, Joe enters the rock place and does not find her; however, "every movement and every leaf shift seemed to be her."

He begs for some sign after he receives no verbal response to his question is that you? "You my mother? Yes. No. Both. Either. But not this nothing" (178). Joe's petition to Wild to say some kind of yes, even if it is no, corresponds to the Yoruba divination system called *obi*, a system of using kola nuts, or in the Americas, four pieces of coconut. John Mason describes the type of answers available. He says when a Yoruba devotee divines with *obi*; he or she is seeking a yes or no answer to a specific question that is asked just one time. "There are three "yes" and two "no" answer possibilities, each of a different quality" (*Four New World Yoruba Rituals* 83).

For example, the three "yes" answers are *alafia*, meaning an emphatic "yes"; next is *ejife*, a more balanced "yes"; and the third *etagua*, an incomplete answer by itself, but combined with another response such as *alafia* or *ejife*, or even another *etagua*, yield a positive affirmation. The answer is yes, but the person will have some difficulty. If pursued, however, with focus and clarity, the results will be sure. The "no" answers are *ocana* or any of the following combinations, *etagua ocana* or *etagua oyekun*. Not having a response to his query, Joe still has unresolved questions.

The third time he tries to find Wild, he is a married man. The tree that he uses this time to locate her is different from the white-oak tree of his previous attempt. Now, his landmark resembles a baobab tree with roots that climb skyward: "Defiant and against logic its roots climbed" (182). The baobab tree is a sacred tree representative of the ancestral impulse, since its roots are both at his foundation and reach toward the sky in the direction of ancestors. Joe's connection with the tree as a site to begin his search corresponds with Dennis Duerden's assertion that "maternal reconnection with ancestors is the journey of the quintessential woodsmen. Hunter's cults have expressed their ambivalent attitude to the matrilineal authority" (119).

When Joe reaches her place—"a natural burrow"—it is "pitch-dark" with a "domestic smell" (183). The narrator reports, "He had come through a few body-lengths of darkness and was looking out the south side of the rock face. A natural burrow. Going nowhere. Angling through one curve of the slope to another. Treason River glistening below. Unable to turn around inside, he pulled himself all the way out to reenter head first. Immediately he was in the open air and the domestic smell intensified" (183). In this ritual re-birth, Joe's subterranean journey resembles the birth process. Climbing through a symbolic birth canal—"a few body lengths of darkness"—and entering a metaphorical womb—a natural burrow or "private place"— Joe experiences a calm anticipation. He feels at "peace." Again, the idea of consumption and eating define Joe's perception. The image of Joe waiting alone, waiting to eat in Wild's private place, with an opening closed to the public" (184), is reminiscent of a fetal Joe deep in Wild's womb, being nourished through the umbilical cord.

The description of Wild's domestic space also coheres with ideas about ecological influences on the lives of people. Wild's home in the rock and its location—where water meets the shore—represent places of great spiritual transition where reeds and other plants grow. From a Kongo spiritual perspective, places where marshes meet the land represent ancestral domains where there is a concentration of power and bisimbi or water spirits. Additionally, some of the items enumerated to describe Wild's residence "a circle of stones for cooking," "a doll," "a bundle of sticks," a "set of silver brushes, and a "silver cigar case" (184) are spiritually significant. For instance, the circle of stones is a recodification of what the Ba Kongo call *makuku matatu* an ancient idea of the three firestones or the physical world linked with the Kongo worldview.[11] Finally, the other items symbolize a variety of memoirs: the doll represents the child she abandoned; the silver items refer to the shine and gleam of the spiritual realm; and a bundle of sticks is symbolic of a type of divinatory practice. Joe locates the presence of her things, but is still incomplete in her absence. His entrance into the *burrow* to track Wild is replicated in the city as he tracks Dorcas from "*borough to borough*" (131, emphasis added). Like Wild, Dorcas does not fit in a role ordained by others and is Wild's correlate located in an urban environment.

From an African perspective, the efficacy of healing is the ability to transcend time both liminal and spatial. In the absence of a spiritual healer, Joe decides to heal himself and transmogrifies or shape-shifts by changing Wild into Dorcas. This choice contrasts to his marriage to Violet. Marriage was her choice, but it provided him a way to escape "all the redwings" (30). While hunting for Dorcas, he refers to her as "Hardheaded" and "Wild" (182). He is able to track her—although she is well camouflaged in her environment. Her aunt, Alice Manfred considers Dorcas prey as well. To prevent Dorcas from being stalked, Alice Manfred attempts to camouflage

Dorcas by hiding her hair in braids. She also "taught her how to crawl along the walls of the buildings, disappear into doorways, cut across corners in choked traffic—how to do anything, move anywhere to avoid a whiteboy, over the age of eleven" (55). Still that does not protect her from Joe's hunting accuracy and the fervor of his search. Joe, who still practices the skills of keen observation in his new environment "knew what a woman looks like moving in a crowd, or how shocking her profile is against the backdrop of the East River" (34), reads the sign of Dorcas's wild nature: "Because he was more used to wood life than tame, he knew when the eyes watching him were up in a tree, behind a knoll or, like this, at ground level" (166).

As mentioned, the chapter that the narrator recounts Joe's search for Wild is the same chapter where he hunts for Dorcas in the City. While searching for Dorcas, Joe "doesn't see the paper ring from a White Owl cigar that sticks to the crown of his cap" (181). Adorned in the regalia of the feathers available in the city—a White Owl cigar wrapper indicates his status as being "crowned" or an archetypal representation of the Òrìsà Ochossi, an Òrìsà *fun fun* or white Òrìsà, like Obatala. Ochossi functions to lead a person toward personal transformation and, like Ifa, helps a person fulfill his or her destiny. Joe's body becomes the threshold between himself and the spirit world conveying the intent of his actions: the hunt. Mary Nooter Roberts and Allen F. Roberts explain that the body is a place where memory is created and preserved (86). They assert that these markings "do not document, describe or represent, or symbolize as much as they dispose." They further state that external signs present a "discourse of power, which becomes meaningful in their elucidation, during the moment of their disclosure" (112).

Additionally, the implication of the owl imagery in *Jazz* corresponds to a foreshadowing of Dorcas's death. In the story of "The Death Owl" the narrator Thaddeus "Tad" Goodson warns:

> Don't you laugh and don't you holler . . . fuh when det' owl holler it's a warning, somebody soul guh enter de sky, somebody guh flap he wings across the burnin' lake. Det owl ain't no wol, and he ain't no bird. Det owl de lost sperrit of a lonesome soul. He de scarified sperrit. An' he ain't got no fren' an' he ain't got no company but de partin' sperrits, and he fly wid {ap}em to de far shore. He rest in de hollow tree, and he live in de night, an he visit de far shore. He de voice of de onrestless sperrit, he de soun of death, an he ain't nothen fer te make game at. (D. Walker 13)

Dressed in his ceremonial dress and carrying the gun as an emblem of his office, Joe begins to transform into the personality of the hunter. He states, "I wasn't looking for the trail. I was looking for me and when it started talking at first I couldn't hear it. I was rambling, just rambling all through the City. I had the gun but it was not the gun—it was my hand I wanted to touch you with" (131). He had lost the trail and picks it up the next day. One of the attributes that assist Ochossi is his telepathy. His power is potent. Joe communicates this to Dorcas, and her comments affirm this spiritual communiqué. She states, "He is coming for me. He is coming for me. Maybe tonight. Maybe here" (190). The narrator adds her insight about the hunt, remarking that he is not tracking her to harm her.

It is interesting to note: Joe's actions not only ignore Henry Lestoy's advice not to kill the young or female, but also the mandate exemplified in the refrain from one of *Ochossi*'s praise songs. The refrain sung for Ochossi is *Ode mata ore ore wole wole* (Hunter don't shoot, enter the house, enter the house). In *Tribal Talk*, Will Coleman notes this restriction from a Fon perspective. According to rules of hunting among the Fon of Dahomey, the *afianku* or antelope should not be killed without making a proper sacrifice of its own request (23).

Morrison presents Joe's pursuit and killing of Dorcas as a logical part of his lifelong search and hunt for Wild. The "tender" Dorcas becomes the incarnate body of Wild and provides Joe the opportunity to be nourished. Furthermore, the appearance of the birds gives him the signal of Wild's presence. He shoots her in a crowd that resembles a "flock of redwings" (131). It is not Joe's intention to harm Dorcas. He wants to stay and catch her, so she will not hurt herself. In a conversation with Alice Manfred, Violet confirms Joe's gentleness: "Joe? No. He never hurt nothing" (81). The intent of his shooting is to capture Wild/Dorcas for the last time. This is the fourth time he has stalked Wild, which is the number of cosmic completion indicating that this time, if he is successful, he will realize the heroic fulfillment that he seeks.

When Joe shoots and kills Dorcas, he bonds with her as a sacrificial victim through the link of blood, a metaphor for the blood relationship that he has sought with Wild. Awolalu remarks that when Yoruba speak or think of sacrifice, it is never in a metaphorical or general sense but always in a religious sense (135). The sacrifice is performed to maintain and restore the relationship of a person to the sacred world (135–36) and has various intents and purposes; however the exchange of blood invokes the pleasure and the blessing of the divinities and the spirits and blots out sins and averts illness and death (178).

*   *   *

> Those who are dead are never gone. They are in the house. The dead are not dead
>
> —Birago Diop

After Joe shoots Dorcas, Violet also pierces her flesh with metal. Violet's cutting of Dorcas's dead face is more a ceremony of marking her for recollection with "a little dent under her earlobe" (91). In spiritual cultures, the body is marked as a site of remembrance. The idea foundational to the cut is memory. For example, should the person return to earth, they will be recognized, remembered. Additionally, Toni Morrison continues her tradition of marked women in her novels: Sula's tattooed eye in *Sula*; Sethe's back in *Beloved*; Pilate's smooth stomach in *Song of Solomon.*

I propose that the framed photograph of Dorcas, a phonetic approximation of the word *sacred* spelled backward, is an *nkisi*, a Kongo concept, which translates into "things that do things." Nkisi also represents a spirit from the land of the dead. Much like the novel's epigrammatic inscription, "I am the name of the sound and sound of the name" taken from the *Nag Hamadi*, the idea of *nkisi* is punned to correspond to both the *name* and *action* illustrated in the root word that connects the *nkisi* as a phenomenon of nature and an act performed by the *nganga* or ritual officiate.[12] MacGaffey explains that an *nkisi* can also be represented as one of the *bidumbu* or cosmograms in the graphic writing systems and can be inscribed on a person or on the ground (*Astonishment and Power* 62). Etymologically, *nkisi* is derived from the infinitive *kukinsa*—meaning "to take care, to cure, to heal, to guide by all means even by ceremony." The *nkisi* takes care of human beings in all aspects of life in the world because people have material bodies that need care by *nkisi* (medicine) and *nganga* (healers). The silver frame with its image captured by light contains the constituent elements from which *nkisi* must be fabricated: mineral (metal), plants (paper), and pigment (earth) (MacGaffey 37). All *minkisi* (plural of *nkisi*) are fabricated things made from wood or other materials to produce desired effects with a will of their own. Within the catalogue of *minkisi* there is a type of *nkisi* called *nkisi nkondi*; *nkondi* means "hunter."

Benjamin C. Ray explains the function of the *nkisi* in detail:

The *nkisi* spirit allows itself to be controlled by a ritual specialist, called an *nganga*, in return for sacrificial offerings and money. The *nkisi*-spirit has to be contained in a material object, usually a gourd, a bag, bark box, or a snail shell; figure sculptures of humans or animals were used in the past for the most powerful and violent *nkisi*. These were called "*minkisi* of the above" because of their association with rain and thunderstorms, in contrast to the benevolent *minkisi* of the below, associated with earth and water. The *minkisi* of the below were used to heal illnesses and to overcome misfortunes; the minkisi of the above were used to attack and destroy people. (124)

MacGaffey remarks on the nature of *nkisi nkondi* as being swift to kill people. This is evident in Dorcas's death. She has already fallen to the ground before anyone hears the report of Joe's gun. The name *nkondi*, derived from *konda*, means to hunt alone at night rather in a corporate game hunt with the purpose of pursuing evildoers (MacGaffey 97). Practitioners of traditional religions depend on *minkisi* to do things for them, even to make life possible. The narrator notes that "the mantel used to have shells and pretty covered stones, but all that is gone now and only the picture of Dorcas Manfred sits there in a silver frame waking them up all night long" (13). The mantel has already been consecrated as a sacred space marked by the placement of the organic shells and pretty-colored stones. For instance, the seashells are minkisi known as *zinga*, which is a pun on the word *kuzinga*, which means to live long. Robert F. Thompson and Joseph Cornet record that seashells represent the "classic Kongo symbol of the spiral journey from one world to the next" ("Siras Bowens" 238).

The photograph of Dorcas mediates the tension between Joe and Violet Trace. This *nkisi* is the name of the thing used to help a person—when sick they obtain health. The *nkisi* hunts down illness and chases it away. As an organic object, it has an in-extinguishable life.[13] Described as "the only living presence in the house" (11), "the picture of Dorcas Manfred sits there in a silver frame waking them up all night long" (13). Janheinz Jahn describes the Bantu concept of this stage of human existence. "When a man dies, therefore his biological life (*buzima*) is in fact over, and his spiritual life (*magara*) also ceases—but something remains, namely that life force" (107).

Although the judgmental narrator's comments are reductive, the silver frame "flashes" spiritual information as a type of *bakulu* discourse transforming a moment of sublime recognition into eternity.[14] Now installed on the shrine, the picture fulfills various needs. For Joe, he derives pleasure because the face is not accusatory. Violet sees a face that is, "an inward face—whatever it sees is its own self." The picture is a type of mirror like one of the *nkisi nkondi* in the Kongo tradition represented by a carved statue (portrait) with a mirror on the stomach. Similar to efficacy of homeopathic medicine, the *nkisi* that causes the problem also supplies the cure.

Joe and Violet also call Dorcas's name in connection with their nocturnal viewings. Their summoning of the spirit personality controlling the *nkisi* situates them as *banganga* (plural of *nganga*) (MacGaffey 27). In her spiritual life or *magara* stage, Dorcas still has the ability to affect the living world.

✳   ✳   ✳

> You just gotta know how to talk to the spirits. They teach you
> everything."
>
>   —Henry Dumas, "Echo Tree"

Attuned to the ancestral world and matters of the spirit, Violet, like Joe, walks in both the physical and spiritual worlds at the same time. She is able to see her other self: "that other Violet that walked about the City in her skin; peeped out through her eyes and saw other things" (89). Throughout the course of the novel, there are signs along the way providing traces of information of her spiritual proclivity, such as Violet's out-of-body experiences—trancelike states when she peered out of her eyes and saw herself astral-projected. Violet also channels spirits. In speaking of her personality the narrator remarks, "Closely examined it shows seams, ill-glued cracks and weak places beyond which is anything. Anything at all" (23).

The openings of which the narrator is speaking establish Violet's being vulnerable when examined from a spiritual perspective and can be read as *interstices* where spiritual information exchanges between dimensions. Moreover, when the narrator questions the illogicity of Violet's language, she observes Violet's extrasensory perceptions as, "the anything-at-all begin in her mouth" and disconnected words (23). This is illustrated when talking about numbers she wants to play, Violet says, "got a mind to double it with an aught and two or three others just in case who is that pretty girl standing next to you?" (24). Another example of this spiritual predilection is when asked if she could do somebody's hair, she replies out of context, "two o'clock if the hearse is out of the way" (24). The influence of something outside of herself is reiterated by her hand's independent actions, the hand "that can find in a parrot's cage a knife lost for weeks" (24).

Violet, like Joe, is also a hunter. After Dorcas's death, "she commenced to gather the rest of the information" (5). Violet begins to retrace the girl's life by hunting down information on her from Malvonne, the woman who rented the "love nest" to Joe for his illicit rendezvous with Dorcas, to Dorcas's beautician, to former teachers at "JHS 139," to, finally, Alice Manfred, Dorcas's aunt and guardian. The narrator observes, "It was like watching an old street pigeon pecking the crust of a sardine sandwich the cats left behind" (6). Other indices of Violet's affiliation with the hunter are physical descriptions of her being dressed in a "fur-collared coat" and capable of a sound that "belonged to something wearing a pelt instead of a coat" (92). This description of her being able to mimic the sound of an animal is a key confirmation of her being a hunter who is a master of animal calls used to entrap prey.

Among other spiritual formulations, the hairdresser, like the midwife, is accorded exceptional status and this sensibility as a form of cultural expression is codified in language unique to African American people. The task they perform, dressing hair, speaks to the way in which African people relate to the head or in Yoruba, *ori*. In fact, this detail extends beyond language to signify spiritual awareness and protection in harmony with the West African cultures. In the same fashion, the person who "dresses" the head in African culture is one who executes a sacred act and participates in the process of body memory, since coiffure is another form of body memory, "a corporeal mode of communicating information about a person's past, personal history, and identity" (Roberts and Roberts 112).

The Òrìsà Oshun's identity is also invoked in the novel in the characters of Wild and Dorcas, as well as in symbolic representation. Particularly important to women seeking to become pregnant and to give birth safely to healthy children, she is praised as Iya Lode (the Great Mother) who gives birth "like a female animal with ease and frequency" (Ray 35)." She is called the "goddess of the 'Living Waters,' the basic substance of life on earth" (Ray 35). Morrison provides significant clues to indicate the presence of the Òrìsà Oshun as a companion to Ochossi, most notably in allusions to singing, laughter, sewing, brass, and the adimu or offerings of honey and oranges emblematic of this river-rain deity. For example, immediately preceding her death as she lies dying, Dorcas sees a dark pile of oranges and says to Felice, "Listen, I don't know who is that women singing but I know the words by heart" (193). These references are to Oshun, the Òrìsà who represents the idea of love—a strong connection to the heart.

Moreover, Toni Morrison emphasizes Oshun's identifying feature of laughter—asserting that a balance between joy and pain must be maintained to live life. Laughter is used as a kind of mask mediating, containing, concealing, and revealing. "Laughter covers indiscreet glances of welcome and promise, and takes the edge off gestures of betrayal and abandon" (64). For example, when Violet attempts to "steal" a baby, "Violet lifted her head to the sky and laughed with the excitement in store when she got home to look. It was the laugh-loose and loud that confirmed the theft for some and discredited it for others. . . . Would a kindhearted innocent woman . . . laugh like that? (20). Violet's laugh has different textures and communicates assorted information. The women ask, "And what kind of laugh was that? What kind? If she could laugh like that, she could forget not only her bag but the whole world" (22). With Alice Manfred's help, Violet discovers "that laughter is serious. More complicated, more serious than tears" (113). When she comes to terms with how ridiculous she must have looked cutting Dorcas at the funeral she laughs so hard, she is healed.

Laughter is also one of the signs to identify Wild. If she is close enough, "she creeps and hides and touches and laughs a low sweet baby girl laugh in the cane" (37). Joe who is ever alert for the signs associated with light and movement is tricked by the laughter: "When he called on Sheila to deliver her Cleopatra order, he entered a roomful of laughing, teasing women" (29). The laughter deceiving him and throwing him off the track, he whispers a forbidden thing in Dorcas's ear. Dorcas replaces Violet to whom he is barely speaking to "let alone laughing together" (36). Dorcas's laugh is comparable to Wild's, which is described as "thick enough to laugh at" and to break Golden Gray's heart (154). Hunters Hunter also recalls Wild's laugh, "He remembered her laugh, though, and how peaceful she was the first few days following the bite" (166). With Dorcas, there is much laughter. The narrator reports that after getting with Joe, Dorcas could "laugh at the things that are right side up and those that are upside-down—it doesn't matter because you are not doing the thing worth doing which is lying down somewhere in a dimly lit place enclosed in arms, and supported by the core of the world" (63). Ultimately, Joe hears laughter like "pealing bells" when he finally arrives at the party, right before he shoots Dorcas (187).

Accompanying the motif of laughter are the multiple references to singing, also associated with the Oshun. Some of the references relate to the sexuality needed to engender fertility expressed as "Songs that used to start in the head and fill the heart had dropped on down, down to the place below the sash" (56) or "The dirty get-on-down music the women sang, the men played, and both danced to" (58). Furthermore, songs with sexual innuendo like "ain't nobody going to keep me down you got the right key baby but the wrong keyhole you got to bring it and put it right here, or else" (60) represent the raw sexuality associated with the Òrìsà of seduction and childbirth.

Principally, one of Oshun's spiritual functions is knitting and sewing society together indicated by her role as a river Òrìsà. The river, Oshun's domain, is a metaphor for the birth of civilizations. Likewise, Joe's search for his mother is symbolic for the missing records of parentage or a genealogical connection. He is not alone in this search; here Morrison implies that Africans in the western hemisphere have felt like motherless children a long way from home. Using the image of the needle (*abere*) and its activity of stitching, Morrison helps not only the characters come to terms with the loose and unraveled ends in their individual lives, but also the readers get a chance to stitch their discontinuous memories. The needle is also connected to the hunter as Bade Ajuwon illustrates in his observation of one of the Ijala chants to Ogun, the primordial hunter. He notes: *abere wonu ofun o raa poo* (a needle that falls in a pit is lost forever) (180). An additional chant is *Abere o ni bale, oro gbongbon* (a fallen needle will never give a loud sound) (180). The needle and stitching are important to the hunter so he can mend his clothes—a necessary expression of his personality.

Interesting to note are the ways in which Toni Morrison employs the metaphor of the needle, also a major symbol of Oshun, to bring together two women who are not mothers: Violet Trace and Alice Manfred. A primary example of healers, motherhood has a vaulted place in the hierarchy of women's power. The Yoruba lineage has conserved the ancestral mother cult, one of the oldest and most persistent within the African spiritual universe. The mother is a collective term and refers to the special powers of women whether elderly, ancestral, or deified. In her pairing of Violet and Alice, Morrison suggests that an alternate way of constructing power and authority in women's space is through harmonious relationships between women. Violet is the granddaughter of True Belle, a competent seamstress who stitched by firelight (101) and Alice is a sewing expert whose "stitches were invisible to the eye" (111). Just as True Belle heals the family after Rose

Dear jumps into the dark well, Alice's spiritual power, contained in the invisible authority of her stitches, can heal Violet.

Having great value although a small object, Morrison emphasizes the needle's significance to repair the cultural breaches of African people rent asunder in North America. After Dorcas is murdered, Alice puts down her needle indicating the duress associated with her loss. Additionally, the concept of stitching represents a type of *nkisi* called *muzazu*, at once the name of something in the natural world, a cocoon (*muzazu*), and a performative activity, stitching together (*zazula*) indicates its potential to comfort and heal (MacGaffey 62). For example, the second time Violet visits Alice the narrator reveals that Alice "was irritated by the thread running loose from her sleeve, as well as the coat lining ripped in at least three places she could see" (82). Alice is able to see through Violet's concealment revealed by the narrator who says, "She was holding her coat lapels closed, too embarrassed to let her hostess hang it up lest she see the lining" (109). The coat's frayed lining is a metaphor for her frayed mind and internalization of the pain associated with her childlessness and her husband's indifference.

From this observation, she realizes that Violet needs healing. Violet is in need of repairing. Alice offers to stitch her dress. Violet, threadbare and broken in spirit, makes her way to the daily appointments with Alice who repairs not only Violet's worn clothes, but also opens up something to heal her own loose threads (mind). With Violet's lining repaired and "her cuffs secure" (83), the reader realizes the extent of her healing through the exchange of life stories between she and Alice. This mending that makes the cuffs secure is achieved by the interface, which is the insertion of a piece of fabric between two other pieces of cloth. This interfacing represents the power of narratives and female union to mediate and heal the sadness and pain associated with the loss experienced by both women. Joe notes the power of women to heal: "It's a way they have of mending you; fixing what they think needs repair" (122).

At the novel's end, Alice, Violet, and Joe are restored. Moreover, the narrator restores her integrity by admitting that she was thrown off the track with Felice's relationship with the Traces. She also declares that she was wrong about Joe running around in bad weather looking for Dorcas, not Wild's chamber of gold. Reiterating the nuances of improvisational jazz, the narrator ventures outside of the comfortable domain of melody, returns to the beginning, and rejoins the melody line after having considered the signs, records, traces, and tracks. To the question asked of the young girl who leaves the baby unattended to retrieve a record, "You left a whole baby with a stranger to go get a record?" (17), Morrison answers, yes; records are important.[15] Answering this question throughout the course of the novel, Morrison affirms the necessity of recording one's own stories, especially for a people whose history has been inscribed by the same people that have delimited their lives. As the refrain from one of *Ochossi*'s songs instructs: *Ko ro Ko ro ko mo de mo ro* (Teach the traditional customs. Teach the traditional customs), *L'aye l'aye ko mode mo ta* (to have the world).

If I'd a Knowed More, I Would a Loved More

Toni Morrison's *Love* and Spiritual Authorship

The love we had stays on my mind.
—The Dells

In her 1993 Nobel Prize for literature lecture, Toni Morrison describes prominent features of the African's encounter in America, lamenting over such disquieting conditions as their not having had a home in this place, the historical occurrence of being "set adrift from the one(s) you knew," and the social situation of being placed "at the edge of towns that cannot bear your company" (28–29). Morrison's unwillingness to surrender commentary concerning the defining attributes of the African American experience recorded in her novels is commendable, and the inexorable references to historical, spiritual, and cultural modes of resistance complements her narrative integrity.[1] With honest courage and commitment to document spiritual traditions of displaced African people through her verbal figurations, Morrison has honored the living memory of Africa and has helped to transform fiction from a site of terror to a place of spiritual power.[2]

By their having taken up residence in the spiritual spaces and cultivating identities "separate" from the Europeans and within the cultural milieu of Africa, African people have challenged the value of whiteness and subverted the intentions of legal separation, which was to deny them access to that perceived space of privilege. The novels examined in this study, when considered collectively represent traditions inspired by a shared spiritual memory. Using narratives that speak of displacement and the renewal of hope, Morrison points to the possibilities for wholeness through the interplay between the individual and community.

Additionally, employing ritual that provides rehabilitation of the soul, she awakens the sleeping giants of myth, and allows silences to be disturbed through the montage of spiritual and cultural events. In *Shadow and Act*, Ralph Ellison comments that "myth and ritual are used in literature to give form and significance to the material" as they are true portraits of how people function in everyday life (174). Similarly, Frantz Fanon explains the way in which a people remove the yoke of cultural estrangement and negation, stating, "The nation gathers together the various indispensable elements necessary for the creation of a culture, those elements which alone can give it credibility, validity, life, and creative power" (245). Language is decidedly one of the "indispensable elements" to which Fanon makes reference. As a major cultural dynamic, language continues to occupy a space of ultimate importance. For example, Morrison begins her eighth novel, *Love* (2003), with the voice of "L," one of the omniscient narrators, lamenting about the injudicious use of language. L exclaims, "Nowadays silence is looked on as odd and most of my race has forgotten the beauty of meaning much by saying little" (3).[3] In her protracted remarks, she chides folks for their lack of discretion. That tongues let loose "work all by themselves with no help from the mind" (3) is not an inconsequential concern. L surmises that the potency and potential of language to "stop a womb or a knife" has been dispirited primarily because of the lack of restraint.

L cannot sanction this imprudent use of Nommo. Janheinz Jahn defines Nommo as "The driving power that gives life and efficacy to all things" and "the physical-spiritual life force which awakens all sleeping forces and guides physical and spiritual life"; its misuse is inexcusable (101). In her earlier novels Morrison establishes the exclusivity of black language. It exists in the trespass of language, such as Hannah's questioning of Eva's maternal affection in *Sula* or in the privileged language of "grown folk" in *The Bluest Eye* when Claudia says, "We do not, cannot know the meanings of all their words, for we are nine and ten years old. So we watch their faces, their hands, their feet, and listen for truth in timbre" (17). It is also located in the words of Baby Suggs that heal African folk in the clearing, which capture the essence of asé to heal the people who have just crossed over the threshold of enslavement in *Beloved*. The shape and content of the spoken word have power. The spoken word can also be deprived of authority illustrated by Baby Suggs's words, "And no, they ain't in love with your mouth. . . . What you say out of it they will not heed. What you scream from it they do not hear" (*Beloved* 88). African people have held firmly to the power of language to create the requisite spiritual realities to sustain life in hostile environments. The same power resident in blood, water, seed, and in everything that quickens life analogous to the Yoruba concept of *asé* and the Kongo idea of *nyama* (vital force) informs language.

Other concerns that perturb L are the changes that have occurred since the legal end of segregation, including the privacy and privilege of culture and the unity they engender. The cultural integrity represented in Eloe, a town in which "no white people live" (*Tar Baby* 172) and "The Bottom" (*Sula*) has been challenged. Since the 1960s and the advent of (dis)integration, what belongs in the catalogue of African culture is diminishing because of cultural appropriation and the transfer of cultural memorates into the province of popular culture. For instance, the concept of high five, *booka* or *yangalala* in Ki-Kongo language, a gesture reproduced in the African American community as remembered and regenerated tradition, has become ubiquitous not only in American society at large, but also throughout the world. As soccer moms slap their raised palms and retired Floridians on golf courses in exclusive country clubs "give some skin," it is only a matter of time when the meaning of the gesture and the knowledge of the gesture's cultural authorship will be forgotten like other African performative expressions such as baton twirling, rapping, scatting, jazz singing, tap dancing, among others too numerous to list.[4]

Assaults to culture are also accompanied by the insistence of people who reside outside the cultural parameters of the black world to determine not only the nature of black culture, but also to attempt ownership and oversight. Toni Morrison laments about this type of cultural confiscation saying, "For a long time, the art form that was healing for Black people was music. That music is no longer exclusively ours; we don't have exclusive rights to it. Other people sing it and play it; it is the mode of contemporary music everywhere. So another form had to take its place" ("Rootedness" 340). Morrison, like other Africans, remains alert and searches for new codes, new ways to express their individual cultural ethos. For Morrison, it is the novel that replicates the orality of narratives passed down intergenerationally; it becomes the restorative medium to communicate the values of the group.

One of the compendium of items in the oral tradition, humming, is highly valued. In *Love*, Morrison's L counters the current state of affairs by reaffirming the power of humming. The power of the hum to calm and still the mind connects L with other "women who know things"—those who rock, hum, and create an aura of spiritual space to center themselves. To those readers familiar with African American worship traditions, Morrison invokes images of women in plumed church hats or dressed in white on first Sundays raising a hymn and moving the words beyond language into the safe space of slow and steady hums. These women turn the wooden benches into decks of ships, inviting us to "Get on board, the Ole' Ship of Zion."[5] The hum beckons and reiterates the sentiments of Ralph Ellison's protagonist in *Invisible Man*, who states that ancestral information is available on the lower frequencies. L's hum "is mostly below range" (*Love* 4), beyond language codes. Like the women who gather in front of the house at 124 Bluestone Road and create the "sound that broke the back of words" (*Beloved* 261), L uses the hum, a language that informs and transcends words. We are prepared to believe L's words and actions and respect her access to information.

However, it is not until the end of the novel, that we, the readers, realize that L's narration, graphically represented in italics, takes place from the realm of the ancestors. L, who like Baby Suggs is deceased when the novel opens, only participates as a disembodied ancestor through the tropes of memory, invocation, and narration. This concluding essay catalogues the spiritual principles that the ancestral voice calls our attention to in *Love* and discusses their significance with a correlative analysis with spiritual ideas presented in other novels, emphasizing the primacy of love.

Structurally, *Love* consists of nine chapters (the symbolic number of the Egungun, Oya, and Aganju) constituting individual remembrances of Bill Cosey, who is deceased when the novel opens. The significance of the structural correlation with these Òrìsà relates to their respective roles of remembrance, change, and the ferrying of ideas across realms of consciousness. Consistent with African belief systems, these recollections are neither ultimately good nor bad. Instead there is an admixture of both attributes.

L states that Bill Cosey could be called a "good bad man, or a bad good man" (200). However, she concludes that even though she believes the "Dark won out," Cosey was "an ordinary man ripped, like the rest of us, by wrath and love."[6] While it may be argued that his marrying his granddaughter's age-mate in her prepubescent years denotes a morally reprehensible act, his restraint in having sexual relations with her until she reaches puberty redeems him. The reader understands that when Cosey wants to have more children, he chooses Heed because she is a virgin. Additionally, Bill Cosey is a man who has "wide hospitality," an African value, which attests to the core value of his having good character.

This is not the first time that Toni Morrison presents characters that elide the severe categories of binary oppositions. In *The Bluest Eye*, she relies on her reader's awareness of the deleterious effects of aesthetic negation on the psyche of a young girl. As a result of this understanding, we forego judgment. Moreover, we understand Pecola's descent into madness, having escaped our own descent or having recently emerged from the abyss of self-dejection formed by internalized messages of racist thinking. Additionally, in *Sula*, Morrison draws Eva Peace as a character who evokes compassion from her readers even though she sets Plum on fire to relieve him of the pain of his heroin addiction. Similarly, we are primed to understand and sympathize with Sethe in *Beloved* for her difficult and desperate decision to commit infanticide on the named, but unnamed, Crawling Already? baby. Finally, in *Jazz*, a teary-eyed Joe Trace wins our hearts as we accompany him through the pain of dejection associated with his displacement to the North and his subsequent untethering from the woods and the sense of psycho-ecological wholeness engendered in that space. We, as readers, forgive Joe for shooting/sacrificing Dorcas because we understand his burden of feeling like a "motherless child a long way from home." With empathy, we fill in the spaces created by that emotional trauma and cross that "deep river" ourselves in an attempt to gain our own healing and psychic stability.

However, we do not exonerate Jadine Childs for her singular ability to be selfish and dismissive of other African people, especially those with earthly ways, such as Aunt Rosa and the folks she encounters in Eloe and on Isle des Chevaliers. She, unlike Sula, lacks spiritual depth, which renders her an unsympathetic character, especially since her behavior is constructed with the values, beliefs, and perceptions of white people. These attributes motivate her to be destructive to not only her lover, but also to her kinfolks Ondine and Sydney. In comparison, while Sula is unruly, she is someone who engenders trust because of her honesty and courage, ideal cultural traits.

Returning to *Love*, the narrative begins with the arrival of Junior Viviane. In *Love*, similar to Sula's arrival to the Bottom after her ten-year sojourn to an undisclosed place, Junior Viviane arrives to Silk accompanied by a "chafing wind." Additionally, like other characters—M'Dear (*The Bluest Eye*), Eva Peace (*Sula*), Thérèse Foucault (*Tar Baby*), Pilate Dead (*Song of Solomon*), Baby Suggs (*Beloved*), Violet Trace (*Jazz*), and Consolata Sosa (*Paradise*)—Morrison introduces Junior as a woman who has the ability to read people. Her method is "to watch for the face behind the face; and to listen for the words hiding behind talk" (28). Furthermore, she is a tree woman, comparable to the *Ajé* who Jadine encounters inhabiting the woods on Isle des Chevaliers.[7]

Once in the house on Monarch Street, Junior feels protected—described as a recurring vision of having a stranger with shiny eyes waiting beneath the trees to rescue her.[8] The picture of Bill Cosey over Heed's bed reassures her. He is the stranger. Her "Good Man" announces his presence by the scent of his aftershave and later becomes a palpable presence in the dream world. Morrison's description of her "sci-fi eyes" with shiny lids, lashes, and irises (114) and having such "beautiful hair, wild" (117) attests to Junior's otherworldly nature and connects her to the uninhibited characters Wild (*Jazz*) and the eponymous Beloved. Her liminality is signified by the description of her: "Junior had no past, no history, but her own" (169). Moreover she writes that Junior is a "strange girl with no purse" (*Love* 23), similar to the women of Ruby (*Paradise*) who do not carry purses.

Although unaware, even to her, Junior's role is to mediate between Christine and Heed, who Christine believes has "robbed her of her past" (*Love* 24). Having been in a protracted feud, the two women need outside help to repair their rift in the same way Sethe needs the circle of Cincinnati women to rescue her from her "too thick love." Prior to her arrival, the women live in the house with the spirit of Bill Cosey, who resides in the portrait located in Heed's room. With her presence as the fourth person in the house, the girl with fins for feet brings the narrative to a level of cosmic completion.

Just like the assemblage of characters in previous novels, the residents of Monarch Street share some of the spiritual features that Morrison has previously employed. For example, the omniscient narrator describes Christine as having "one gray eye" (19), linking her to the double-eyed men who walk in two realms such as Cholly Breedlove, Joe Trace, Ajax (A. Jacks), Son Green, and Stamp Paid. Continuing this description, Morrison writes, "Twelve rings on three fingers of each hand snatched light from the ceiling fixture and seemed to elevate her task from drudgery to sorcery" (20). Heed is also similar to characters drawn from Morrison's spiritually situated imagination. Portrayed as a woman who moves from a world of mud to white sand, Heed is described as smelling like "butter-rum candy, grass juice, and fur" (24) with hands "like fins" (28) and skin with a memory of "seafoam" (78). As readers who have made prior visits to Morrison's imaginative world, we are primed to expect concepts and behavior and have come to accept these depictions as ordinary.

The occupants of Monarch Street are not the only women who speak spirit. Consistent with her cultural cataloguing of ideas, Morrison also iterates the power of cultural memorates that have traveled from Africa such as an awareness of the heightened spiritual power of all African women. For example, Vida Gibbons tells her grandson Romen, "I don't want you eating off her stove" (17). Her admonishment to Romen does not reflect her concern that he might be poisoned; instead it corresponds to the African idea that by ingesting food from people—especially women—who are ill-intentioned, one might also ingest a spiritual malevelonce that has been placed in the food. We have witnessed this occurrence in *Sula*, where it is suggested that the root-working mother of Ajax is the cause of Sula's demise.

Additionally, in *Love*, as in preceding novels, Morrison employs spiritual signs, such as the motif of the Kongo cosmogram. In her description of Christine's stopping the car to brake for a turtle crossing the road, Morrison repeats the Kongo cosmogram motif used in all of her earlier novels. Morrison writes, "She stopped and looked in the *rearview* mirrors—*left* one, *right* one, and *overhead*" (87; emphasis added). The four cardinal directions of the *dikenga dia Kongo* serve as a major conceit for the remembered tradition of the Kongo reiterated in this novel. Moreover, Morrison's account of Christine's looking into the mirror recalls the layout of the town of Ruby in *Paradise*.

Additionally, Morrison's description of Christine's recognition of the turtle's spiritual significance is telling. Intuitively, Christine leaves the car and runs back down the road. Morrison writes, "[She] did not ask herself why her heart was sitting up for a turtle creeping along Route 12" (87).[9] In Kongo tradition the turtle's carapace (*lolo ina nombe*) represents the founding ancestor and invokes an awareness of spirituality. Morrison uses this motif of the turtle in *Beloved*, described as "four placed plates under a hovering motionless bowl" as a means of substantiating Beloved's spiritual identity (105). Among the Dogon, turtles possess mystical power symbolizing ancestral lineage. The encounters that both Christine and Denver have with the turtles come at a turning point in their emotional lives, when they need the direction of divine forces to intervene.

Morrison suggests that these signs are coded in the spiritual DNA and in the matrix of the soul and are accessible when one needs the requisite information. This information occurs not at the cellular, but at the soulular level. Her response also suggests the practice of communicating with nature in order to receive messages consistent with the folkloric idea of being able to hear something "from the grapevine," or the expression "a little bird told me something," or understanding the disconcerting feeling one has about wind that does not produce rain, an idea that we encounter in *Sula*.

There are also other instances of remembrances of nature and the esteem in which African people recollect that sacred connection. Like Joe Trace and Son Green, who are both archetypes of woodsmen, Sandler misses the trees peopling the land where he lived before Bill Cosey rescued them from their lives in the swamp. Morrison also laments about the ecological changes, a conversation that she begins in *The Bluest Eye* and reiterates in each of her subsequent novels. L laments the changes in nature. She states in *Love*:

> The sky is empty now, erased, but back then the Milky Way was common as dirt. Its light made everything a glamorous black-and-white movie. No mater what your place in life or your state of mind, having a star-packed sky be a part of your night made you feel rich. And then there was the sea. (105)

In the world of black people, the moon can be a personal friend, a person can become a star, according to Son Green (*Tar Baby*), sand is a comrade, and as Pauline Breedlove has told us in *The Bluest Eye*, june bugs not only light up a tree leaf, but can also inspire a life.

In Toni Morrison's novels, separation from the land creates such a psychological disjuncture in the personalities of characters that some never recover. This disconnection serves as a metaphor for the dislocation of African people from the African continent. It continues to sign itself as a trope of remembrance of that iniquitous history.

Just as she attempts in preceding literary efforts—and like her literary ancestors whose literary figurations indict the oppressors—Morrison ensures that history is documented, no matter how horrifying the nature of those recollections. Just as she lifted the veil concerning the horrors of enslavement and the inhumanity of chain gangs in *Beloved* and recorded the social, political, and economic displacements in all of her novels, Morrison is careful to document the latest episodes in the serialized epic of America's racial terror. In her description of the resort, she notes that besides being a place for recreation and leisure activities, it is a place where African people could debate "death in the cities, murder in Mississippi" (*Love* 35). She further details events of the time, such as children blowing "apart in Sunday school" (80), re-recording the bombing of the church in Birmingham and the resultant murder of four little girls who were attending the church at the time of the bombing. Furthermore, she also includes a reference to the murder of Emmet Till: "As early as 1955, when a teenager's bashed-up body proved how seriously whites took sass" (81). Morrison also shows that times never really change as far as the brutal ways in which white supremacist ideology plays out on the text of black bodies. For instance, times have not changed from Sandler Gibbons's time, where "his boyhood had been shaped by fear of vigilantes," to the present, where the police in "dark blue uniforms . . . did the work of the posses" (15).

Not only are there the continued haunting of oppressive forces, there are interactions with spirits similar to the contact between Pilate and her father Macon Dead, Sethe's and Denver's relationship with Beloved, and Violet's connection with Dorcas's spirit in *Jazz*. Characters in the novel *Love* have encounters with apparitions. For example, May's ghost is described as being "helmeted and holstered" as well as to be "gaining strength" (82). At the novel's end the two women who were separated in life, reunite and renew their friendship in death, much like Sula and Nell. Christine tells Romen who is on his way to take Heed to the morgue, "take a blanket. She might get cold" (198). Even in Bill Cosey's description of the death of his only son Billy, Cosey says, "When I lost him . . . it was like somebody from the grave reached up and grabbed him for spite" (43). Here Bill broaches the topic of the dead being able to interact and exert influences on the living, and idea that Morrison inscribed repeatedly in her novels in a variety of narrative settings.

The final point to discuss here is Toni Morrison's novelistic preoccupation with the concept of love. Love according to Morrison is verifiable through the five senses—as well as through spiritual channels. For example, at the end of *Jazz*, Morrison iterates the power of love and forgiveness to ferry one across the deep abyss of despair. Joe and Violet have re-captured their love for one another. The narrator of Jazz ends her narration remarking, "I envy their public love" (229). In *Love*, being smitten causes a glistening in Romen that the narrator describes as a "moist radiance" (109). In *Love*, Morrison defines love as being "soul-chained" (112)—an expression that relates to the feeling Connie Consolation experiences with "the living man" in *Paradise.*

Besides romantic love and its attending passions, love has different faces and takes on different personalities. For Heed and Christine, the rift in their love occurs when Bill Cosey chooses Heed. Their relationship suffers even more after Christine is sent off to boarding school. Brought together by Heed's death, the reader is assured that their renewed relationship will be stronger and will resume where they left off as children. Christine is able to communicate her feelings to Heed before her death. Unlike Sula and Nell, Christine and Heed have the opportunity to mend and recover their ruptured love before Heed makes her spiritual transition.

Morrison discusses the power of love in a 1989 interview with Bill

Moyers. She says, "Love, we have to embrace ourselves. Self-regard. James Baldwin once said, 'You've already been bought and paid for. Your ancestors already gave it up for you. You don't have to do that anymore. Now you can love yourself.' It's already possible" (266–67). She continues, "Some of it's very fierce. Powerful. Distorted" (267). Through a consideration of love, most of the characters in Morrison's novels change in the course of the novel's plot action and come to realize some powerful life lessons. By this, I am referring to a dynamism that allows the characters to go through an ordeal, learn lessons about themselves, about others, about the nature of being human with all their personal foibles, and come through those challenges fulfilled and re-centered. Experiencing love, characters not only discover meaning, but also healing.

In *Love*, Morrison informs readers that love is enabling and elemental to wholeness, wellness—and is the ultimate expression of one's being a full human being. Because African people were denied the right to love each other in healthy ways, in stable family units uninterrupted from the parceling out and selling of African people that occurred under chattel enslavement, this expression takes on new challenges, given these external hostilities. As Baby Suggs reports, "Yonder they do not love your flesh. They despise it. They don't love your eyes; they'd just as soon pick em out. No more do they love the skin on your back. Yonder they flay it" (*Beloved* 89). In her novels, Morrison not only indicts white people for their ignoble actions, she also records the destructive effects of withholding love and rejecting one's own in *The Bluest Eye*. For example, in *The Bluest Eye*, because of her sense of rejection, Pecola searches for maternal love, similar to both Joe and Violet Trace's pursuit, based on departures of their own mothers, through abandonment and the other through suicide, respectively. Punctuating this experience is Dorcas's own maternal yearnings after the murder of her father and her mother's burning during the St. Louis race riots.

Notwithstanding the muffling of the sustained notes of love in the chorus of African life in North America, Morrison's words fill the compressed spaces of identity, push against oppression, and create openings and potentialities that allow the reader to grow and find new ways of being, new ways of loving. This is especially important in the socially suboptimal environment of America where African people have had to live on avenues of uncertainty near the intersections of whatever whim and whatever horror prevailed in the unbridled imaginations of their oppressors.

However, that being said, the themes of Toni Morrison's novels imply that as long as we can say we have loved, we have lived: that is the measure of a life. At the end of Pilate's life, when she lies dying, she tells Milkman, "I wish I'd knowed more people. I would have loved 'em all. If I'd a knowed more, I would a loved more" (*Song of Solomon* 340). In *Love*, as in all of her novels, Morrison's spiritual authorship makes the point decidedly clear: that no matter what African people in America have faced, love is the true power of our lives. Echoing Baby Suggs's words, Morrison's novels insist, "Love your heart. For this is the prize" (*Beloved* 89).

Glossary

Yoruba Terms

Abara meji: Owner of two bodies.

Abere: Sacred needle used by Oshun to mend and heal her devotees.

Abiku: A child that is "born to die." An *abiku* is a spirit who continually dies and is continually reborn.

Adimu: Offerings to Òrìsà that do not include blood sacrifices. *Adimu* can include fruit, liquor or *oti*, grains, or cloth.

Aganju: Aganju is the Òrìsà who embodies the essence of fire. One of the Òrìsà considered as the father of nature, he assists human beings by ferrying them toward their destinies. He is petitioned to transform the fire within, which is sometimes realized as anger, into passion and psychic empowerment. Represented by the sun, he reminds human beings of the potential of each day and helps them work toward the fulfillment of their destinies.

Agogo: A bell used to communicate with Òrìsà. The *agogo* is also used to invoke a priest into an altered state of consciousness to then be possessed by the Òrìsà that crowns his or her head. It also is used to spiritually clean an environment.

Ajé: In the Lukumi Yoruba spiritual tradition, the Ajé or *awon iya wa* (our mothers), are also referred to as *Iyami Osoronga*. These wise women with extraordinary power make people both revere and fear them because of their dense concentration of Asé. They exist in the African American tradition and are called Ma Dear, Other Mother, or Big Momma.

Apataki: Stories that illuminate a situation that delivers a moral tale. Apataki accompany the *odu* being read during the divination and contributes to the person's understanding of the archetypal idea being communicated in the odu.

Asé: Asé is the divine power that innervates all life forces. As the spiritual essence of God, it can be exchanged through *ebo* when a person's life force becomes diminished. The power that makes things happen or the spiritual energy of Olodumare in the universe, it is the performative power of spirit. All things are accomplished through asé. There are places on the body and on the earth the have concentrations of *asé*.

Asedi: The monetary component of a sacrifice. The money reinforces the sacrifice and underscores the ritual's intent.

Ayé: The earth and the world of the living.

Babalawo: A *babalawo* is a male initiate of Orunmila who performs Ifa divination. *Babalawo* literally translates as "the father of secrets."

Babaluaiye: Father of the world who carries diseases into the world and cures them. This limping Òrìsà is the owner of balance. He reminds human beings to maintain the balance between the spiritual and material realms.

Ebo: Sacrifice or offering to one of the Òrìsà, ancestors, or Iyami to elevate and strengthen the devotee, to assist them with a problem or to propitiate the deity or spirit to whom the offering is made. This offering can be a blood offering, but may consist of any of the formulary offerings within the Yoruba tradition. The idea of *ebo* is exchange, giving something to receive something.

Egun: Egun are the ancestors. They protect us from malevolent forces and spirits. They are the link between the spiritual and the material realms. The foundation of all people, *egun* dwell among us and continue to influence the lives of their descendants.

Egungun: A form of *egun* worship performed through masquerade. The *egungun* maskers help the community to understand their symbiotic relationship between themselves (the living) and those who have transitioned the physical realm into the land of spirits.

Ejila: Ejila *shebora* is the *odu* represented by the number 12. The refrain is "the soldier never sleeps."

Ejioco: One of the *odu* in the Yoruba divination system of *merindilogun*. The metaphoric refrain is the "arrow between brothers."

Eleda: A person's head. The head represents God.

Elese meji: A person's feet.

Ekundayo: The joy that comes after pain.

Elegba: The messenger of God who represents the beginning and ending of all things. Elegba helps human beings to reach their destinies by offering choices to determine one's life. Elegba is the idea of choices and change who delivers messages to the other Òrìsà on behalf of human beings who acknowledge and petition him.

Emi: Breath and lungs.

Eniyan: A human being.

Ese: Traditional stories.

Ewe: Various plants and herbs used for healing and making *ebo* and *osain.*

Fifeto: A *fifeto* ritual is performed to spiritually clean and cool down the energy engendered from the use of knives and the heat of the blood offered in ritual sacrifices.

Fun fun: The color white. *Fun fun* also refers to the Òrìsà that are considered cool such as Obatala.

Gbere: Incisions or *gbere* in Yoruba language are protective cuts made in the skin signaling the invisible transformations of persons.

Gelede: Performed by men, this masked performance honors the power of women.

Ibae: A term of respect when speaking about the dead.

Ibeji: The Òrìsà who are twin deities who represent balance between the interstices. The children of Sango and Oshun, Ibeji are powerful representations of the bounty of life and remind us of the potential available at the intersections of the realms. They comprise the three children who are born after them. The first twin is called Taiwo, the second is Kehindé, the third is Idowu, the fourth child is Alaba, and the fifth is Idogbé.

Ifa: A form of divination, the Ifa corpus has 256 signs with a variety of stories attached to them. These stories deliver a moral story to help devotees cope with life's challenges.

Ifunpa: Amulets sewn in a packet.

Ijala: A type of chant performed for hunters.

Inu: The internal self.

Iré: Blessings and good fortune or positive influences.

Ita: *Ita* is a divinational reading with the *merindilogun* the third day after a person's initiation into the priesthood.

Iyalòrìsà: Female priest in the Lukumi system and the mother of Òrìsà.

Iyawo: A person who is an initiate into the priesthood. In this liminal state, the person is not who they were and not who they will become.

Iwa: Character. In the nondoctrinal Yoruba spiritual tradition, the goal to be reached in one's lifetime is the achievement of good character (*iwa pele*).

Lukumi: Lukumi is the name of the Yoruba tradition that developed in Cuba during the enslavement era. A variation in spelling is Lucumi. The Lukumi people originate in southwestern Nigeria and Benin and Togo.

Mae de Santo: Mae de Santo is the mother of saints and a female priest in the Candomblé system of Brazil. Her office is similar to that of the Iyalorisa.

Mae pequena: Literally, little mother, this Iyalorisa assists the Mae de Santo. In Yoruba language she would be called Iya Kekere or Oju Ebona Kan (Ojubona Kan).

Matanza: the ritual sacrifice of animals to birth the Òrìsà.

Merindilogun: Translating into sixteen, the *merindilogun* (*dilogun*) is a type of divination using sixteen cowrie shells. These ritually charged *dilogun* yield patterns, generate *odu*, and recollect associative *apataki*.

Mojuba: The *mojuba* are elegiac prayers that accompany all rituals. Besides being foundational to all ceremonies, these prayers are recited daily to greet the day and reinforce the interconnectedness of God, Òrìsà, the ancestors, the divine forces of nature, one's sanguinal parents, God parents, and the community of Òrìsà worshippers.

Ogbanje: An Igbo word describing children who are born to die; similar to *abiku*.

Obba: The true wife of Shango, this warrior Òrìsà is the defender of women. She represents the cemetery.

Obatala: The deity of creation and the chief representative of Olodumare on earth, Obatala is the highest in the hierarchy of Òrìsà. Obatala is the creator of the first human beings. The owner of the white cloth, he is the guardian of morality recognized as good character.

Obi: Obi ata is a system of divination that one employs to communicate with the Òrìsà. Using four lobes of coconut meat to ascertain yes or no answers to a series of questions, the supplicant is able to get guidance on various issues.

Ochossi: Ochossi is the Òrìsà of hunting and is associated with ethical righteousness. He is the Òrìsà that assists devotees in achieving goals and helps them to achieve their destiny.

Odidé: Parrot sacred to Ochossi.

Odu: A sacred corpus of knowledge elemental to one of the sixteen ideas of the *merindilogun*.

Ogun: Ogun is the Òrìsà of iron and creativity who owns the world. He owns all sacrifices and is the patron of blacksmiths and hunters. Considered an elder Òrìsà, he has been on the earth since the earth's creation.

Ojiji: A person's shadow.

Oju inu: Insight.

Oké: Child enclosed in a caul at birth.

Okan: Heart.

Olodumare: The primary name used to refer to god, the Supreme Being of the universe. Other names used to refer to god are Olorun ("owner of heaven") and Olofi.

Olokun: Olokun is the deep part of the ocean or the bottom of the sea. He represents history and shared memories. A primordial Òrìsà, Olokun assists people in healing themselves from the suppression of memory, which holds the key to their liberation from the lesions and breaches of the past.

Olòrìsà: An initiated devotée dedicated to a specific Òrìsà.

Oni l'oni aiye: Owners of the world.

Ori: Ori translates into head and represents a person's destiny.

Oriki: A praise poem chanted during public celebrations.

Orile: A particular type of *oriki* that stresses the accomplishment of family members and lineage ancestors.

Ori inu: A person's destiny.

Òrìsà: Òrìsà are the divinities in the Yoruba spiritual tradition. They may be Irunmolé created by Olodumare at the beginning of the world or deified human beings who, having distinguished themselves during their lifetimes, have been elevated to the status of an Òrìsà. The Òrìsà are manifestations of the natural world and interact on earth with the living. Through interaction with the Òrìsà human beings gain an understanding of the Olodumare.

Orita Meta: An intersection. Referred to as three roads that come together. It is a symbolic representation of the intersection between *ayé* and *orun* depicted as a cross within a circle. When drawn it creates a spiritual portal.

Oromadie: Oromadie are roosters sacrificed to Elegba as propitiary sacrifices or *ebo*.

Osain: An Òrìsà or sacred aspect of God that is hidden in the leaves and plants and roots of trees. He is the Asé found in the phytonutrients of organic matter. There can be no ceremony or initiation without Osain's invocation through the ritual washing of leaves and plants. As sacred medicine, he washes away pain and sickness and renews all who invoke his power.

Oshun: Oshun is a female Òrìsà who is also referred to as Iya Lode, the great mother. This river deity represents the "blood that flows in the veins." She is the Òrìsà of society, love, beauty, and family. She is primary to the notion of development since all civilizations depend on the fresh water sources of rivers to generate and sustain societies.

Oshun Ibukolé: This road or aspect of Oshun is represented by the buzzard and is responsible for saving the world from destruction.

Ota: Divine force that lives in stones, they are the memory of the earth.

Oya: Oya is the warrior Òrìsà who gave Shango thunder and lightning. She is the wind before the storm and the guardian of the spirits of the dead. Her domain is the gate of the cemetery. Oya is the mother of the *egungun*.

Oyeku meji: Oyeku meji concerns the relationship of dark spaces and individual actions and their ultimate connection to spiritual elevation.

Shango: Shango is the Òrìsà who represents the office of king and the seat of authority. A historical person who was the fourth Alaafin of Oyo, Shango is the idea of passion, truth, and the life force that empower human beings to achieve greatness in their lives.

Tibi Tire: Good and bad luck together.

Yemonja: The mother of all Òrìsà, Yemonja is the owner of the sea. Yemonja is also the Òrìsà of motherhood. The merciful Òrìsà is petitioned when seeking comfort and spiritual deliverance. Like the ocean, her grace is wide and deep and devotees understand that there is no problem too great for her to handle.

Yoruba: A group located in West Africa. Historically, the Yoruba lived in kingdoms and city-states. A highly developed civilization with unparalleled artistic and cultural achievements, the Yoruba are well known for their spiritual and technological accomplishments. In North America, the spiritual tradition of the Yoruba is often referred to as "Yoruba" as well.

Kongo Terms (Bantu)

Baana ba nlongo: Born abnormally and having precocious spiritual sensibilities.

BaKuba: Literally the people of lightning, the BaKuba live in the Kasai area of the Kongo.

Bakulu: The *bakulu* are deceased ancestors who continue to interact with human beings. Residing below the *kalunga* line, the *bakulu* or venerated ancestors dwell under the surface of living waters as manifestation as well as memory.

BaLuba: The Luba people or BaLuba live in the southeastern part of the Democratic Republic of the Congo and are renowned for their highly evolved material and spiritual technologies.

Ba Manianga: A subgroup of the BaKongo, located in lower Kongo.

Banganga: Plural of *nganga*.

Bantu: Plural term for people. (Muntu, singular person.) It also represents a large group of people and a language family that includes Kiswahili, Xhosa, Chiluba, Ki-Kongo, and hundreds of languages.

Bisimbi: Plural form of the word *simbi*, these water spirits found at the intersection where water meets the earth are vital forces of nature. They are the guardian and protective spirits.

Booka: Booka or *yangalala* is a spiritual gesture that accompanied Africans to the western hemisphere. The gesture now called "high five" transports feelings of good will when the two palms touch.

Buta: Family.

Buzima muzazu: At once the name of something in the natural world, a cocoon (*muzazu*), and a performative activity, stitching together (*zazula*) indicates the *nkisi's* potential to protect and heal.

Candomblé: A term that refers to the organization of religious practices. It translates from the Ki-Kongo language as "house of initiation," from *ka* a diminutive, *ndumbe* (initiate); and *mbele* (house).

Dikenga dia Kongo: The Kongo cosmogram represents the journey of the soul of a person. Its four points represent the life crises stage of existence: Pre-birth/birth, puberty, marriage, and death. The four stages are marked as *musoni, kala, tukula,* and *luvemba.*

Dingo dingo: Process.

Izilo ze Nkosi: Beasts of the King were often used to test the courage of men who were to be promoted to the next level of status.

Kala: Kala means black and represents the second phase of a person's existence. Kala and *zima* collectively represent the notion of duality in Kongo traditional beliefs.

Kalunga: The principle of change.

Kanda: Community.

Kimyumba: Deceased.

Kini: The invisible body.

Kitenta: Motifs or spirit capitals.

Konda: To hunt alone.

Koyija kibundi: This refers to washing the village after something catastrophic has occurred. In a general sense, this washing purifies the village and its inhabitants of the negative forces associated with the disaster.

Kinzu: Kinzu is the structural motor of the universe that is the prime mover of all energy.

Lolo ina nombe: In Kongo tradition the turtle's carapace represents the founding ancestor and invokes evokes an awareness of spirituality.

Lukasa: The memory grid that subsequently became the prototype of the computer's motherboard. *Lukasa* is a mnemonic device employed in traditional African cultures such as the *lukasa* sculptures of the Ba Luba; each board is a commemorative site where readers can participate in recollecting buried knowledge to refortify and restore a sense of identity and cultural connectivity. A conceptual map of fundamental aspects of Luba culture used to trace memory and recall genealogies and arcane knowledge to pass on to subsequent generations. Each board is unique and represents the divine revelations of a spirit medium expressed in sculptural form.

Lwengisa: A foreshadowing of a significant event.

Magara: Spiritual life of a person. This idea also includes the force of spiritual intelligence engendered by the ancestors.

Makuku matatu: Represents the three firestones foundational to creation.

Mamoni: Lines painted around the eyes of the Nganga that help her to see the hidden and dangerous things of the world such as sickness and evil.

Mpemba: Also known as *luvemba*, *mpemba* is kaolin or white clay representing the dead. The realm of the ancestors, this community of the dead is called Mpemba, and its residents are called *bakulu*. *Kongo pembas* are the graphic symbols drawn on the floor or walls to invoke the presence of the spirit.

Minkisi: Plural of *nkisi*.

Moyo: The members of one's family matrilineally descended.

Muntu: Singular person.

Musoni: The first phase of life's journey represented by the color yellow. Musoni represents the realm of prebirth or the beginnings of a person's life process on the *dikenga dia Kongo* or wheel of eternity. Musoni is the stage where a human being is instructed to become a true knower of one's destiny.

Mwela: The soul. *Mwela* can also express portals between the material and spirit realms.

Ndoki: This term is associated with the word *kindoki*, which means power or force. Ndoki is a person with power or force. This term is especially used to describe someone who has spiritual or "invisible" power. As with all power in the hands of a person, a kindoki can be used benevolently or malevolently by the *ndoki*. *Bandoki* is the plural form.

Nganga: Master teacher, priest, and ritual officiate. An *nganga* is a specialist, a true knower, a master. Other functions include being a physician, a visionary, and a priest.

Ngina: Literally, a seed. It can also represent generations. I am the seed of a seed, of a seed, of a seed.

Nkisi: Singular of *minkisi*. An *nkisi* is a form of traditional medicine made from animal or mineral, which, under the guidance of an Nganga, helps to heal people from illness or any other imbalance. An *nkisi* makes it possible to approach a spirit. In the Western hemisphere, the Bantu of Brazil refer to the Kongo deities as Nkisis.

Nkisi nkondi: An *nkondi* is an *nkisi*, which means hunter. This nkisi hunts down the source of the problem. It is a diagnostic device as well as a prescriptive tool.

Nitu: The physical body.

Nommo: Nommo also refers to the power of speech to create, organize all that exists.

Nsi: Land.

Ntu: A Bantu concept that represents the innervating power of existence. In the language it forms the noun class of words. For example: *muntu* (a person), *kintu* (things), et cetera.

Nyama: Vital force.

Nza: The universe.

Semba: Punish.

Tukula: The northern node of the dikenga dia Kongo cosmogram, *tukula* represents the maturation cycle of the person and is signified by the color red.

Tambukusu: The genetic code as a memory of creation.

Togu na: House of words. Speech.

V: The basis of all realities.

Vanga: Vanga means to perform or do.

Vangama: Vangama is the formation of the person.

Vaika: Vaika represents the existence stage, to be, to exist, to rise.

Vezima: Flash of light representing the interaction between the physical and spiritual realms.

Vunda: Vunda means death both natural and unnatural.

Zinga: The seashell used as an *nkisi*. Kuzinga is an infinitive, which means to live long. Seashells represent a major Kongo symbol of the spiral journey from one world to the next.

Other Terms

Amma: Dogon supreme deity.

Bukra: Bukra is one of the terms that African people in North America employ to refer to white people.

Damballah Ouido: A principal deity in the Fon tradition. Alternately Damballah Wedo.

Dogo so: Dogon idea of speech. Speech is divided into four categories: *giri so* (front speech), *bolo so* (back speech), *bene so* (side speech), and *so dayi* (the language of knowing reserved for initiates).

Loa: The deities of the Vodun (Voodoo) tradition. Alternately, the spellings are Lwa.

Fon: People from Benin, formerly Dahomey, and parts of Togo. The Fon tradition birthed the Vodun spiritual tradition of Haiti and Brazil. It is also one of the antecedents of the African American hoodoo tradition. In Brazil their descendants worship the Vodunsi, while the Haitians worship the Loa.

Maafa: A term coined by Marimba Ani, which means the great disaster of captivity, transport, and subsequent enslavement of African people.

Malochia: The "evil eye." The intent of the gaze is to cause psychic harm. One can protect oneself from harm using talismans or other apotropaic means such as asafetida worn in cloth around the neck, similar to Aunt Jimmy in *The Bluest Eye*.

Nommo: In the Dogon cosmology, Nommo or twins refer to mythological ancestors, and to one's own lineage.

Palo Monte: Also referred to as Regla Congos, this system of worship is a derivative of Kongo spiritual traditions recodified in the western hemisphere.

Sangoma: South African female traditional healer.

Umuntu umuntu nagabuntu: A person is a person because of people. This philosophical statement refers to the complementary nature of the collective.

Vévé: The iconographic pattern used as a site to invoke the presence of the Loa (deities) in the ritual space of Vodun ceremonies.

Yala: Meaningful images or symbolic icons in the Dogon language.

Yingim and Danyim: Funeral events held annually among the Dogon of Mali to honor all the deaths that have occurred in the village throughout the year.

Notes

Preface: Dancing between Two Realms

1. In the preface of *African Rhythm and African Sensibility*, Chernoff explains that the fundamental aesthetic in Africa is participation, stating that "without participation there is no meaning." Illustrating the importance of dance to music, he says, "When you ask a friend whether or not he 'understands' a certain type of music, he will say yes if he knows the dance that goes with it. The music of Africa invites us in the making of a community" (23). Chernoff, *African Rhythm and African Sensibility*, 23.

2. The Kongo cosmogram, *dikenga dia Kongo*, is represented in many ways in African American material and performance culture. See Tobin and Dobard, *Hidden in Plain View*. Also, see Gundaker, ed., *Keep Your Head to the Sky*. Thompson has documented the repeated influence in painting, quilt-making, yard decorations, funerary art, performance styles, and body gestures. The repetition of this structure is a variant of the ring shout, a Kongo sacred dance that African people retained in America. See Thompson, *Flash of the Spirit*. Also, see Thompson and Cornet, *Four Moments of the Sun*; and Thompson, *Faces of the Gods*.

In its re-codified form as a popular dance, the Kongo cosmogram is performed as the "Electric Slide" (a testament to its Kongo origins of which a subgroup of people are referred to as Ba Kuba (the people of lightning). The dance consists of four 90-degree turns counterclockwise (360 degrees), which re-creates the *dikenga dia Kongo* and signs the remembrance of the matrix or spiritual structure of the circle representing the soul's journey. Sterling Stuckey posits that the ring shout helped to consolidate African's identity in North America. See Stuckey, *Slave Culture*, 12.

It is significant that memorates were kept in musical and dance forms as symbolic modes of cosmic perception in the United States of America owing to the manner in which the particularly harsh conditions of American enslavement denied African people access to little other than their physical bodies. Since dance does not have a material artifact as the product, it allowed Africans to not be completely submerged by Euro-American concepts (Baraka, *Blues People* 16.) Dance is a major archival resource of African people and exists as "symbolic restatements of something sacred the history of which may still be remembered or may have been forgotten" (Idowu, *Olodumare* 115). See Fabre, "The Slave Ship Dance" in *Black Imagination and the Middle Passage*. According to Fabre, in dance performances Africans expressed coded kinships and loyalties, references to the spirit world and claims of African identity (40).

Through the creation of sacred space, Africans re-presented belief systems using the body to inscribe the cultural worlds east and west of the Atlantic. Like the *dikenga dia Kongo*, the Yoruba worldview is also described as a circle with intersecting lines. The circle with a cross has a representation in Yoruba spiritual culture as *orita meta* or the crossroads, the intersection between the cosmic realms. As such, *merindilogun* divinations performed with sixteen cowrie shells begin with the inscription of this sacred sign to open the channels to pass information between the realms.

3. In this study I employ the term *spirituality* as a multivalent term that includes, but is not limited to, notions of philosophy, religion, belief systems, ritual practices, kinship, and community formation representative of a clustering of African identities. Moreover, in my application of the term I am creating a spiritual inquiry across distinct cultures and disciplines within the historical, cultural, and spiritual context of the African diaspora. Undergirding this approach is a theoretical alliance with the ideas that Olupona expresses in the foreword to *African Spirituality*. I concur with Olupona, who asserts that "African people continue to express an essential element in the formation and sustenance of modern cultures in various parts of the globe consistent with African meaning in the modern, post-colonial world" (xv). His edited volume explores how Africans in the diaspora and on the African continent have maintained the possibilities of making and deriving meaning relative to the spiritual world.

Introduction: There's a Little Wheel a Turnin' in My Heart: Cultural Concentricities and Enduring Identities

1. For the purpose of this study I am defining African peoples as a confederation of various nations of people captured and brought to the western hemisphere. Additionally, I am using the term *African* in its broadest sense to include all people of African descent, regardless of national origin. I am not employing the term *traditional* to separate time, but to demonstrate the harmony between historical and contemporary realities, which connect the present with infinite time consistent with African cosmologies. Nell Irvin Painter argues that being "'African'" Americans is part of a New World identity. Naming people by the continent of their origin and ignoring their ethnic identity is a consequence of distance in time and space" (*Creating Black Americans* 5). Although this generic term lacks the particularity of ethnic delineation, it references a common site of origin.

2. Louisiana was the only state in America where drums were not outlawed for use by African people. Subsequently, a distinct musical and cultural heritage persists unparalleled on the American landscape. Not limited to Congo Square, jazz funerals, "second line parades," and Mardi Gras, Louisiana culture represents an intense and dynamic cultural example of Africa in America

3. Although most biographical information records Toni Morrison's birth name as Chloe Anthony Wofford, her mother states that she named her Chloe Ardelia Wofford after Morrison's maternal grandmother, Ardelia Willis. In an interview in

the *Lorain Journal*, Morrison's mother says that Morrison changed her name to Toni after having converted to Catholicism while at Howard University. Saint Anthony was the name that Morrison selected for her confirmation name. It was subsequently shortened to Toni and adopted as her first name. Ansberry, "Toni Morrison's Mom Recalls Storytelling Days in Lorain."

4. Lecture at the Goree Institute, July 19, 2002, as part of the UNCF Mellon 2002 Faculty Seminar at the Goree Institute, Goree Island, Republic of Senegal, July 15–23, 2002. In this seminar, titled "Gods, Knowledge and Modernity" and led by Nobel laureate Wole Soyinka, I examined the belief structures and worldviews of the Yoruba, Dogon, Baule, Igbo, and other groups' spiritual traditions as the bases for exploring modernity and the humanities within an African frame. As a result of participating in this seminar, I developed many of the ideas presented in this study.

5. In Curtin's *The Atlantic Slave Trade*, the author gives the figures of 24.5 percent of enslaved Africans transported to North America from Angola, or the Royal Kingdom of Kongo, which is approximately 109,214 Africans transported from the Angola region alone (157). Gomez revises Curtin's number in his germinal study, *Exchanging Our Country Marks*, remarking that 26.1 percent or 125,253 enslaved Africans were brought to British North America and Louisiana (29). As significant as those calculations are, they are still conservative. However, evidence of the cultural and spiritual influences of Kongo culture remains one of the most influential systems of ideas in the western hemisphere. Heywood assembles an impressive group of scholars, all of whom attest to the influence of Central African people in the American diaspora. See Heywood, ed., *Central Africans and Cultural Transformations*. Also see Thornton, *Africa and Africans in the Making of the Atlantic World, 1400–1800*, for a discussion of the stability of Kongo identity in "a bundle of traits" including language, religion, aesthetics, as well as material culture, which could be appreciated and adopted by the "larger community than the one that originally created it" (208).

6. In the African American sense, music, dance, drama, and language are spiritual practices as there are no clearly drawn lines dividing notions of sacred, secular, or profane.

7. *Maafa* is a term coined by Marimba Ani that refers to the great physical and psychic despair resulting from the capturing of African people, their subsequent transport to the western hemisphere, and continuous experience of oppression consistent with the values of white supremacist values.

8. An alternative spelling is Lucumi. The Lukumi people originate in southwestern Nigeria and, to a lesser extent, portions of Benin and Togo.

9. See Blassingame, *The Slave Community*. Blassingame notes the ability of culture to bolster "self-esteem, courage, and confidence" as well as a means to "defend against personal degradation" (76). See also Stuckey, *Slave Culture*; Heywood, ed., *Central Africans and Cultural Transformations*; and Gomez, *Exchanging Our Country Marks*.

10. See T. Washington, *Our Mothers, Our Powers, Our Texts*. In Yoruba language, *ayé* is the word for earth. Fundamentally, the power of the earth connects to the

power of the Ajé, those older women who have the ability to see through different eyes, shape-shift, as well as the ability to confidently wield spiritual power. See an extended discussion of the Ajé in my examinations of *The Bluest Eye* and *Tar Baby*.

11. I am employing the term *cosmology* as the body of conceptions that enumerate and classify the phenomena that compose and order the universe as well as the norms and processes that govern it. Accompanying these conceptions are embedded myths and other collective representations.

12. Similar ideas about the nature of African spiritual practices equal to the hyperbolic analysis in Conrad's *Heart of Darkness*, where Kurtz has been entrusted to make a report to the "International Society for the Suppression of Savage Customs" in order to facilitate "weaning those ignorant millions from their horrid ways" (45).

13. Jung and Kerenji, *Introduction to a Science of Mythology*, 101. Quoted in Soyinka, *Myth, Literature and the African World*, 35.

Chapter 1. I's Got the Blues: Malochia, Magic, and the Descent into Madness in *The Bluest Eye*

1. In this essay, all references to *The Bluest Eye* refer to the 1994 Plume edition and will consist of pagination in parenthetical format.

2. Waliggo quoted in the foreword to Magesa, *African Religion*, xii.

3. The asafetida bag replicates the Kongo concept of an *nkisi*, a visual implement that has the power to heal, protect, and deflect harm. See MacGaffey, *Religion and Society in Central Africa*. Also see Thompson, *Flash of the Spirit*.

4. See an extended discussion of the role of Banganga (plural of *nganga*) in the *Song of Solomon* essay.

5. The color of the marigolds—yellow—corresponds to the Kongo delineation of *musoni*, representing the realm of prebirth or the beginnings or the prelude to the life process on the *dikenga dia Kongo* or wheel of eternity.

6. By adding the money or (*asedi*) to the sacrifice, the ritual is ensured a higher degree of efficacy. The money reinforces the sacrifice or exchange. This idea of reciprocity underscores the intensity of the ritual intent.

Chapter 2. Always: The Living Ancestor and the Testimony of Will in *Sula*

1. All references to *Sula* are from the 1973 Knopf paperback edition and will consist of pagination in parenthetical format.

2. See *Song of Solomon* and *Jazz* chapters for further discussion of the epic contours in Morrison's novels.

3. Birenbaum asserts that the most important thing that a hero does is to travel, which is a traversing of mythic space. See Birenbaum, *Myth and Mind*, 55.

4. See Adjaye, *Time in the Black Experience*, as well as Fu-Kiau's description of time as the Kongo propose in the essay on *Jazz*.

5. See essay on *Jazz* for a more detailed discussion of this idea.

6. Morrison's introduction of a male character as the first focal point of her narrative is a pattern initiated in *Sula* that is repeated in *Tar Baby* and *Song of Solomon*.

Also significant is his name. Shad is the name of a member of the herring family that ascends rivers in the spring to spawn. It also suggests shadow.

7. The use of the terms *eccentric* and *peculiar* are not confined to their usual connotations and are not meant to be pejorative. In the context of this study, the term is extended to and describes those who primarily listen within and attend to the dictates of the spiritual realm, or to those who are in touch with the natural world.

8. See the chapter on *Beloved* for a more detailed idea of the river as a matrix of memory.

9. The word *medallion* further solidifies the idea of rank. As a cognate of the word *medal*, it indicates an acknowledgment of something of consequence to be duly noted. It is also the physical equivalent of a title.

10. The idea that his grandfather is not mentioned by name, but referred to as "long time dead," is an appellation referencing the ancestors and hints that his grandfather who lived on the river may have been a river priest of Oya as well. He also lived at the edge of town and made his living on the river. Most of the character's names in Morrison's novels suggest significant attributes of the characters' personalities.

11. This trio of women is another leitmotif that Morrison uses. In *The Bluest Eye* there is the trio of prostitutes: China, Poland, and the Maginot Line living under one roof. Claudia, Frieda, and Mrs. Macteer are another trio of women. In *Song of Solomon* there is Ruth, First Corinthians, and Magdalene (called Lena). In that same novel, Pilate's house consists of Pilate, Reba, and Hagar. In *Beloved*, the house at 124 Bluestone Road consists of the female occupants Sethe, Denver, and Beloved. There are multiple significations in the ascription of trios of women. For example, there is a story for each of the women—or a story in every name. These narratives help to erase the stereotypes or basic stock characters that form a major part of the African American literary tradition. Also, because these households for the most part consist of intergenerational women, Morrison engenders a sense of continuity subverting the disruptions created by the historical enslavement of African people and provides a context for understanding the traditions of the past and a clear direction for the future. Samuels and Weems add, "By including distinct communities of women, Morrison allows us to see individuals who refused to be destroyed by external definitions of the other" (25). In addition to the three women, there are other trios such as the three Deweys, the date of Suicide Day (the third of January), the three ritual implements that Shadrack uses, and the three beets that motivate Eva's journey of survival.

12. In this novel, as in *Beloved*, there are significant references to Oya. For example, the number eighteen reduces to nine and represents the amount of time Eva spends away from her family making her sacrifice. When making offerings to Oya, the supplicant provides nine or any multiple of nine items, since nine is Oya's emblematic number. Plum's name is significant because it represents one of the fruits that are ritually given to her when a devotee makes an *ebo*, or offering, because of its purple color's association with Oya. Also, note the connection of Eva's motivation for her journey as being down to her last three beets, also representative of Oya's color.

13. See discussion of this Yoruba Òrìsà in *The Bluest Eye* and *Song of Solomon* chapters.

14. Feeding the hole is a Yoruba ritual performed to strengthen one's body and spirit along with one's relationship with the earth and the ancestors.

15. For example, because Tupac Shakur's body was cremated, an enduring conversation exists concerning the slain rapper's not being dead. However, the death of his contemporary Christopher Wallace, aka The Notorious B.I.G. or Biggie Smalls, whose body was paraded through the streets of the Bedford Stuyvesant section of Brooklyn, has not generated any rumors of his still being alive.

16. Their identities as intermediaries or *bisimbi* spirits are intimated by their description. MacGaffey notes that *bisimbi* are the tutelary spirits of special children ("Twins, Simbi Spirits" 213). The Deweys are described as three boys who, under the influence of Eva, have merged into one personality: "They spoke with one voice, thought with one mind, and maintained an annoying privacy" (39). They have even begun to look alike so that even their mothers cannot tell them apart. These Deweys "who went wild at the thought of water" resemble Kongo *bisimbi*. This transformation and their identity suggest the meaning of their collective name. The word *dew* derives from the Indo-European base that produced words that mean flow, run, wash, and brook. In the novel's culminating ritual, they are presumed dead because their bodies are not found (162). Failure to find them suggests they have returned to their source.

Chapter 3. I've Got a Home in Dat Rock: Ritual and the Construction of Family History in *Song of Solomon*

1. Nicolaisen argues that naming is intimately tied to narration, which together represents "two of the most essential speech acts." The name as an identifying reference gives structure to a chaotic world, while the story creates the past to help negotiate the present realities (260).

2. Subsequent references to this novel refer to the 1977 American Library paperback edition of *Song of Solomon* and will consist of pagination in parenthetical format.

3. These circles are emblematic of the missing navel (circle) on Pilate's smooth stomach, whose absence is so remarkable that the verbal commentary by other characters creates a type of presence analogous to the ruptures and displacement of African people to the western hemisphere, which engenders a re-creation of Africa more dynamic than the geopolitical space called Africa.

4. I am employing the concept of the reiterated self to refer to the African ontological impulse to recover the ethos, values, and mores of Africa in order to remain whole. This spiritual/cultural insistence subverts the force of white supremacy and its accompanying hegemonic practices, which insist upon fragmenting the African personality and disrupting liberation.

5. See Diedrich, Gates, and Pederson, eds., *Black Imagination and the Middle Passage*, 11.

6. See Lawal, *The Gelede Spectacle*. Lawal states that the Yoruba idea of *oju inu*, or inner eye, can be expressed as the ability to look beyond the present moment and therefore connotes the concept of intuitive imagination.

7. In a linear-defined reality, this return phase signals the completion of the epic journey. However, when situated in the African world, it also signals the beginning as the community receives new information to act upon. This is consistent with the importance of community survival within an African context.

8. The idea of flight is a recurring trope in African American literature documented in enslavement spirituals. Undergirding that belief is the hope of returning to Africa and being released from bondage and an abiding understanding of transmogrification or shape-shifting informed by a worldview that supports the notion of a person actually taking the form of a bird. For more examples of this cultural narrative see, *Drums and Shadows: Survival Studies among Georgia Coastal Negroes*, a 1940 publication by the Georgia Federal Writers' Project. In one of the many accounts of flying in the collection, a former enslaved African from Tin City, near Savannah, Georgia, recounts: "Duh ole folks use tuh tell as chillun duh story bout people dat flied off tuh Africa. I blieb um about flyin" (18). In "Suicidal Tendencies," Daniel Walker notes the coalescence of African notions of transmigration and the African American "preoccupation" with flight.

9. This is Toni Morrison's date of birth.

10. The return to Africa, a recurring mytheme, provides a fixed point for the symbolic return of the fully realized self. This repossessed self experiences a synthesis with the truncated parts of the personality in the return and becomes whole. Eliade discusses the importance of a fixed point or center being elemental to the "founding of the world." It is at this point, he argues, that the "real unveils itself and the world comes into existence" (*Sacred and the Profane* 63).

11. Pilate reminds Ruth of what Milkman had to endure in order to be born. She says, "He come in the world tryin to keep from getting killed" (140). Consistent with the heroic mytheme, which demarcates the arduous birth of the hero, Milkman has to "fight off castor oil, knitting needles, and being blasted with hot steam" (*Song of Solomon* 140).

12. In his review of Okpewho's *The Epic in Africa*, Kunene states, "every human society has a clear view of what constitutes the heroic, the epic the extraordinary" (552). Kunene calls for African scholars to note the parameters of this expressive behavior. Clearly the use of music, dance, and the heightened emphasis of the performance make definitive statements concerning the cultural specificity of the African epic.

13. In this analysis of *Song of Solomon*, the idea of folklore and African spiritual continuities are used coterminously. In *Long Black Song*, Baker notes that folklore stands at the "foundation of the Black literary tradition" (18). Although African spiritual continuities inform what would be known as folklore, I assert that a process of relexification occurred, which only changed the word and not the deep structure of meaning. That is folklore became the inclusive term to house concepts of African be-

lief, verbal significations, and traditions without referencing particular African spiritual traditions. I am conflating the two terms in order to not engage in a protracted discussion tangential to this present study.

14. See discussion of the significance of the woods in the essay on *The Bluest Eye* in this work.

15. While conducting research on spiritual technologies of the Bantu people of South Africa in July 2002, a Sangoma or traditional female priest informed me of the significance of feet as spiritual signs.

16. Morrison would repeat this idea of a building being untethered from its foundation in her seventh novel, *Paradise*. The significance of this idea concerns the notion of spiritual transcendence and is an indication of the spiritual status of the house's occupants.

17. In "Art or Accident: Yoruba Body Artists and Their Deity Ogun," Drewal notes that although *aye* and *orun* are distinct concepts, they are fluid and interpenetrable (257).

18. In a personal conversation with Iya Stephanie Weaver, a priest of Obatala in the Lukumi/Yoruba tradition, Weaver notes that feet—*elese meiji*—are the spiritual points for the Yoruba that are more reliable for establishing spiritual identity than even the physical face.

19. See discussion of *ebo* in the *Jazz* chapter.

20. See a lengthy discussion of the four moments of the sun or the *dikenga dia Kongo* in the preface to this study.

21. The subtitle, *Maneno ya melele,* is Kiswahili language, which I am employing to mean forever words or words of forever.

22. All word translations are from Turner's, *Africanisms in the Gullah Dialect*, 68.

23. Among the Dogon two multiday events occur: the *yingim* and the *danyim*, which are held annually to celebrate all the deaths that have occurred in the village during the year. See Davis, "Dogon Funerals," 68.

24. Milkman's leap into "Solomon's Leap" is described as being "As fleet and bright as a lodestar" (341). This exchange of energies balances out Pilate's death and repays the cosmic debt incurred by Solomon's flight and "abandonment" of Ryna and his twenty-one children. He does not leave a "body behind" like his great-grandfather. Instead, as a ritual interchange, he joins her in the spirit world, the world of Africa. This time he exchanges the authentic life that Pilate gave him for his true life. The stars for the Dogon are inspirited components of a dynamic whole among which there is a constant exchange of energies as they are concerned with the metaphysical and physical realities of the universe. See Griaule and Dieterlen, *Pale Fox*, 15.

Chapter 4. Dancing with Trees and Dreaming of Yellow Dresses: The Dilemma of Jadine in *Tar Baby*

1. All references to *Tar Baby* refer to the 1987 Penguin paperback edition and will consist of pagination in parenthetical format.

2. Although many sources refer to Oya and Oshun as two of the three wives of Shango, according to Iyalosa Oseye Mchawi, Obba Nani was Shango's only true wife.

3. In this collection titled, *Maternal Divinity Yemonja*, Weaver and Egbelade present eleven *ese*, or traditional stories, representing Yemonja, the Òrìsà who is considered to be "God the Mother" (xvi).

4. Ayé is the Yoruba word for earth. Fundamentally, the power of the earth is connected to the power of the Ajé—older women who have the ability to see through spiritual eyes.

5. See *Song of Solomon* for the significance of climbing rocks from the Dogon spiritual perspective.

Chapter 5. In(her)iting the Divine: (Consola)tions, Sacred (Convent)ions, and Mediations of the Spiritual In-between in *Paradise*

1. For this essay, all references to the novel are from the 1998 Knopf hardback edition of *Paradise* and will consist of pagination in parenthetical format.

2. In the preface of his book, *Myth, Literature and the African World*, Soyinka chides African people for accepting doctrines originating from cultural spaces outside themselves. He asserts that African people should check to see if they can elicit those ideas from their own cultural frames (xii).

3. Morrison begins this idea of racial indeterminacy in her short story, "Recitatif" (1991). In this story, Morrison encodes the assumptions, premises, and other determiners of racial identity in dialogue guiding readers to determine the racial identity of the characters. In order to make the determination, the readers have to read the signs and test them against the assumptions of race they bring to the text. Morrison argues that all American texts encode highly nuanced language loaded with racial, political, cultural, and gendered meaning.

4. In *Myth and Mind*, Birenbaum suggests that the division of the world into opposites creates opportunities of choice between the polarities (32).

5. This idea of two brothers shooting each other mirrors a Yoruba *odu*, or spiritual pattern, called *ejioco* whose metaphoric refrain is the "arrow between brothers." The number two represents the pattern for this *odu* and is also emblematic of Ibeji or twins within a Yoruba frame.

6. The "Disallowing" is the defining event in the construction of the family history of the townspeople of Haven and Ruby. The core experience of having been turned away by "the blue-eyed, gray-eyed men in good suits" (193) helped them to establish themselves as insiders and everyone else as outsiders. The nine patriarchs who established the town signify the Dogon's cosmological number of creation consisting of God, Amma, and the eight original ancestors of the Dogon creation.

7. The original motto affixed to the iron stove was, "Beware the Furrow of His Brow." Subsequently, to match the self-righteous attitudes of Ruby's inhabitants, who believed that the "hard-won heaven [was] defined by the absence of the unsaved, the unworthy, and the strange," the motto changes to "Be the Furrow of His Brow."

Finally, after the massacre of the women, the motto morphs into, "We are the Furrow of His Brow," indicating the displeasure of God concerning their actions.

8. In 2001, my Iyalosa and I visited several Dogon villages and witnessed the particular layouts of the various communities: Kani Kambole, Teli, Ende, Begnimatu, and Djiguibombo are all consistent with Griaule's description recorded in *Conversations with Ogotemmeli* and Griaule and Dieterlen's, *The Pale Fox*.

9. The concept of "8-rock" represents the coal-colored men of Ruby, who along with their descendants band together and form their own settlement, excluding other African Americans through the practice of intragroup discrimination. The name corresponds to the number of Dogon ancestors in the Dogon cosmology. Moreover, the number eight represents the number of men on the Dogon leadership council who act on behalf of the village. Additionally, there are eight symbolic seeds that represent the organization within the body of human beings realized as the microcosm of the world. The eight is derived by combining the four elements and the four cardinal directions (Griaule and Dieterlen 54).

10. From the Yoruba perspective, *abiku* refers to a child who is "born to die." For more information about this concept see, Okri, *The Famished Road*. See also, Soyinka, *Ake*. See also, Osundare, "The Poem as a Mytho-linguistic Event," in Jones, Durosimi, and Jones, eds., *Oral and Written Poetry in African Literature Today*. The space where *abiku* reside while they wait to take another body is in the interspace between the spirit world and the living. Sometimes they take long breaks between coming to earth and dying and remain in the in-between (Okri 5). Additionally, *abiku* children are marked by incisions to their flesh and piercings so their parents will recognize them when they return.

11. The Candomblé tradition of Brazil consists of representation from the following nations: the Nago/Ketu people of Nigeria, the Fon or Jeje people from Benin, the Kongo/Angola from the Bantu groups of Angola and the Democratic Republic of Kongo, and the indigenous people of Brazil—the Amerindians called Caboclo.

12. This female-centered focus of divinity was maintained in the Catholic structure, which has female saints and other female ideas of spiritual power, unlike the Protestant obliteration of the female spiritual presence. See, Lopes, "Sobrevincias e Recreacões Bantas no Rio de Janeiro," 69–75.

13. In a conversation with my Iyalosa (Godmother), Oseye Mchawi, Priest of Obatala, she mentions the idea of the protective nature of Oshun, Iyalode, and Yemonja—the Great mother, to safeguard and defend their children, all people. On another note, I see a parallel with the guarding of the Ibeji as an allegory for African people in the western hemisphere charged with the responsibility of keeping the living traditions of Africa alive. Sustained by the re-codifications and continued dynamic re-inventions, they safeguard what they cannot afford to forget so far removed from the geophysical space of continental Africa.

14. The narrator provides the discrepancy between the two versions of the story. In the first instance, the narrator passes judgment regarding the nature of cultural imposition by the Catholic nuns by calling the nuns' action a "kidnapping," while

Consolata, whose voice is indicated by the words *hurt* and *soil*, has an appreciation for her rescue and provides a different narrative.

15. Connie attempts to consecrate that unity when she bites Deacon's lip. Since she has been taught that the blood is the life, from a Catholic perspective her biting and licking of Deacon's blood is her attempt to sacralize their union (Holy Communion).

16. *Dogo so* is the Dogon word for language.

17. In *The Cultural Unity of Africa*, Diop notes the dissolution of the matriarch as a major cultural disruption that served as a precursor to the invasion of Africa by the Arabs—and subsequently the Europeans.

18. See Rocha, *Cadernos de Teologia Negra: Deus na Roda Com a Gente.*

19. See the discussion of Iyami Osoronga or Ajé in the chapters on *The Bluest Eye* and *Tar Baby* in this study.

20. In his essay titled "The Immortal Child," DuBois discusses America's disallowing in his rendering of the career of British musical genius, Samuel Coleridge-Taylor. He states that in America his talent "might never have been permitted to grow." He continues, "We know in America how to discourage, choke, and murder ability" (97). See DuBois, *Darkwater.*

Chapter 6. Living with the Dead: Memory and Ancestral Presence in *Beloved*

1. Morrison, *Beloved*, 274–75. Subsequent references to the novel refer to the 1987 Knopf hardcover edition and will consist of pagination in parenthetical format.

2. For African people, the necessity to acknowledge the "sixty million" is evident, especially when the suppressed memories transform into a denial of their own history. For instance, in Crouch's review of *Beloved* in the *New Republic*, he notes, "*Beloved* above all else, is a blackface holocaust" (40) and an "appropriation of a holocaust tale" (42). This anachronistic statement affirms the necessity for Morrison to tell the story of the "sixty million" or more. An African American, Crouch dismisses the validity of the African captivity experience in his reductive statement, "sixty is ten times six" (40). He intimates that Morrison has taken Jewish history and has attempted to trump it to elicit sympathy and to compete in a "big-time martyrs rating" (40). See also, Morrison, interview with Angelo, "The Pain of Being Black," 120–23. In this interview Morrison discusses the idea of "sixty million" as being a conservative estimate of the lives lost in the Middle Passage.

3. See the discussion of the concept of the "in-between" in *Paradise* in Chapter 5 of this book.

4. Russell notes, "The end is a constantly recurring theme" of apocalyptic writing. For him it is the end that gives meaning to the present and the past and in which all things, on heaven and earth and in heaven, will receive their deserved reward" (21–22).

5. This construction of time consists of time and space as well as accompanying events occurring in overlays, or the collapsing of time in three dimensions (past, present, and future). See a compilation of essays for a discussion of the complex

nature of time from a variety of African cultural perspectives. See Fu-Kiau, "Ntangu-Tanda-Kolo: The Concept of Time," 3–34, and Kokole, "Time, Identity, and Historical Consciousness in Akan," 35–77, in Adjaye, ed., *Time in the Experience*. See an extended discussion of the concept of Hantu in Jahn, *Muntu*, and Pennington, "Time in African Culture," in Asante and Asante, eds., *African Culture*, 123–39.

6. Morrison explains why she opens the novel in media res noting, "I wanted the compelling confusion of being there as they (the characters) are; suddenly, without comfort or succor from the 'author' with only imagination, intelligence, and necessity available for the journey" (33). The audience invited to participate with the heroes on their journey vicariously becomes a hero. See Morrison, "Unspeakable Things Unspoken," (33).

Chapter 7. Tracing Wild's Child Joe and Tracking the Hunter: An Examination of the Òrìsà Ochossi in *Jazz*

1. Epic, defined as a genre of literature, contains poetic language, is narrative, heroic, and uses legendary characterization. In addition, it is a multifunctional idea dealing with cultural and traditional transmission in a didactic fashion and embodies a multigenre approach including legends, genealogy, song, praise poems, and incantations. See Johnson, "Yes Virginia, There Is an Epic in Africa," 308–26.

2. For the discussion of human sacrifice throughout this chapter, I am using the Yoruba idea of *oluwo* or *oluo* as described by Awolalu. He notes the practice of human sacrifice before the arrival of the British before the nineteenth century. Awolalu explains that it was better to sacrifice one life for the good of the community than for all to perish. See Awolalu, *Yoruba Beliefs and Sacrificial Rites*, 168–69.

3. All references to *Jazz* are from the 1992 Knopf paperback edition and will consist of pagination in parenthetical format.

4. Fu-Kiau explains that the *muntu* is encircled by Buta (family); Moyo (the member's of the family from one's mother's descent); Mwelo-nzo (extended family); Kanda (community); Nsi (land, region, or country). All radiate outward and are bordered by the last circle, Nza, representing the universe (*African Cosmology* 41). See the chapter on *The Bluest Eye* for a more detailed explanation of this concept.

5. Among the Dogon there are seven initiation societies that correspond to the body's seven main joints: the ankles, the knees, the hips, the necks, the shoulders, the elbows, and the wrists.

6. Morrison is dismissive about the changes that white Americans have viewed as progress. For a discussion of how events of the 1960s influenced her fiction, see Jean Strouse's "Toni Morrison's Black Magic," 52–57.

7. I view the quality of the change-up as a way to culturally survive. The change-up quality becomes evident when other groups attempt to expropriate African world culture.

8. Joe's two-eyedness references his relationship to the Yoruba *odu ejioco*, the representational *odu* of the hunter deity.

9. Ijala chants are performed at gatherings or meetings of hunters. The purpose

of the chants is to salute and invoke the presence of Ogun, the patron deity of hunters. Ijala chants are performed at gatherings or meeting of hunters. See Babalola, "A Portrait of Ogun as Reflected in Ijala Chants," in Barnes, ed., *Africa's Ogun*, 147–72.

10. As part of his hunting arsenal, Ochossi is familiar with *ewe* (various plants and herbs including poison).

11. See the chapter on *Tar Baby* for a more extended discussion of these ideas.

12. In the nineteenth-century narrative, *Incidents in the Life of a Slave Girl*, Jacobs notes the presence of *minkisi* in her reference to the preacher's castigation of the enslaved African's practice of "tying up little bags of roots to bury under the door-steps to poison each other with" (69).

13. A looted people, our artifacts, too, have been expropriated. For some, *minkisi* are interesting nail-embedded souvenirs whose operative structures are dormant. Displayed in travelers' living rooms they have been turned into conversation items.

14. For more clarification, see the discussion of this idea in the *Song of Solomon* chapter in this book.

15. The Okeh record company was one of the first music publishing companies to record what was then called race music. They recorded blues and early R&B.

Chapter 8. If I'd a Knowed More, I Would a Loved More: Toni Morrison's *Love* and Spiritual Authorship

1. Resisting the imposition of hyphenation and the hybrid identity imposed by that "dash," I refer to African people in North America as African Americans, no hyphen, or African people in America.

2. See her commentary on the depiction of African people as background in the nihilistic figurations of European-American writers. Metonymically displaced, the presence of Africans provided an ontological space for Europeans to be self-fashioning. See Morrison, *Playing in the Dark*.

3. All references to the novel are from the 2003 Knopf hardback edition of *Love* and will consist of pagination in parenthetical format.

4. In the catalogue accompanying the Musée Dapper's 2002 exhibition, *Le Geste Kongo*, Thompson chronicles spiritual gestures such as the Kongo sign, called *booka* or *yangalala*. Described as holding one hand above the head, this gesture's purpose is to transport feelings of good will from one person to another. Thompson chronicles that the *booka* sign belongs to a Kongo spiritual society. With the fingers apart the gesture becomes spiritually charged and represents the rays of the sun. This particular sign is recognized and "signed" throughout the world. Moreover, two hands raised in this manner represent a level of spiritual possession. See Thompson, "Le Gestuelle Kongo," 177–78. See also Major, ed., *Juba to Jive*, 420. Major notes that the gesture originates in Africa and represents solidarity between men and serves as a compliment for an accomplishment.

5. I recall being at a Bernice Reagon concert when she began singing the hymn "Tis the Ole Ship of Zion." When the African women in the audience did not join in this communal performance, she chided them saying, "You better sing, or hum if

you don't know the words." Afterwards, she told the group that the song was one to remember, she continued, "Who knows, something might go down and this song might be the access code to get to safety."

6. This is both a reference to the nature of Bill Cosey's character and to the spiritually bankrupt behavior of his father, Daniel Robert Cosey, also known as DRC or "Dark."

7. The term *Ajé* not only refers to the concept of spiritually powerful women but also to the spiritual power itself. This power is resident in all women, but when developed signifies a select group of women. As women age, the power increases and engenders both fear and respect. Many Yoruba believe that the Ajé must be placated and offered propitiary sacrifices to gain their support. Often called *awon iya wa* (our mothers) in the Lukumi Yoruba spiritual tradition, they refer to these women as Iyami Osoronga and salute them in the *mojuba*, or prayers that proceed all ritual activities.

8. As Morrison's faithful readers, we never question why Junior sees herself in a tree. In Morrison's literary vistas, Junior's being positioned in a tree seems to be as natural an occurrence as saying she is walking.

9. The turtle is a familiar of the Òrìsà Sango. The significance of the number twelve has already been discussed in the chapter on *Tar Baby*. Additionally, the number twelve is represented by the *odu ejila*, whose refrain is "the soldier never sleeps," a reference to Sango's singular and unfailing ability to defend his devotees.

Works Cited

Adams, Edward C. L. *Tales of the Congaree*. 1927. Edited by Robert G. O'Meally. Chapel Hill: University of North Carolina Press, 1987.

Adjaye, Joseph K., ed. *Time in the Black Experience*. Westport, Conn.: Greenwood Press, 1994.

Ajuwon, Bade. "Ogun's Iremoje: A Philosophy of Living and Dying." In *Africa's Ogun: Old World and New*, edited by Sandra T. Barnes, 173–98. Bloomington: Indiana University Press, 1997.

Ani, Marimba. *Yurugu: African Centered Critique of European Cultural Thought and Behavior*. Trenton, N.J.: Africa World Press, 1994.

Ansberry, Clare. "Toni Morrison's Mom Recalls Storytelling Days in Lorain." *Lorain Journal*, January 12, 1982, 5:1.

Armah, Ayi Kwei. *Two Thousand Seasons*. London: Heinemann, 1979.

Awkward, Michael. "Negotiations of Power: White Critics, Black Texts, and the Self-Referential Impulse." *American Literary History* 2, no. 4 (1990): 581–606.

Awolalu, J. Omosade. *Yoruba Beliefs and Sacrificial Rites*. Brooklyn: Athelia Henrietta Press, 2001.

Babalola, S. A. *The Content and Form of Yoruba Ijala*. Oxford, Britain: Clarendon Press, 1966.

———. "A Portrait of Ogun as Reflected in Ijala Chants." In *Africa's Ogun: Old World and New*, edited by Sandra. T. Barnes, 147–72. Bloomington: Indiana University Press, 1997.

Baker, Houston A., Jr. *Long Black Song: Essays in Black American Literature and Culture*. Charlottesville: University of Virginia Press, 1990.

———. *Workings of the Spirit*. Chicago: University of Chicago Press, 1991.

Bakerman, Jane S. "Failures of Love: Female Initiation in the Novels of Toni Morrison." *American Literature* 52 (1981): 549.

Bambara, Toni Cade. *The Salt Eaters*. 1980. New York: Vintage, 1992.

Baraka, Amiri. *Blues People*. New York: Perennial, 1998.

Bell, Bernard W. *The Afro-American Novel and Its Tradition*. Amherst: University of Massachusetts Press, 1987.

Bell, Catherine. *Ritual Theory, Ritual Practice*. New York: Oxford University Press 1992.

Berry, Mary Frances, and John Blassingame. "Africa, Slavery and the Roots of Contemporary Black Culture." In *Chant of Saints*, edited by Michael S. Harper and Robert B. Stepto, 241–56. Chicago: University of Illinois Press, 1979.

———. *Long Memory: The Black Experience in America*. New York: Oxford University Press, 1982.

Bhabha, Homi K. *Nation and Narration*. New York: Routledge, 1990.

Biebuyck, Daniel P. "The African Heroic Epic." *Journal of the Folklore Institute* 13 (1979):18.

———. *Hero and Chief: Epic Literature from the Bayanga (Zaire Republic)*. Berkeley and Los Angeles: University of California Press, 1978.

Birenbaum, Harvey. *Myth and Mind*. Lanham, Md.: University of America Press, 1988.

Blackburn, Sara. "Sula." Review of *Sula* by Toni Morrison. *New York Times*, December 30, 1973, 3.

Blassingame, John W. *The Slave Community: Plantation Life in the Antebellum South*. 1972. New York: Oxford University Press, 1979.

Bloom, Harold, ed. *Modern Critical Views Toni Morrison*. New York: Chelsea, 1990.

Bockie, Simon. *Death and the Invisible Powers: The World of Kongo Belief*. Bloomington: Indiana University Press, 1993.

Bontemps, Arna. "A Black Man talks of Reaping." In *Cavalcade: Negro American Writing from 1760 to the Present*, edited by Arthur P. Davis and Saunders Redding, 332. Boston: Houghton Mifflin, 1971.

Bradshaw, John. *Bradshaw On: the Family: A Revolutionary Way of Self Discovery*. Deerfield Beach, Fla.: Health Community, 1988, 2. Quoted in Laurenti Magesa, *African Religion: The Moral Traditions of Abundant Life*, 170–71. Maryknoll, N.Y.: Orbis, 2002.

Brown, Ras M. "Walk in the Feenda: West-Central Africans and the Forest in the South Carolina-Georgia Lowcountry." In *Central Africans and Cultural Transformations in the American Diaspora*, edited by Linda M. Heywood, 289–317. New York: Cambridge University Press, 2002.

Byerman, Keith. "Beyond Realism." In *Toni Morrison: Critical Perspectives Past and Present*, edited by Henry Louis Gates Jr. and K. Anthony Appiah, 100–125. New York: Amistad, 1993.

Campbell, Jane. *Mythic Black Fiction: The Transformation of History*. Knoxville: University of Tennessee Press, 1986.

Chernoff, John Miller. *African Rhythm and African Sensibility: Aesthetics and Social Action in African Musical Idioms*. Chicago: University of Chicago Press, 1981.

Christian, Barbara. *Black Women Novelists: The Development of a Tradition*. Westport, Conn.: Greenwood Press, 1980.

———. "Somebody Forgot To Tell Somebody Something: African-American Women's Historical Novels." In *Wild Women in the Whirlwind: Afra-American Culture and the Contemporary Literary Renaissance*, edited by Joanne M. Braxton and Andree Nicola McLaughlin, 326–41. New Brunswick: Rutgers University Press, 1990.

Chukwunyere, Kamalu. *Person, Divinity, and Nature: A Modern View of the Person and the Cosmos in African Thought*. Lawrenceville, N.J.: Red Sea Press, 1988.

Clarke, John Henrik. "Pan-Africanism: A Brief History of an Idea in the African World." In *Presence Africaine*, 26–37, 1988.

Clemons, Walter. "A Gravestone of Memories." *Newsweek*, September 28, 1987, 74–75.

Cloke, Paul, and Owain Jones. *Uprootings/Regroundings: Questions of Home and Migration*. New York: Berger, 2003.

Coleman, Will. *Tribal Talk: Black Theology, Hermeneutics and African/American Ways of "Telling the Story."* University Park: Pennsylvania University Press, 2000.

Conrad, Joseph. *Heart of Darkness*. 1902. New York: Dover, 1990.

Creel, Margaret Washington. "Gullah Attitudes Toward Life and Death." In *Africanisms in American Culture*, edited by Joseph E. Holloway, 69–97. Bloomington: Indiana University Press, 1992.

———. *A Peculiar People: Slave Religion and Community-Culture among the Gullahs*. New York: New York University Press, 1988.

Crouch, Stanley. Review of *Beloved* by Toni Morrison. *New Republic* 19 (October 1987): 38–43.

Cullen, Countee. "Heritage." In *The Vintage Book of African American Poetry*, edited by Michael S. Harper and Anthony Walton. New York: Vintage, 2000.

Curtin, Phillip D. *The Atlantic Slave Trade: A Census*. Madison: University of Wisconsin Press, 1969.

Davis, Cynthia A. "Self, Society, and Myth in Toni Morrison's Fiction." In *Modern Critical Views Toni Morrison*, edited by Harold Bloom, 7–25. New York: Chelsea, 1990.

Davis, Shawn R. "Dogon Funerals." *African Arts* 35, no. 2 (Summer 2002): 67–77.

Diop, Cheikh Anta. *The Cultural Unity of Africa*. 1959. Chicago: Third World Press, 1978.

Diop, Yande Christiane. Foreword. *The Surreptitious Speech: Presence Africaine and the Politics of Otherness, 1947–1987*, edited by V. Y. Mudimbe. Chicago: University of Chicago Press, 1992.

Drewal, Henry John. "Art or Accident: Yoruba Body Artists and Their Deity Ogun." In *Africa's Ogun: Old World and New*, edited by Sandra T. Barnes, 235–60. Bloomington: Indiana University Press, 1997.

Drewal, Henry John, and Margaret Thompson Drewal. *Gelede: Art and Female Power among the Yoruba*. Bloomington: Indiana University Press, 1990.

Drewal, Henry John, Margaret Thompson Drewal, and John Mason, eds. "Ogun and Body/Mind Potentiality: Yoruba Scarification and Painting Traditions in Africa and the Americas." In *Africa's Ogun: Old World and New*, edited by Sandra T. Barnes, 332–52. Bloomington: Indiana University Press, 1997.

Drewal, Henry John, Margaret Thompson Drewal, John Pemberton III, and Roland Abiodun, eds. *Nine Centuries of African Art and Thought*. New York: Henry Abrams, 1989.

Drewal, Margaret Thompson. *Yoruba Ritual: Performers, Play, Agency*. Bloomington: Indiana University Press, 1992.

DuBois, W.E.B. *Darkwater: Voices from within the Veil*, edited by Henry Louis Gates Jr. The Oxford W.E.B. DuBois Series. New York: Oxford University Press, 2007.

———. *The Souls of Black Folk*. 1903. New York: Penguin, 1982.

Duerden, Dennis. *The Invisible Present: African Art and Literature*. New York: Harper and Row, 1971.

Dumas, Henry. *Goodbye Sweetwater: New and Selected Stories*, edited by Eugene B. Redmond. New York: Thunder's Mouth Press, 1988.

———. "Rites." In *Knees of a Natural Man: The Selected Poetry of Henry Dumas*, edited by Eugene B. Redmond, 5–6. New York: Thunder's Mouth Press, 1989.

———."Root Song." In *In Search of Color Everywhere: A Collection of African-American Poetry*, edited by E. Ethelbert Miller, 15. New York: Stewart, Tabori and Chang, 1994.

Eliade, Mircea. *The Myth of the Eternal Return, or Cosmos and History*. 1954. Translated by Willard R. Trask. Bollingen Series, no. 44. Princeton, N.J.: Princeton University Press, 1971.

———. *The Sacred and the Profane: The Nature of Religion*. 1959. Translated by Willard R. Trask. New York: Harcourt, 1987.

Ellison, Ralph. *Invisible Man*. New York: Signet, 1952.

———. *Shadow and Act*. New York: Vintage, 1972.

Evans, Mari, ed. *Black Women Writers (1950–1980): A Critical Evaluation*. Garden City, N.Y.: Anchor, 1984.

Fabre, Geneviève. "The Slave Ship Dance." In *Black Imagination and the Middle Passage*, edited by Maria Diedrich, Henry Louis Gates Jr., and Carl Pedersen, 33–46. New York: Oxford University Press, 1999.

Fabre, Geneviève, and Robert O'Meally, eds. *History and Memory in African American Culture*. New York: Oxford University Press, 1994.

Fanon, Frantz. *Black Skin, White Masks*. New York: Grove Press, 1968.

———. *The Wretched of the Earth*. Translated by Constance Farrington. New York: Grove, 1968.

Ferreira, Anthony. *Eshu*. New York: Athelia Henrietta Press, 2000.

Frye, Northrup. *Anatomy of Criticism*. Princeton, N.J.: Princeton University Press, 1973.

Fu-Kiau, Bunseki K. *African Cosmology of the Bantu-Kongo: Principles of Life and Living*. Brooklyn: Athelia Henrietta Press, 2001.

———. "Ntangu-Tanda-Kolo: The Concept of Time." In *Time in the Black Experience*, edited by Joseph K. Adjaye, 3–34. New York: Greenwood Press, 1994.

———. *Self-Healing, Power, and Therapy: Old Teachings From Africa*. New York: Vantage, 1993.

Gaines, Ernest J. *The Autobiography of Miss Jane Pittman*. New York: Bantam, 1971.

Gates, Henry Louis, Jr. *The Signifying Monkey: A Theory of African-American Literary Criticism*. New York: Oxford University Press, 1987.

Gbadegesin, Segun. *African Philosophy: Traditional Yoruba Philosophy and Contemporary African Realities*. New York: Peter Lang, 1991.

Georgia Federal Writers' Project. *Drums and Shadows: Survival Studies among Georgia Coastal Negroes.* 1940. Athens: University of Georgia Press, 1986.

Gleason, Judith. *Oya: In Praise of an African Goddess.* New York: HarperCollins, 1987.

Gomez, Michael A. *Exchanging Our Country Marks: The Transformation of African Identities in the Colonial and Antebellum South.* Chapel Hill: University of North Carolina Press, 1998.

Griaule, Marcel. *Conversations with Ogotemmeli: An Introduction to Dogon Religious Ideas.* London: Oxford University Press, 1970.

Griaule, Marcel, and Germaine Dieterlen. *The Pale Fox.* 1965. Translated by Stephen C. Infantino. Chino Valley, Ariz.: Continuum, 1986.

Grimes, Ronald L. *Beginnings in Ritual Studies.* London: University Press of America, 1982.

Grossberg, Lawrence. "The Space of Culture, The Power of Space." In *The Post-colonial Question: Common Skies, Divided Horizons,* edited by Iain Chambers and Lidia Curti, 169–88. London: Routledge, 1996.

Gundaker, Grey, ed. *Keep Your Head to the Sky: Interpreting African American Home Ground.* Charlottesville: University of Virginia Press, 1998.

Gyekye, Kwame. *Tradition and Modernity: Philosophical Reflections on the African Experience.* New York: Oxford University Press, 1997.

Hall, Julien. "Negro Conjuring and Tricking." *The Journal of American Folklore* 10, no.3 (1897): 241–43.

Hallen, Barry. *The Good, the Bad, and the Beautiful: Discourse about Values in Yoruba Culture.* Bloomington: Indiana University Press, 2000.

Harris, Trudier. *Fiction and Folklore: The Novels of Toni Morrison.* Knoxville: University of Tennessee Press, 1991.

Hernton, Calvin. *Sex and Racism in America.* New York: Grove Press, 1988.

Heywood, Linda M., ed. *Central Africans and Cultural Transformations in the American Diaspora.* New York: Cambridge University Press, 2002.

Hogue, W. Lawrence. "Literary Production: A Silence in Afro-American Critical Practice." In *Within the Circle: An Anthology of African-American Literary Criticism from the Harlem Renaissance to the Present,* edited by Angelyn Mitchell, 329–47. Durham: Duke University Press, 1994.

Holloway, Joseph E., ed. Introduction to *Africanisms in American Culture.* Bloomington: Indiana University Press, 1990.

hooks, bell. *Yearning: Race, Gender, and Politics.* Boston: South End, 1990.

Horvitz, Deborah. "Nameless Ghosts: Possession and Dispossession in *Beloved.*" *Studies in American Fiction* 17, no. 2 (1989): 157–68.

Hughes, Langston. "Jukebox Love Song." In *The Collected Poems of Langston Hughes.* New York: Vintage, 1995.

Idowu, E. Bolaji. *Olodumare: God in Yoruba Belief.* New York: A&B Books, 1994.

Jacobs, Harriet. *Incidents in the Life of a Slave Girl,* edited by Jean Fagan Yellin. Cambridge: Harvard University Press, 1987.

Jahn, Janheinz. *Muntu: African Culture and the Western World*. New York: Grove Weidenfeld, 1961.

Johnson, John W. "Yes Virginia, There Is an Epic in Africa." *Research in African Literatures* 11 (Fall 1980): 308–26.

Jones, Le Roi (Amiri Baraka). *Blues People: The Negro Music in White America*. New York: William Morrow, 1963.

Jung, C. G., and C. Kerenji. *Introduction to a Science of Mythology*. Translated by R.F.C. Hull. London: Routledge and Kegan Paul, 1970.

Kokole, Omari H. "Time, Identity, and Historical Consciousness in Akan." In *Time in the Black Experience*, edited by Joseph K. Adjaye, 35–77. New York: Greenwood Publishing Group, 1994.

Kunene, Mazisi. "Toward a Poetics of the Oral Performance." Review of *The Epic of Africa* by Isidore Okpewho. *Research in African Literatures* 11 (1980): 552–57.

Landes, Ruth. *The City of Women*. Albuquerque: University of New Mexico Press, 1994.

Lawal, Babatunde. *The Gelede Spectacle: Art, Gender, and Social Harmony in an African Culture*. Seattle: University of Washington Press, 1996.

Levine, Lawrence W. *Black Culture and Black Consciousness: Afro-American Folk Thought from Slavery to Freedom*. New York: Oxford University Press, 1977.

Lopes, Nei. "Sobrevincias e Recreacões Bantas no Rio de Janeiro." *Estudos Afro-Asiáticos* 15: 69–75.

Lyotard, Jean-Francois. "The Post Modern Condition: A Report on Knowledge." 1979. In *Theory and History of Literature*, translated by Geoff Bennington and Brian Massumi. Minneapolis: University of Minnesota Press, 1984.

MacGaffey, Wyatt. "The Eyes of Understanding: Kongo Minkisi." In *Astonishment and Power*, edited by Wyatt MacGaffey and Michael D. Harris, 21–103. Washington, D.C.: National Museum of African Art, 1994.

———. *Kongo Political Culture: The Conceptual Challenge of the Particular*. Bloomington: Indiana University Press, 2000.

———. *Religion and Society in Central Africa: The BaKongo of Lower Zaire*. Chicago: University of Chicago Press, 1986.

———. "Twins, Simbi Spirits, and Lwas in Kongo and Haiti." In *Central Africans and Cultural Transformations in the American Diaspora*, edited by Linda M. Heywood, 211–26. New York: Cambridge University Press, 2002.

Magesa, Laurenti. *African Religion: The Moral Traditions of Abundant Life*. Maryknoll, N.Y.: Orbis, 2002.

Major, Clarence, ed. *Juba to Jive: A Dictionary of African American Slang*. New York: Penguin, 1994.

Maloney, Clarence, ed. *The Evil Eye*. New York: Columbia University Press, 1976.

Martin, Jacky. "From Division to Sacrificial Reconciliation in Toni Morrison's Novels." *Obsidian II* 2, no. 5 (1990): 80–99.

Mason, John, and Gary Edwards, eds. *Black Gods: Òrìsà Studies in the New World*. Brooklyn: Yoruba Theological Archministry, 1985.

———. *Four New World Yoruba Rituals*. Brooklyn: Yoruba Theological Archministry, 1985.

———. *Idana Fun Òrìsà: Cooking for Selected Heads*. Brooklyn: Yoruba Theological Archministry, 1999.

———. *Orin Òrìsà: Songs for Selected Heads*. Brooklyn: Yoruba Theological Archministry, 1992.

Maus, Marcel. *The Category of the Person*. Translated by W. D. Halls. Edited by Michael Carrithers, Steven Collins, and Steven Lukes. Cambridge: Cambridge University Press, 1985.

Mbiti, John S. *African Religion and Philosophy*. London: Heinemann, 1969.

———. Introduction to *African Religion and Philosophy*. 2nd rev. ed. London: Heinemann, 1991.

McCauley, Robert N., and E. Thomas Lawson. *Bringing Ritual to Mind: Psychological Foundations of Cultural Forms*. London: Cambridge University Press, 2002.

McDowell, Deborah E. "The Self and the Other: Reading Toni Morrison's *Sula* and the Black Female Text." In *Critical Essays on Toni Morrison*, edited by Nellie McKay, 77–89. Boston: G. K. Hall, 1988.

Mchawi, Oseye. Personal communication. December 2005.

Memmi, Albert. *The Colonizer and the Colonized*. New York: Orion Press, 1965.

Mintz, Sidney W., and Richard Price. *The Birth of African American Culture: An Anthropological Perspective*. Boston: Beacon Press, 1976.

Mobolade, Timothy. "The Concept of Abiku." *African Arts* 7, no.1 (Autumn 1973): 62–64.

Moffett, Ida. Introduction to *The Pale Fox*, by Marcel Griaule and Germaine Dieterlen. 1965. Translated by Stephen C. Infantino. Chino Valley, Ariz.: Continuum, 1986.

Morrison, Toni. Afterword to *The Bluest Eye*. 1970. New York: Plume, 1993.

———. *Beloved*. New York: Knopf, 1987.

———. "Behind the Making of The Black Book." *Black World* 23 (February 1974): 86–90.

———. "Black Woman Women's Lib." *New York Times Magazine*, August 23, 1971, p. 63.

———. *The Bluest Eye*. 1970. New York: Plume, 1994.

———. "Home." In *The House That Race Built*, edited by Lubiano Wahneema. New York: Vintage 1998.

———. "Lecture and Speech of Acceptance upon the Award of the Nobel Prize for Literature." Stockholm. December 19, 1993. New York: Knopf, 2000.

———. "The Pain of Being Black." Interview with Bonnie Angelo. *Time*, May 22, 1989, 120–23.

———. *Conversations with American Writers*. Interview with Charles Ruas. New York: McGraw Hill, 1984. Reprinted in *Conversations with Toni Morrison*, edited by Danille Taylor Guthrie, 93–118. Jackson: University Press of Mississippi, 1994.

———. *Presence Africaine*. Interview with Christina Davis. *Presence Africaine: Revue*

Culturelle Du Monde/ Cultural Review of The Negro World 1145. 1988: 141–50. Reprinted in *Conversations with Toni Morrison*, edited by Danille Taylor Guthrie, 223–33. Jackson: University Press of Mississippi, 1994.

———. "Toni Morrison." Interview with Diana Cooper-Clark. In *Interviews with Contemporary Novelists*, edited by Diana Cooper-Clark, 191–211. New York: St. Martin, 1986.

———. "The Seams Can't Show: An Interview with Toni Morrison." Interview with Jane Bakerman. *Black American Literature Forum* 12.2 (Summer 1978): 56–60. Reprinted in *Conversations with Toni Morrison*, edited by Danille Taylor Guthrie. Jackson: University Press of Mississippi, 1994.

———. "In the Realm of Responsibility: A Conversation with Toni Morrison." Interview with Marsha Darling. *Women's Review of Books* 5 (March 1978): 5–6. Reprinted in *Conversations with Toni Morrison*, edited by Danille Taylor-Guthrie, 246–54. Jackson: University Press of Mississippi, 1994.

———. "An Interview with Toni Morrison." Interview with Nellie McKay. *Contemporary Literature* 24, no. 4 (1983): 413–26.

———. "The Language Must Not Sweat: A Conversation with Toni Morrison." Interview with Thomas LeClair. In *Toni Morrison: Critical Perspectives Past and Present*, edited by Henry Louis Gates Jr. and Kwame Anthony Appiah, 369–77. New York: Amistad, 1993.

———. *Jazz*. New York: Knopf, 1992.

———. *Love*. New York: Knopf, 2003.

———. "Memory, Creation, and Writing." *Thought* 59 (1984): 385–90.

———. *Paradise*. New York: Knopf 1998.

———. *Playing in the Dark: Whiteness in the Literary Imagination*. New York: Knopf, 1990.

———."Recitatif." In *The Norton Anthology of American Lierature*, Shorter 7th edition, edited by Nina Baym, 1461–75.

———. "Rediscovering Black History." *New York Times Magazine* 11 (August 1974): 14–18.

———. "Rootedness: The Ancestor as Foundation." In *Black Women Writers (1950–1980): A Critical Evaluation*, edited by Mari Evans, 339–45. New York: Anchor Books, 1984.

———. "A Slow Walk of Trees (As Grandmother Would Say), Hopeless (As Grandfather Would Say)." *New York Times Magazine*, July 4, 1976, 104.

———. "The Site of Memory." In *Out There: Marginilization and Contemporary Cultures*, edited by Feruson et al., 299–306. Cambridge: Massachusetts Institute of Technology, 1990.

———. *Song of Solomon*. New York: American Library, 1977.

———. *Sula*. 1973. New York: Plume, 1987.

———. *Tar Baby*. New York: Penguin, 1987.

———. "Unspeakable Things Unspoken: The Afro-American Presence in American Literature." *Michigan Quarterly Review* 28 (1989): 1–34.

Mudimbe, V. Y. *The Invention of Africa: Gnosis, Philosophy, and the Order of Knowledge*. Bloomington: Indiana University Press, 1988.

Murphy, Eddie. "James Thunder Early." In *Dreamgirls*. Directed by Bill Condon. Performed by Jamie Foxx, Beyoncé Knowles, Eddie Murphy, and Jennifer Hudson. Dreamworks and Paramount Pictures, 2006.

Murray, Albert. *The Hero and the Blues*. University of Missouri Press, 1973.

Mutwa, Credo V. *My People*. London: Penguin, 1971.

Nascimento, Abdias Do. "Padê De Exu Libertador" In *Orixás: Os Deuses Vivos Da África*, 13–18. Rio de Janiero: IPEAFRO/Afrodiaspora, 1995.

Neal, Larry. "The Black Arts Movement." In *Visions of Liberated Future: Black Arts Movement Writings*, edited by Michael Schwartz, 62–78. New York: Thunder's Mouth Press, 1989.

———. "Fragments from the Narrative of the Black Magicians." In *Hoodoo Hollerin' Bebop Ghosts*. 1968. Washington, D.C.: Howard University Press, 1974.

Needham, Rodney. *Symbolic Classification*. Santa Monica: Goodyear 1979.

Niane, Djibril Tamsir. *Sundiata: An Epic of Old Mali*. 1965. Translated by G. D Pickett. New York: Addison-Wesley, 1995.

Nicolaisen, F. H. "Names and Narratives." *Journal of American Folklore* 97, no. 385 (1984): 259–72. March 16, 2005. *Questia.com*. www.questia.com/search.

Nora, Pierre. "Between Memory and History: Les Lieux de Mémoire." In *History and Memory in African-American Culture*, edited by Geneviève Fabre and Robert O'Meally, 284–300. New York: Oxford University Press, 1994.

Nzegwu, Nkira. "Art as Time-Lines: Sacral Representation in Family Spaces." In *Sacred Spaces and Public Quarrels: African Cultural and Economic Landscapes*, edited by Ezekial Kalipeni and Paul T. Zeleza, 172–95. Trenton, N.J.: Africa World Press, 1999.

Oduyoye, Mercy A. *Hearing and Knowing: Theological Reflections on Christianity in Africa*. New York: Orbis, 1986.

Ogunbile, David O. "Eerindilogun: The Sacred Shells and Stones." In *Osun across the Waters: A Yoruba Goddess in Africa and the Americas*, edited by Joseph M. Murray and Mei Mei Sanford, 189–212. Bloomington: Indiana University Press, 2001.

Ogunyemi, Chikwenye Okonjo. "An Abiku-Ogbanje Atlas: A Pre-Text for Rereading Soyinka's *Ake* and Morrison's *Beloved*. African American Review 36 (2002): 663-73.

———. "Sula: A Nigger Joke." *Black American Literature Forum* 12 (1979): 130–33.

Okpewho, Isidore. *African Oral Literature: Backgrounds, Character, and Continuity*. Bloomington: Indiana University Press, 1992.

———. "The Anthropologist Looks at Epic." *Research in African Literatures* 11 (1988): 429–48.

———. *The Epic in Africa: Toward a Poetics of the Oral Performance*. New York: Columbia University Press, 1979.

Okri, Ben. *The Famished Road*. New York: Anchor, 1991.

Olatunji, Olatunde O. "The Yoruba Oral Poet and his Society." *Research in African Literatures* 10, no. 2 (1979): 179–207.

Olupona, Jacob K., ed. *African Spirituality: Forms, Meanings, and Expressions.* New York: Crossroad Publishing, 2000.

Osofsky, Gilbert, ed. *Puttin' On Ole Massa: The Slave Narratives of Henry Bibb, William Wells Brown, and Solomon Northrup.* New York: Harper and Row, 1969.

Osundare, Niyi. "The Poem as a Mytho-linguistic Event: A Study of Soyinka's 'Abiku.'" In *Oral and Written Poetry in African Literature Today*, edited by Eldrid Jones, Eustace Palmer Durosimi, and Marjorie Jones. Trenton, N.J.: Africa World Press, 1989.

Otten, Terry. *The Crime of Innocence in the Fiction of Toni Morrison.* Columbia: University of Missouri Press, 1989.

Page, Philip. *Reclaiming Community in Contemporary African American Fiction.* Jackson: University of Mississippi Press, 1999.

Painter, Nell Irvin. *Creating Black Americans: History and Its Meanings, 1619 to the Present.* Oxford: Oxford University Press, 2006.

———. *Sojourner Truth: A Life, a Symbol.* New York: W. W. Norton, 1996.

Patterson, Orlando. *Rituals of Blood: Consequences of Slavery in Two American Centuries.* New York: Basic Civitas Books, 1998.

Peel, J.D.Y. *Religious Encounter and the Making of the Yoruba.* Bloomington: Indiana University Press, 2003.

Pennington, Dorothy L. "Time in African Culture." In *African Culture: The Rhythms of Unity*, edited by Molefi K. Asante and Kariamu Welsh Asante, 123–39. Trenton, N.J.: Africa World Press, 1990.

Pryse, Marjorie. "Pattern against the Sky: Deism and Motherhood in Anne Petry's 'The Street.'" In *Conjuring: Black Women, Fiction, and Literary Tradition*, edited by Marjorie Pryse and Hortense Spillers, 116–31. Bloomington: Indiana University Press, 1985.

Raboteau, Albert J. *Slave Religion: The Invisible Institution in the Antebellum South.* New York: Oxford University Press, 1978.

Ray, Benjamin C. *African Religion, Symbol, Ritual, and Community.* Englewood Cliffs, N.J.: Prentice Hall, 1976.

Redmond, Eugene. Telephone interview. October 10, 1993.

Reed, Ishmael, ed. *19 Necromancers from Now.* New York: Doubleday, 1970.

———. *Mumbo Jumbo.* New York: Atheneum, 1988.

Richards, Donna Marimba. *Let the Circle Be Unbroken: The Implications of African Spirituality in the Diaspora.* Trenton, N.J.: Africa World Press, 1989.

Roberts, John W. *From Trickster to Badman: The Black Folk Hero in Slavery and Freedom.* Philadelphia: University of Pennsylvania Press, 1998.

Roberts, Mary Nooter, and Allen F. Roberts. *Memory: Luba Art and the Making of History.* New York: Museum for African Art, 1996.

Rocha, Geraldo. *Cadernos de Teologia Negra: Deus na Roda Com a Gente.* Rio de Janeiro: Pilar, 1994.

Rodrigues, Eusebio L. "The Telling of *Beloved*." *Journal of Narrative Technique* 21 (1991): 153–69.

Russell, D. S. *Apocalyptic: Ancient and Modern*. Philadelphia: Fortress, 1978.

Samuels, Wilfred D., and Clenora Hudson Weems. *Toni Morrison*. Boston: Twayne, 1990.

Schechner, Richard. "Ritual in/and Performance Studies." Unpublished seminar materials. Faculty Resource Network. New York: New York University, June 1998.

Segy, Ladislas. *African Sculpture Speaks*. New York: De Capo Press, 1969.

Seydou, Christiane. "A Few Reflections on Narrative Structures of Epic Texts: A Case Example of Bambara and Fulani Epics." Translated by Brunhilde Biebuyck. *Research in African Literatures* 14 (1983): 312–31.

Silva, Jacimar. *Todos os Segredos de Oxum*. Rio de Janeiro: Technoprint, 1995.

Somé, Patrice Malidoma. *The Healing Wisdom of Africa: Finding Life Purpose through Nature, Ritual, and Community*. New York: Tarcher, 1998.

———. *Of Water and the Spirit: Ritual, Magic, and Initiation in the Life of an African Shaman*. New York: Putnam, 1994.

Soyinka, Wole. *Ake: The Years of Childhood*. London: Heinemann, 1981.

———. "Gods, Knowledge, and Modernity." UNCF Mellon Faculty Seminar. Goree Institute, Dakar, Senegal. July 19, 2002.

———. *Myth, Literature and the African World*. New York: Cambridge University Press, 1976.

———. "Theatre in African Traditional Cultures: Survival Patterns." In *Death and the King's Horseman*, edited by Simon Gikandi, 89–103. New York: Norton, 2003.

Smith, Barbara. "Toward a Black Feminist Criticism." In *The New Feminist Criticism*, edited by Elaine Showalter. New York: Pantheon, 1985.

Smith, Valerie. *Self-Discovery and Authority in Afro-American Narrative*. Cambridge, Mass.: Harvard University Press, 1987.

Stein, Karen F. "Toni Morrison's *Sula*: A Black Women's Epic." *Black American Literature Forum* 18 (1984): 146–50.

Stewart, Carlyle F., III. *Black Spirituality and Black Consciousness: Soul Force, Culture and Freedom in the African-American Experience*. Trenton, N.J.: Africa World Press, 1999.

Strouse, Jean. "Toni Morrison's Black Magic." *Newsweek* 97 (March 1981): 52–71.

Stuckey, Sterling. *Slave Culture: Nationalist Theory and the Foundations of Black America*. New York: Oxford University Press, 1981.

Sullivan, Brenda. *Spirit of the Rocks*. Cape Town: Humdu and Rousseau, 1995.

Sweet, James H. *Recreating Africa: Culture, Kinship, and Religion in the African-Portuguese World, 1441–1770*. Chapel Hill: University of North Carolina Press, 2003.

Tate, Claudia, ed. *Black Writers at Work*. New York: Continuum, 1988.

Thomas, H. Nigel. *From Folklore to Fiction: A Study of Folk Heroes and Rituals in the Black American Novel*. Contributions in Afro-American and African Studies, no. 118. New York: Greenwood Press, 1988.

Thompson, Robert Farris. *Face of the Gods: Arts and Altars of Africa and the African Americas*. New York: Museum for African Art, 1993.

———. *Flash of the Spirit: African and Afro-American Art and Philosophy*. New York: Vintage, 1984.

Thompson, Robert Farris, and Joseph Cornet. *Four Moments of the Sun: Congo Art in two Worlds*. Washington, D.C.: National Gallery of Art, 1983.

———. "Kongo Influences on African American Artistic Culture." In *Africanisms in American Culture*, edited by Joseph Holloway, 148–84. Bloomington: Indiana University Press, 1990.

———. "Le Gestuelle Kongo." *Le Geste Kongo*. Translation by Nathalie Laverroux et Valerie Merlot. Paris: Musee Dapper, 2002.

———. "Siras Bowens of Sunbury, Georgia: A Tidewater Artist in the Afro-American Visual Tradition." In *Chant of Saints*, edited by Michael S. Harper and Robert B. Stepto, 230–40. Chicago: University of Illinois Press, 1979.

Thornton, John. *Africa and Africans in the Making of the Atlantic World, 1400–1800*. New York: Cambridge University Press, 1998.

Tobin, Jacqueline L., and Raymond G. Dobard. *Hidden in Plain View: A Secret Story of Quilts and the Underground Railroad*. New York: Anchor, 2000.

Toomer, Jean. *Cane*. 1923. New York: Liveright, 1975.

Turner, Darwin T. Introduction to *Cane*, by Jean Toomer, ix–xxv. New York: Liveright, 1975.

Turner, Lorenzo Dow. *Africanisms in the Gullah Dialect*. 1949. Ann Arbor: University of Michigan Press, 1973.

Turner, Victor. *The Forest of Symbols: Aspects of Ndembu Ritual*. Ithaca, N.Y.: Cornell University Press, 1967.

———. "Liminality and Communitas." In *The Ritual Process: Structure and Anti-Structure*. Chicago: Aldine, 1969.

Van Gennep, Arnold. 1908. *Rites of Passage*. Chicago: University of Chicago Press, 1960.

Waliggo, John Mary. Foreword to *African Religion: The Moral Traditions of Abundant Life*, by Laurenti Magesa. Maryknoll, N.Y.: Orbis, 2002.

Walker, Alice. *In Search of Our Mothers' Gardens*. New York: Harcourt Brace Jovanovich, 1983.

Walker, Daniel E. "Suicidal Tendencies: African Transmigration in the History and Folklore of the Americas. *Griot* 18, no. 2(1999): 10–18.

Walker, Margaret Alexander. "We Have Been Believers." In *This Is My Century: New and Collected Poems*. Athens: University of Georgia Press, 1989.

Walker, Sheila S. "Are You Hip to the Jive? (Re)Writing/Righting the Pan-American Discourse: African Roots/American Cultures." In *Africa in the Creation of the Americas*, edited by Sheila S. Walker, 1–44. New York: Rowman and Littlefield Publishers, 2001.

Washington, Margaret, ed. Introduction to *Narrative of Sojourner Truth*. New York: Vintage Classics, 1993.

Washington, Teresa N. *Our Mothers, Our Powers, Our Texts: Manifestations of Ajé in African Literature.* Bloomington: Indiana University Press, 2005.

Wa Thiongo, Ngugi. *Writers in Politics.* London: Heinemann, 1981.

Weaver, Lloyd, and Olukunmi Egbelade. *Maternal Divinity Yemonja: Tranquil Seas Turbulent Tides.* New York: Athelia Henrietta Press, 1999.

Weaver, Stephanie Thomas. Personal communication. January 2007.

Welsing, Frances Cress. *The Isis Papers: The Keys to the Colors.* Chicago: Third World Press, 1991.

West, Cornell. Lecture given at Wesleyan University, May 1988. Quoted in *History and Memory in African American Culture*, edited by Geneviève Fabre and Robert O'Meally, 3. New York: Oxford University Press, 1994.

Wheatley, Phillis. "On Being Brought from Africa to America." In *The Collected Works of Phillis Wheatley*, edited by John Shields. New York: Oxford University Press, 1988.

Wilson, Amos. *The Falsification of Afrikan Consciousness: Eurocentric History, Psychiatry, and the Politics of White Supremacy.* New York: Afrikan World InfoSystems, 1993.

Wiredu, Kwasi. *Cultural Universals and Particulars: An African Perspective.* Bloomington: Indiana University Press, 1996.

Work, John W., ed. *American Negro Songs and Spirituals.* New York: Bonanza Books, 1940.

Zauditu-Selassie, Kokahvah. "I Got a Home in Dat Rock: Memory, Òrìsà, and Yoruba Spiritual Identity in African American Literature." In *Orisa: Yoruba Gods and Spiritual Identity in Africa and the African Diaspora*, edited by Toyin Falola and Ann Genova, 367–84. Trenton, N.J.: Africa World Press, 2005.

———."Women Who Know Things: African Epistemologies, Ecocriticism, and Female Spiritual Authority in the Novels of Toni Morrison." *Journal of Pan African Studies* 1, no.7 (March 2007): 38–57.

Index

Kokahvah Zauditu-Selassie is a Yoruba priest of Obatala and a Mama Nganga in the Kongo tradition. She has been a National Endowment for the Humanities scholar, a Fulbright-Hays fellow in Cairo, Egypt, and South Africa, a National Council for Black Studies fellow at the University of Ghana, Legon, and a Scholar in Residence at New York University. She has lived, studied, and traveled extensively throughout Africa, South America, and the Caribbean. Her teaching specialization is African American literature, while her research focuses on African spiritual culture in literature and popular culture. Currently, she is professor of English at Coppin State University, Baltimore.

CPSIA information can be obtained
at www.ICGtesting.com
Printed in the USA
BVHW030217120521
607120BV00006B/201